UZO EGONU

An African Artist in the West

UZO EGONU

An African Artist in the West

Olu Oguibe

KALA PRESS
LONDON

First published in 1995 by
KALA PRESS, PO BOX 3509, LONDON NW6 3PQ

ISBN 0 947753 08 7

British Library Cataloguing in Publication Data
A catalogue record for this book is available
from the British Library

This book is published under
the Arts Council of England's
Publishing Franchise for INIVA

Design: Rasheed Araeen
Typeset: Emset, London
Printing: ABC Printers, England

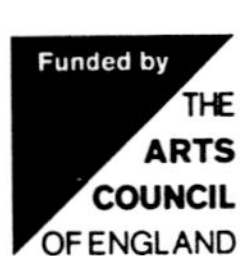

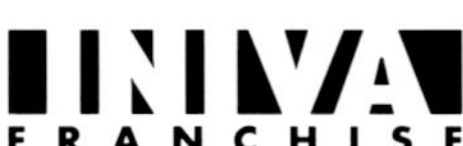

Contents

Cover: *Landscape with Yellow Bridge* 1981
Screenprint 65 x 91 cm

Dimensions of works illustrated are approximate

For my seven sisters
and for Liz Small

Introduction

In 1983 the International Association of Art admitted Uzo Egonu into its league of life counsellors, placing him in the fellowship of such noted artists of the 20th century as Henry Moore, Joan Miró, and Louise Nevelson. The critic George Whittet situated his work "on a level rarely met in contemporary European styles since the death of Paul Klee".[1] A few years later the African painter and scholar Obiora Udechukwu described Egonu as "perhaps Africa's finest painter".[2] These occasions appropriately summarise Egonu's unique place in history: a contemporary master in Europe, and an artist of great significance in his own part of the world.

A true professional who has dedicated himself to his work and depended entirely on his studio practice, Egonu worked in a society and a moment in history which were hardly conducive for artists of non-occidental origins in the West. He arrived in Britain at the end of the war and at the beginning of his teens. His origins quickly marked him out from his contemporaries, but also lent his vision and work something quite unique in contemporary art. His training was in European art, especially the methods and techniques of the High Renaissance, with a particular leaning towards the Flemish tradition favoured by the Camberwell College of Arts and Crafts during the time of his studentship. After college he broadened his knowledge by visiting the great galleries of Europe to understudy the masters not only of the Renaissance but also of modernism.

However, Egonu was a private person, aware of his uniqueness. Never unduly fascinated by any of the stylistic currents around him, he had a natural inclination to construct himself somewhat outside of prevailing streams and to pursue his own vision. Working on his own gave him space to pursue this vision, building on his wide knowledge of European traditions and a conscious and often meticulous recollection of his African origins.

Difference, of course, has played a key part in the orthodox narratives of contemporary art, and the tendency to write out of its history artists of non-European descent, especially those who chose the West as the theatre of their practice. Europe has had difficulty engaging Egonu and his work not only for reasons of his origins, but also because he placed them at the centre of his concerns and his work. Throughout the 1960s he dedicated his work to the contemplation and narration of the pains of emergent nationhood in his home country and on his continent. In the late 1970s and the 1980s he returned to the same questions, engaging through his work the difficult questions of the demise of the state. All of these were connected to a life and reality quite distinct from the esoteric cerebralism of much of the art produced during those periods. Today art freely engages in the mapping of national and political terrains and boundaries in postcolonial aesthetics, as well as in postmodernism. But in his formative years, Egonu's engagement in this difficult preoccupation had genuine parallels only in literature, and only in recent years has critical theory begun to develop a discourse around it. At best, therefore, his work received only peremptory attention from a critical establishment ill-prepared to deal either with his preoccupations or with artists of his background.

And yet, Egonu cannot strictly be described as an artist of the margin, for, although he was denied a place in the centre, he indeed operated and survived within the boundaries of that centre. So that, although he was 'invisible' — and he occasionally speaks of this invisibility — at the same time he lived on a certain level of assured patronage and an, albeit inconsistent, access to the structures of the establishment.

I was introduced to Egonu's work as a young art student at the University of Nigeria, which in 1982 hosted a historic exhibition of his prints. The encounter was breath-taking. The forceful eloquence of the work was almost indescribable, as was the incredible simplicity of its language. The painfully stringent lyricism of Egonu's forms and the power of his rhetorical devices effectively turned me away from my fascination at that time for Jim Dine and the 1980s New York art scene. Seven years later, in the autumn of 1989, I arrived in England as a British Foreign and Commonwealth Office scholar, with the specific aim to study and document Egonu's work. For the next two years we met regularly, weekly at first, then every other week, and spent numerous mornings and afternoons looking together at his career and work. Although his health has been fragile since the early Eighties, he and his wife gave freely of their time and shared their views and unique experiences.

In this book I have attempted to pull Egonu's career into a critical frame, drawing both on his work and on insights gained during my conversations with him. While it would be tempting to apply to Egonu's work the plethora of discursive frames thrown up by the shattering of the modernist monocle, I have avoided this because its greatness lies in the artist's general disregard for movements and prevailing aesthetic strategies, and in his pursuit of techniques appropriate for his own vision and circumstances.

I acknowledge the enormous help of both the artist and his wife. My appreciation also goes to Obiora Udechukwu who recommended me for the Foreign and Commonwealth Office scholarship which made this study possible. Thanks to Nike Odediran who helped transcribe some of my conversations with the artist, and to John Picton of the School of Oriental and African Studies, University of London.

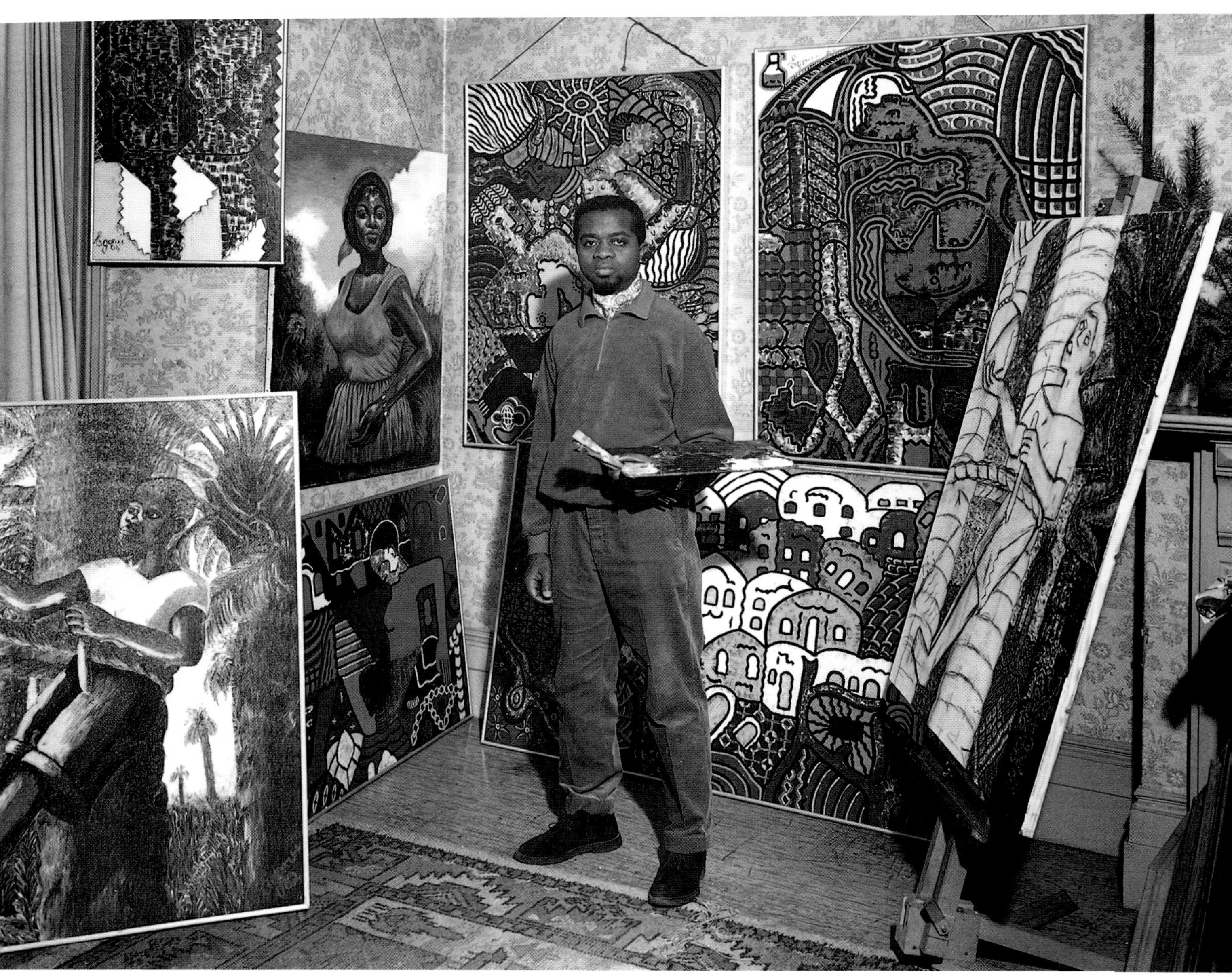

Uzo Egonu in His Studio, 1964
Photo: Stewart Bale

Egonu: The Life

William Uzo Egonu was born on Christmas Day, 1931, in the commercial city of Onitsha on the bank of the Niger, to Henry Chukwuma Egonu, a civil servant with the British colonial administration in Nigeria, and Alice Atibese Nanna Egonu who came from among the minority people of Koko in the lower Niger delta in what is today Nigeria. His father had studied at the highly respected Fourah Bay College, Freetown, and was a well-travelled man and an aesthete who designed his own house and subscribed to fashion magazines from England.

Onitsha in 1930 was not only the "high road to the heart of the Ibo nation", as The Reverend Crowther described it in 1857,[1] but also a spectacular modern city. The novelist Chinua Achebe tells the story of an exotic and sprawling metropolis where all cultures and peoples from across West Africa met and mingled, each people bringing with them their own exuberances and excesses. "Whenever I think of it," writes Achebe, "a phrase from Frantz Fanon comes to my mind: 'a zone of occult instability'."[2]

Despite its tragic encounters with the British prior to colonial pacification, Onitsha remained a strategic, dynamic and regenerative melting pot of peoples and cultures, with an aggressive commercial inclination as well as an eye for the innovative, the progressive, even the eccentric. The city and its people determinedly engaged with the missionaries and European trading posts. By 1930 Onitsha boasted a highly reputed grammar school, a number of elementary schools, a prominent bookshop, as well as "one great church with a regular congregation of 1000 Ibo Christians".[3] Its most important feature beside the Niger river, however, was its market, the "biggest and most spectacular market in the whole world".[4]

A popular section of the neighbourhood where the market was located was the Hausa quarter on the banks of the Niger, so named because it was inhabited by migrants from northern Nigeria. The migrants brought produce from the savannah as well as their religion and cultures, succeeding where the great Jihads or holy wars of the previous century had failed. The peoples of the lower Niger also sailed up the river in their boats to trade their produce and to settle in Onitsha. In addition there were the evangelists and civil servants from Freetown, Sierra Leone, who ran the schools and Christian mission establishments and showed off their European apparel and shiny bicycles. There were the white administrators and missionaries who fed tales of miracles and otherworldly happenings in the city. And there were the arrogant and fiercely material local people with their elaborate and intractable aristocracy.

A maze of colours, peoples, habits, temperaments, Onitsha made perfect home for the bizarre, the eccentric and the exceptional: street performers, fraudsters, stray Europeans seeking the end of the world. Among the latter was the memorable English gentleman, Stuart Young, "scholar, mystic, trader, single-handed fighter against the new European monopolistic cartels",[5] and lover of the legendary mermaid of the Niger who lavished wealth on him and forbade him romantic relationships with mortals. Young was adopted by the people, and would appear half a century later as one of the 'Heroes and Heroines of Onitsha'.[6] Achebe recalls another prominent figure in Onitsha in the 1930s, a half-demented minstrel named Okoli Ukpor:

> If you went to Onitsha in those days and did not run into Okoli your visit was somehow incomplete. He played for money on his flute, whistling and blowing his instrument alternately: "Man and woman, whoever holds money, let him bring." Occasionally, he would raise an additional half-penny by blowing each nostril into the open drain — in time with his beat. Rumour had it that Okoli was as sober as the next man, that he had two wives and a barn full of yams in his hinterland home, and only came to Onitsha during the slack moments in the farm to raise quick cash from amused charity by pretending to be light-headed.[7]

There were magicians, acrobats, quack technicians and inventors of myriad products and gadgets, pedlars of Oriental elixirs and aphrodisiacs, prophets and fortune-tellers. And at the centre of everything was the market and the immigrant quarter where Egonu was born.

Alongside the whirling eccentricities of modernisation were the particularly sophisticated traditions of the Onitsha, held tightly in place by the King, his chiefs and an elaborate structure of age-grades, societies, title-holders and priests. Each enactment of the Kingdom's rituals, each outing of an ancestral spirit, each regatta on the Niger to celebrate the Queen of the Seas, was a great spectacle. Such was the richness of Onitsha: an eccentric patterning of colour and ebullience, which Egonu would draw upon later in life.

Uzo Egonu began his schooling at St Joseph's Infant School, built on property which his grandfather provided for the purpose at the turn of the century. His parents' marriage had broken up following the birth of his younger brother, Hugh, after which his father moved to Calabar on the coast, where he continued his job with the colonial administration. Living with relations, Uzo was a lonely and withdrawn child for whom school provided warmth and relief.

After three years in the infant school, he enrolled in the Holy Trinity Elementary School, a Catholic mission school whose head teacher, Mr Odogwu, was a friend of his family and relative of the sculptor and painter Ben Enwonwu. In some ways Holy Trinity was also fun in so far as it took him away from the restrictions of his grandmother and aunts. The environment was strict, however, and the activities hardly memorable. Local teachers eager to impress their white inspectors and clergy who keenly policed the schools brought down the whole weight of their high-handedness on the children. Corporal punishment was the rule and it was not rare for a teacher to push the limits beyond the acceptable. It was in Onitsha at the turn of the century that a Sierra Leonian school teacher flogged his housemaid to death with the aid of his school children because the little girl took food without permission.[8] In his own day Egonu recalls cane-wielding teachers keeping guard every morning to thrash latecomers and truants.

His happiest recollections from this period are of the festivities of Empire Day, the colonial celebration when all the schools in the region gathered at the government headquarters and the colonial administrators took their salute of allegiance to the British Empire. The fun was more in the sporting events, however, and in the colourful displays, the performing bands of the schools and the colonial paramilitary, and the cultural dances and enactments which took place every Empire Day:

> It used to be a grand thing indeed. Naturally, the whole thing had a more or less propaganda purpose because what happened was, there used to be competition between the Catholics and the Protestants. Competition for shields... First of all, in the morning, there would be a march past. The local Resident would take the salute with the Union Jack. Then, all the children would appear with their paper hats and so forth. First of all the infants. Then the Holy Trinity School, the St Mary's School, the Protestants... There would be a brass band. Big do, yes. In the afternoon, the sports would start.[9]

Empire Day, despite the drudgery of the march past the Resident Officer, was always an event to look forward to since it recreated the esotericism of an Onitsha market day with the added eccentricities of the Europeans in their all-white attire and helmets.

Egonu's favourite class at Holy Trinity was nature study, in which he excelled, for by now he had already begun to show a unique artistic talent. Before infant school his creative inclinations emerged slowly and painfully. Without the close attention of his mother, or even of his father with whom he recalls never spending much time, his creativity was regarded with suspicion by his relatives. In his moments of loneliness he occupied himself by leafing through the illustrated pages of his father's fashion and furniture catalogues, and soon began to reproduce the illustrations. At his age this was not merely precocious to those around him but ominous. On one occasion, while staying with an aunt, he drew a human figure the accuracy of which astonished the aunt. Believing the child to be possessed by an evil spirit, she took him to see a diviner and, as expected, the diviner confirmed he was a spirit child. "He kept knocking on my head, knocking," Egonu recalls. The trauma of this experience was to remain with him for a long period, during which he began to believe it was wrong to draw and indeed that he was an abnormal child, and it was a while before he found the courage to return to drawing. Nature study at Holy Trinity gave him the opportunity to draw again and to continue to improve his skill.

In 1942, Egonu's father introduced him to a young, local teacher and artist, John Okechukwu, with whom he began to take art lessons. Okechukwu was self-taught and the art teacher at the Teacher Training College in Onitsha where, his profile as an artist already on the rise, his work was bought by the church. He had had a childhood much like Egonu's, having lost his parents at an early age and grown up in the care of an aunt. Independently he developed a skill in draughtsmanship and sculpture in the classical canon. His ceramic pieces were sent to Britain for glazing, and some of his most accomplished works included a crucifix for the chapel of the Catholic Church in the city. He is also believed to have designed the Bishop's house at Holy Trinity, Onitsha.

An artist of Okechukwu's reputation seemed the right master for the young Egonu. Not only was he accessible but his youth and confidence were reflected in his unique teaching methods. He combined his instructions with conversations on the cultural heritage of colonised people and took time to impress upon his ward that this was in no way inferior to European culture. He tutored the young artist on professional practice, teaching him the basics of visual literacy and draughtsmanship, how to think beyond the object and to exercise his imagination. Egonu recalls:

> We'd go for a walk, a long walk, and he won't say anything to me more or less, sometimes for a long time... from time to time we'd stop, looking at that and so forth. Later he would say, well, he would like to see my impression of what we'd seen, what impressed me... so, it was not a question of my going back because I had to think about it, you see. I had to think.[10]

Okechukwu introduced him to watercolour, modelling in clay and still-life study, providing him with a sound grounding for the future.

In addition to his lessons with the art teacher, Egonu recalls being taken to masking events where, with his developing awareness, he would spend the time on his father's shoulders trying to work out the peculiarities of each masquerade. About the same time, there was another positive influence on his determination to continue with art. This was in the person of the young and enigmatic artist, Ben Enwonwu, then a pupil of the itinerant British art instructor Kenneth C Murray, who was to be the founder and first director of the Nigerian Department of Antiquities. Enwonwu's obvious talent, his flamboyant nature and his reputation as perhaps the brightest of the Murray pupils, gave him prominence in the city and made him an object of admiration. Egonu showed him his drawings and received advice and criticism. Enwonwu's dedication to a career in art, in a way, fortified Egonu's growing inclinations.

In 1944 Egonu left Onitsha to join his father in Calabar. It was the elder Egonu's wish that his son should be trained under Professor Eyo Ita, a renowned educationalist who was then at the Methodist Hope Waddell Institute in Calabar. Eyo Ita had made his name through his unique teaching methods and a fierce nationalism which reflected his dedication to self-dependent technology. Henry Egonu discussed Eyo Ita's uniqueness with his son who, though he could have known little of the teacher then, still recalls him with unqualified admiration.

For a brief period Egonu was enrolled at the Institute where his talents were quickly noticed by the art teacher, Mr Ekanem. His time at Hope Waddell, however, was very brief, before he was transferred to Sacred Heart College in Calabar. From the new school he entered the first all-Nigeria junior art competition on the advice of his former art teacher, Ekanem, who was also the principal organiser and judge of the competition. When the results came out in 1945, Egonu was already far away from Calabar and Sacred Heart College, but his entry was awarded first place.

Henry Egonu not only provided his son with the best instruction and material, and as favourable an environment for his talent as was possible, he also promoted his work, proudly showing his watercolours and drawings to his colleagues in government and in high society. Among those who were highly impressed by the boy's talent was a manager with the United African Company (UAC), Mr Gee, a generous young man from Little Snoring in Norfolk. Gee not only felt that the younger Egonu needed greater encouragement, he also felt the boy should be sent out of the country, as was the practice at the time, to an environment where he could realise his already obvious future. Like Henry Egonu, whose generation had had to go to Lagos or Freetown for an education comparable to that of the Europeans, Gee felt that the younger Egonu needed to go abroad for better art training and a career in the arts. This, for Gee, meant going to England.

Modern art education in Nigeria was at the time in its embryonic stage, despite the efforts of pioneer modern art teachers Aina Onabolu, Kenneth Murray and the many others whom they trained. It seemed natural that a man of Henry Egonu's standing would prefer to have his son educated in England. But given his fascination for and faith in Professor Eyo Ita and his philosophy of greater independence and self-reliance, he must have also felt slightly reluctant and unsure about sending Uzo abroad, especially since he was still so young, rather thin and frail, and given to solitude. However, the practice of sending young boys to England on their own to study was already fairly popular among the Nigerian élite. Around this time, the well-known transport and produce mogul, and Knight of the British Empire, Sir Odumegwu Ojukwu, had sent his own son to England at the age of thirteen. The Ojukwu boy, Chukwuemeka Odumegwu-Ojukwu, would later become an army general and leader of the ill-fated Republic of Biafra. Also, Uzo Egonu's young hero Ben Enwonwu, as Kenneth Murray's top student, had already sailed for England. So that when Gee put the idea forward and in addition offered to have the young Egonu live with his family in Little Snoring until he was ready for art college, it probably was not very difficult for his much travelled father to concede.

Egonu arrived in England late in 1945, aged 13. The war in Europe was coming to an end, although he recalls that the Japanese were still at war and the allied presence in Britain was heavy. He was taken into the Gee family house in Little Snoring, and enrolled in a private school. Being the only African person in the town was a fairly uncomfortable experience, especially at the beginning. However, being very young, and one who had already begun to develop a certain independence and ability to cope with his environment, the reserved Egonu saw the whole period as a passing phase which prepared him for a life he knew would be played out elsewhere.

In the small private school run by the Macmillans in Little Snoring he studied academic subjects as well as art. He recalls the art teacher knowing a lot less than her students. She would set up a still life for drawing and disappear, only to return the next week merely to look at the drawings. After his period as a student of Okechukwu back in Nigeria, this was of course somewhat disappointing. But the Gees were particularly supportive. In 1948 Egonu finished school and the next year he left Little Snoring for London.

London in 1949 was a vast, bleak city, still convalescing from the disasters of war. The fact that in the colonies subjects now heckled for independence with a new brazenness and fury did not help matters. Also, immigrants began to arrive from the colonies, as if to claim a right in the Empire, and were gratefully received by a country that needed labour to reconstruct itself.[11] It was the same year that the flamboyant Francis Newton Souza arrived England from Goa, and settled into poverty.[12]

Although a lively practice thrived for some artists under the state-sponsored war artists' scheme, Cyril Connolly in his last editorial in *Horizon* summed up the spirit of the times thus: "From now on an artist will be judged by the resonance of his solitude and the quality of his despair." Connolly summarised the advent of a new existentialism which shifted thematic preoccupation from social responsibility to individual introspection. It was in this atmosphere of post-war *angst* that Egonu entered art college. The 'kitchen sink' school of realism was beginning; at Borough Polytechnic young artists gathered around David Bomberg, whilst close to Camden Town, where Egonu soon found lodging, was situated the influential Euston Road Group and perhaps, most importantly, Victor Pasmore, who also taught at Camberwell School of Arts and Crafts.

The two major figures of the war artists' scheme, Henry Moore and Paul Nash, still held stylistic sway over London. The war situation had demanded a stark realism which drove abstraction into the background, signified, as Simon Wilson has observed, in the "geographical and artistic" isolation of the Hepworth-Nicholson group and its self-banishment to Cornwall.[13] The other central figure of the period was Graham Sutherland whose *Thorn Tree* paintings of 1946 were triggered by a St Matthew's Church commission in 1944 for a painting of the crucifixion, itself a metaphor for the agony, desolation and despondency of the war and post-war years. Perhaps the only significant departure from figuration during the period was Pasmore's controversial switch to pure abstraction in 1948 after his move to Blackheath.

In January 1949, Egonu registered in the departments of Fine Art and Typography at Camberwell School of Arts and Crafts. The decision to go to Camberwell was influenced by his father who wanted him to study not merely art but something else which could assure him a job on his return to Nigeria, as was their plan. In the 1940s one could not hope for a well-paid job in Nigeria with merely a certificate in art; the only openings with such a qualification were in school teaching. The elder Egonu would have deemed his boy worthy of a more lucrative job with greater security than teaching could guarantee, if not in the civil service then some form of self-employment. Perhaps his concern was also informed by his state of health which was not revealed to his son, and he needed assurance that, in his absence, his children would be able to fend for themselves. His friends suggested printing in addition to art, and Camberwell was not only the place to find printing and art together, but also where his friends had the right connections to make the requisite arrangements.

Besides, Camberwell had a reputation as one of the finest art colleges in Europe with its traditional European orientation under L J Daniels. Under Gilbert Spencer, who taught painting and drawing, life drawing was given great emphasis, as was also the study of old masters. In the printing department, under W J Wright, Egonu studied several subjects including typography. Despite the college's credentials, Egonu's Camberwell years were not particularly inspired, although he worked at his studies and his art with considerable diligence both to please his father, who kept a watch through his friends and the principal, and because he saw the sense in the arrangement made for him.

Egonu commuted from Camden Town to Camberwell, made very few friends, and only a few teachers made impressions strong enough for him to remember them. Among these was Spencer Daniel who, like his brother Stanley, would later become a Royal Academician. Daniels paid particular attention to Egonu's work, a relationship he found encouraging and useful.

In Camden Town, Egonu lived not far from the West Africa Students Union. The Union was particularly helpful in keeping him in touch not only with other African students but also with the general air of the period, the excitement of impending independence for the colonies, and all its prospects. The Union was the place to read newspapers and get news from home, to engage in long discussions about the times, to avoid the chill and occasional boredom of London, and generally to feel at home. His accent, which had been anglicised during his period in Norfolk, regained a marked Nigerian slant which he has since maintained. This shift in accent is most important for not only did it signify a conscious identification with his origins, it also marked the beginning of a process dealing with the alienation which had begun to characterise his life in England. It was invariably the signal for a mental and political recovery, as well as a redefinition of individual identity.

Egonu graduated from Camberwell in October 1951[14] with qualifications in printing and painting. His testimonial, reissued and signed by Wright in 1962 after he apparently lost the original with other documents in Finland in 1958, shows no indication that he was an exceptional student at Camberwell but remarks that he was "hard-working and made satisfactory progress in his studies". Egonu himself has said that although he worked hard at his studies, his mind was in fact "elsewhere". The outside world was where to prove himself, and this knowledge preoccupied him more than his immediate environment at Camberwell.

Shortly after leaving Camberwell Egonu was taken to meet the sculptor Jacob Epstein, a meeting which in its tremendous impact on Egonu recalls Epstein's own meeting with Brancusi in the latter's Paris studio in 1912. From the meeting he learnt a lot which would be meaningful in his career as an artist in Britain. He had gone to visit a friend, meeting there an engineer who had an appointment with Epstein for the following week, and who invited the young artists

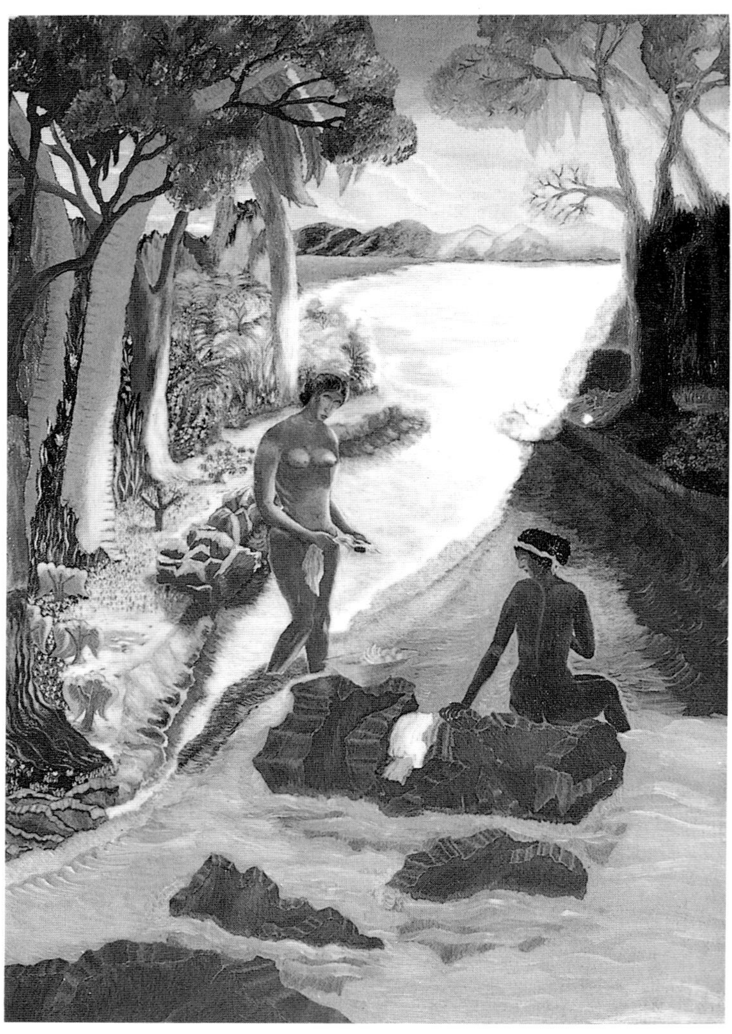

***Two Women Bathing*, 1952 (Painting from a drawing by Egonu aged twelve years).**

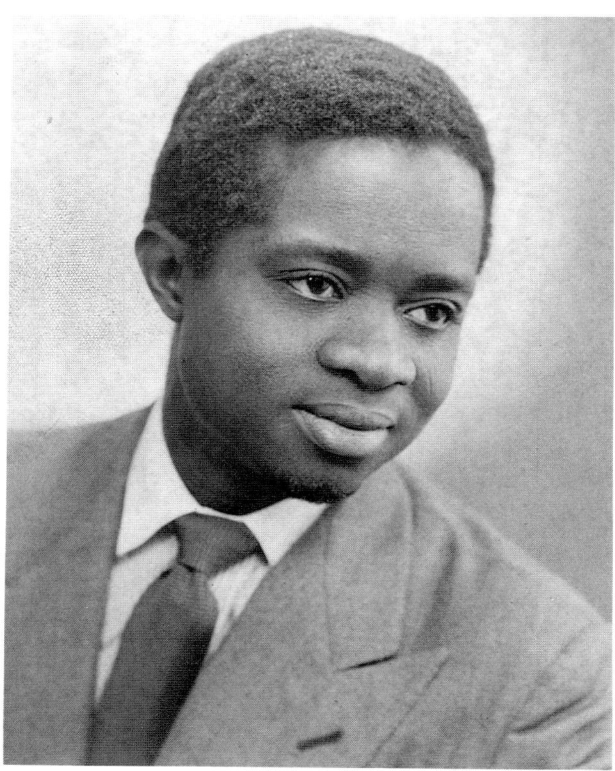

Uzo Egonu in Paris, 1955

to accompany him. Egonu recalls the meeting in Epstein's studio:

> Epstein asked me during conversation what my intention was, whether I will be going back home or staying and working here. Well, naturally I said that, of course my intention was to go back, but one never knows; I might stay. I still remember what he said to me. Because he was a Jew. He said to me, well, that if it was in my thinking to stay in Europe, I must not forget that it won't be enough just to be as capable as a local artist. That's one. The other is that one just gets so far, and then finds it difficult to go further because there'll be greater obstacles. Those were his words. I still remember.[15]

During this period Egonu lived on occasional sales of watercolours and drawings while he sized up the situation. In 1953 he moved to Paris where he lived for a year before returning to London. In Paris he spent his time in the museums and galleries, but especially in the Musée de l'Homme, looking at collections of African art. His particular interest with respect to European masters was the Flemish School, Caravaggio and the Post Impressionists. On the streets of Paris

Egonu made friends with a Ghanaian engineering student who knew a few buyers and introduced him and his work to them. Unfortunately, it has not been possible to trace his Paris watercolours especially since they were sold during a period of relative obscurity. In 1954 his father died in Nigeria, leaving him to support himself. It was apparent that he was beginning to contemplate the possibility of remaining in Europe. His excuse for not returning immediately to Nigeria was a growing anxiety that he might have to split his time between art and a job. Although he was interested in teaching art in his country, he had been informed that there were no openings. This, of course, was not the case. It is likely too that his enthusiasm was dampened by thoughts of missing the few fascinations he was beginning to discover in Europe. He needed the resources which the numerous museums and galleries in Britain and Europe offered, and he was absorbed in discovering African art in their collections. He also needed the company of a community of young artists working in a similar manner as himself. This, he believed, would be unavailable in Nigeria.

Although the prospects of a young African artist in Europe were not at all reassuring, and life was rough and treacherous, Egonu felt more professionally secure in Europe at this formative stage in his career. He feared circumstances at home might force him to become a 'Sunday only' painter and thus harm his development. The competitive atmosphere in Europe he found healthy for a young artist, especially since, as an African he required in his words "three times more hard work" before he could hope for success. His countryman Ben Enwonwu, whose career he followed closely, had himself stayed back awhile in England to practice, earning and executing important commissions and building up his position in the art world. It was indeed his well-established profile in Europe that earned him a high government position upon his return to Nigeria. Also, with the death of his father Egonu's strongest tie with home was somehow severed. Although he was in touch with his mother, he had hardly known her. It is equally possible that he was terrified of his family responsibilities and needed a sense of security and a status befitting an eldest son before he could return home.

After his return to London in 1954, he continued to work in his Camberwell style, selling occasional drawings and watercolours and moving from gallery to gallery to deposit his work for sale. Without financial support from Nigeria he had to strive harder to survive. His paintings from the second half of the decade suggest that he worked on cheap, low quality paper and lived quite frugally.

Sometime in 1954, an incident took place which not only improved his means considerably for some time but also placed him on a more solid professional ground. This was his meeting with Mr Bah, which he has described as marking the beginning of his 'journey' as an artist. He had gone out sketching one afternoon, and on his return was walking along Charing Cross Road when it began to rain, wetting the portfolio under his arm. A car drew up, and the driver beckoned him and offered him a ride. The man at the wheel turned out to be a well-known business man, a club owner and greyhound-racer whose dog, Mr Bah's Choice, was, according to Egonu, very popular in dog-racing circles across Britain. Mr Bah, a Gambian, quickly took to the young artist, and what began as a ride developed into a deep friendship and patronage which continued for the next three years.

Although Bah was not very well educated, he was nevertheless fascinated by the work and professional determination of his young friend and, in the years that they were close, commissioned paintings and drawings, introduced him to his friends, helped organise exhibitions of his works in libraries and other small venues, and found him

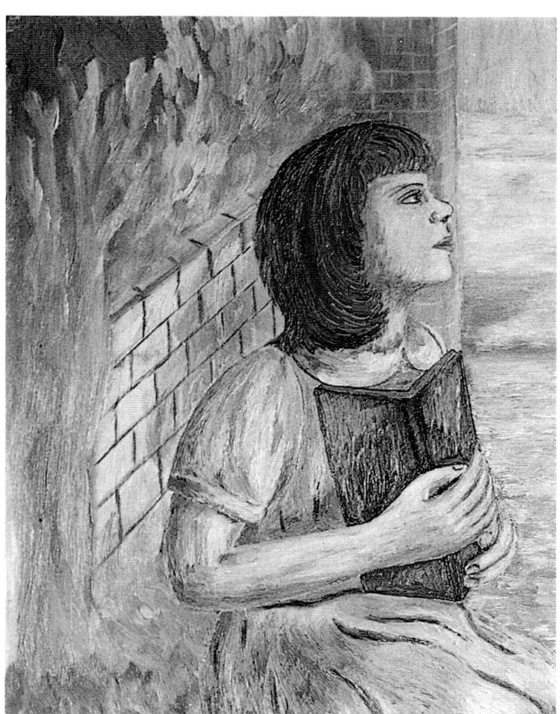

The daughter of Mr Bah's Friend**,** early 1950s

clients. Bah became more than a patron, playing the role of the father he had only known closely for such a brief length of time.

During this period Egonu earned enough both for his upkeep and for further trips to the continent. He hung out with other struggling young artists and they would move from one artist's little room to another's, or cramp up in someone's studio. Through Egonu, Bah also helped the others, getting his friends to buy their work and helping them survive.

In 1958 Egonu travelled for two months in Finland, visiting museums and galleries in Helsinki, Turku and Tampere, and making small watercolours and landscape sketches. While in Tampere he became a sensation as the first black person most people in the city had ever seen. It was during this trip that he lost the little suitcase with his documents and treasured correspondence. The same year he visited Sweden and Denmark. Upon returning he moved to South Hampstead, finally beginning to settle down as a professional artist.

In 1959, however, he registered as an evening student at St Martin's School of Art to study life drawing. His travels in Europe and his fascination for the old masters had, in a way, exposed his weakness

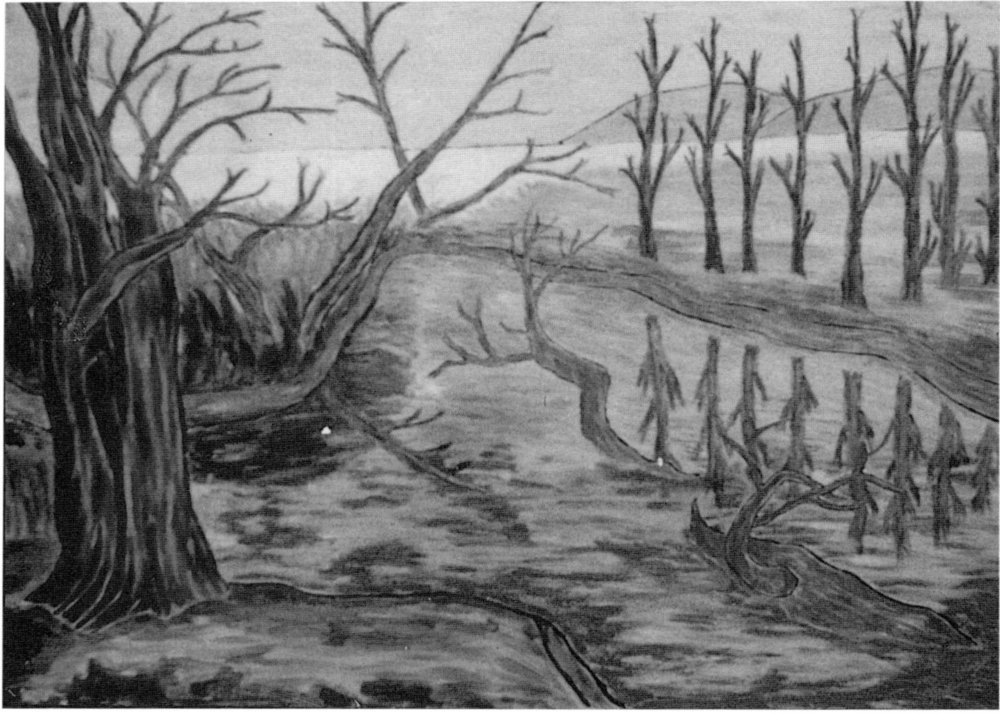

***Pond in Kenwood*, 1961**
Oil on canvas
107 x 145 cm

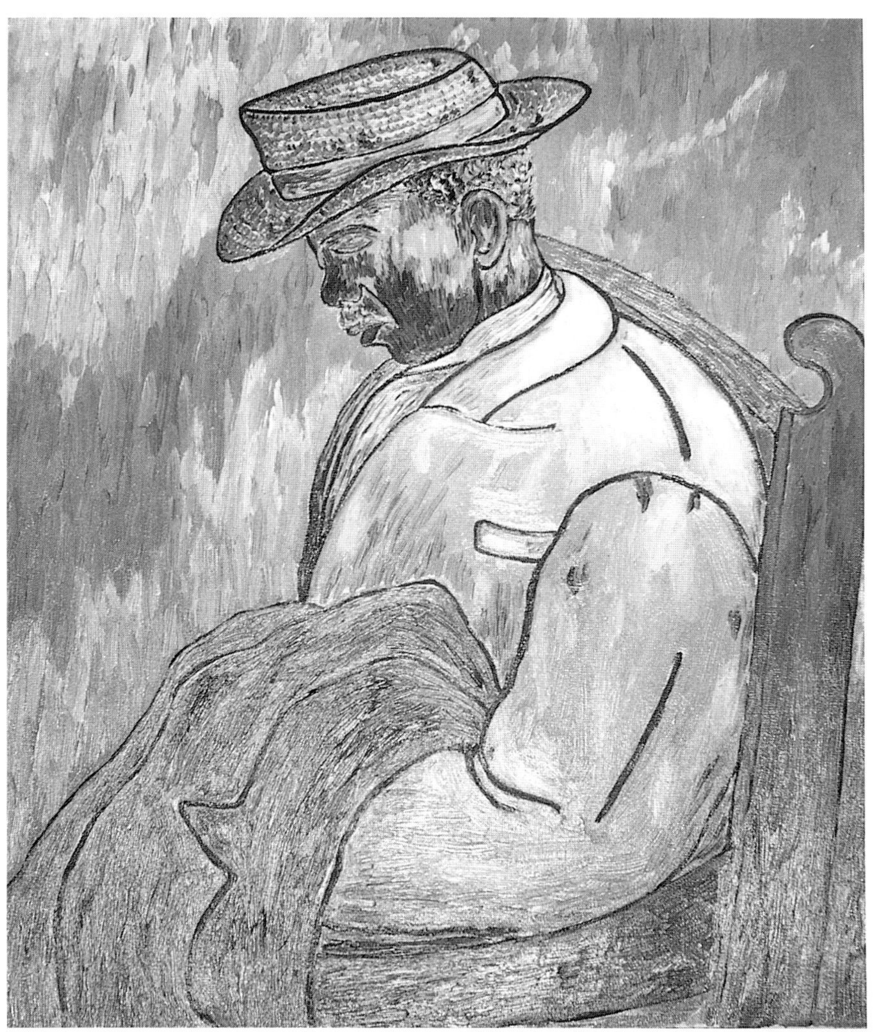

***A Man Resting*, 1962**
Oil on canvas
76 x 64 cm

in drawing. His training at Camberwell had been deficient in certain respects, particularly in anatomy, but since he could not afford to pay a model, he decided to enrol in college where he would have access to one.

Earlier, Egonu had applied to the Nigerian government for financial aid for further study. He had not completely given up his ambition to return eventually to Nigeria, especially with the excitement of the country's impending independence from Britain. He had developed a fascination for printmaking and its enormous possibilities, and he felt it would be of particular value in a developing nation. But his application was turned down with a polite acknowledgement and, very much later, an apology. Egonu was very disillusioned by this, and further unsuccessful attempts. He began to feel sceptical about the new dispensation in his country and its prospects.

For this reason, and others, he decided to remain in Europe. He took evening classes for two years at St Martins, making do with the life study classes because he did not have the finance to take a full specialist course. Works surviving from this period, although they show no exceptional departures from his earlier work, reveal a growing dissatisfaction and agitation, perhaps a disillusionment, personal as well as stylistic. Living was still difficult and he occasionally had to recycle canvas supports to keep painting. On one occasion, he immersed over thirty canvases in the bath and had his girlfriend scrub off the paint so that he could dry and re-use them.[16]

1960 signalled the artist's second break, bringing him his first major public commission and press attention. In September, as part of the setting up of diplomatic structures for the new Nigerian nation, the brewing firm of Whitbread & Company wanted a painting for Nigeria House in London. Egonu met with the advertising company, A N Holden Ltd, who were acting on behalf of Whitbread, and they agreed to look at sketches for a painting on Nigerian life. He submitted sketches and proposals for a painting of a market scene, which was accepted in October 1960 for a fee of 70 guineas.

The same year Egonu approached the Reverend Patrick Brock of St Martin-in-the-Fields in London to show his work in the church, which was agreed for a period of five or six weeks starting October 9, 1961, but on condition that he would not be able to display prices on the work or in the exhibition catalogue and that he would be required to pay some unspecified charge for the 'stewarding' of the exhibition which would be provided by the church.

Egonu was approached soon after by a group of Ghanaians in London to do a portrait of Kwame Nkrumah, the nationalist Prime Minister of Ghana. He did numerous sketches for the commission, working in a neo-classical, heroic style. Nkrumah was portrayed in the sketches as the benevolent philosopher king, a Christ figure stretching a hand of blessing over his flock. The concept may have been informed by the politician's cult name, Osagyefo, the Great Teacher, and the infectious fervour he inspired in his admirers, including the artist. When Nkrumah visited London in 1961 Egonu had a brief audience with him and was allowed to do life sketches for the painting.

The Nkrumah portrait, however, was eventually rejected by the

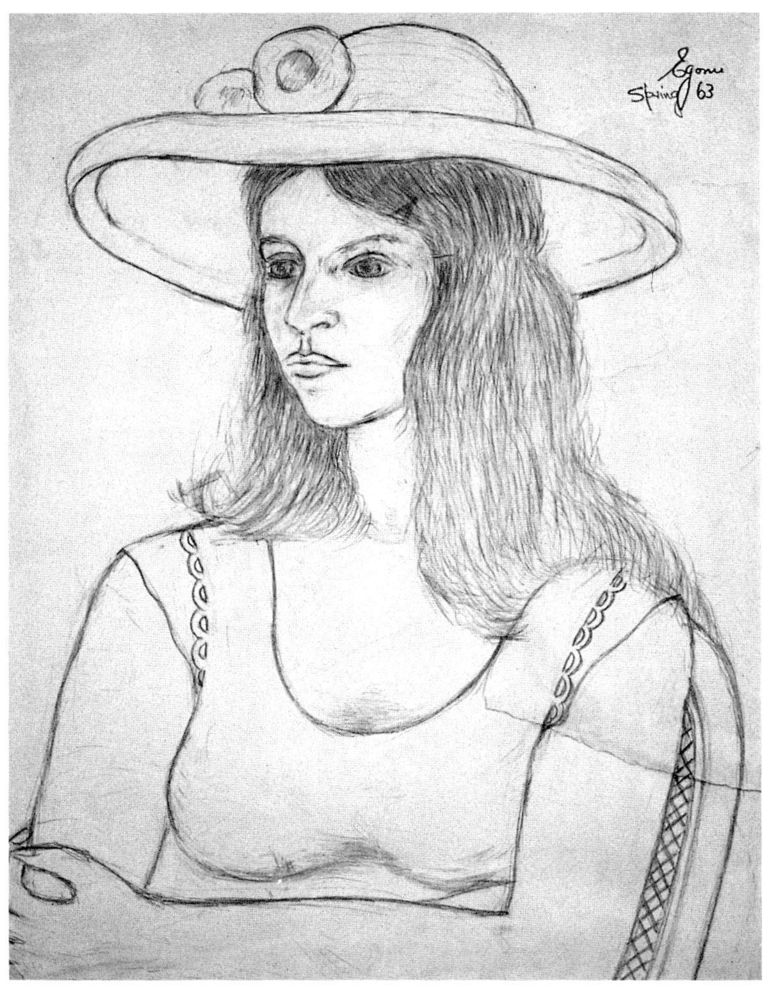

***Hiltrud in Summer*, 1963**
charcoal on paper
51 x 38 cm

clients who had expected a level of verisimilitude which they found lacking in the finished painting. A heated debate erupted over the appropriateness of the image and the artist's concept, and, disillusioned by what he considered to be the aesthetic half-wittedness of most of the clients, Egonu decided to keep the painting which remains in his collection.

He got on with other things, seeking buyers and approaching galleries. In 1962 he showed in the Pan African Council exhibition in London. The following year he joined the newly formed Free Painters and Sculptors group, exhibiting with them at the FBA Gallery. He also showed in the winter salon of the Royal Institute Galleries. The dissatisfaction he had begun to have with his work some years earlier persisted, coupled with a very deep nostalgia which began to show in his paintings. His growing stature and gradual acceptance in England contrasted with the lingering feeling of rejection by his own country which the unsuccessful bursary applications of 1959 had stirred. He succeeded in transforming his yearning for physical return into a series of paintings on African themes and subjects: portraits of Africans, landscapes and anecdotal compositions which drew on childhood memories.

Nationalist pride sustained Egonu's private vow to devise a form of individual cultural nationalism and to manifest this in his work. Although his physical contacts with home were not particularly strong and numerous, he followed events closely, and thus remained part of both the euphoria of the period, if guardedly so, and the concrete movement towards political and cultural redefinition in the country. 1962 to 1965 marked what he has described as 'the Bridge' in his art. This was the period of his final transition from nostalgia and mere gestural identification with home, to self-definition and maturity in his technique and style.

In September 1964 Egonu was given his first one-person show at the Woodstock Gallery in London. The response was mild but significant. Art critics and journalists registered minor reservations with the naivety of the paintings, most of which were genre, as well as the artist's handling of paint. But all were united in observing a talent to watch.

The Woodstock show came at the head of a wave of pluralist receptivity, as ambivalent as it was short-lived, that would sweep through Europe in the wake of the American hijacking of European art spaces and discourse. Together with a growing interest in foreign literature, the British art establishment seemed willing to admit anything but more American influence or dominance. There was also curiosity over the true nature of the peoples of the newly liberated colonies and the nature and context of presentation of their work witnessed a slight change, beginning to be seen less as colonial trophies, and more as evidence of living cultures.[17]

There was also a liberal and Fabian-socialist response to a growing political intolerance in British society towards settlers. The somewhat unexpected collapse of the Empire coincided with the influx of peoples from the colonies, and when this was no longer seen in a positive economic light, it began to arouse considerable resentment among the British. This culminated in the 1962 Commonwealth Immigration

Law, followed by another, even more stringent, in 1965. Improved tolerance in sections of the British art world run by young liberals reflected their own defiance of the establishment; this created a semblance of openness and receptivity which continued to the end of the decade before it was reversed. The atmosphere somehow empowered artists of non-European descent to utilise the few spaces available to them and to initiate collaborations with the liberal fringes of the establishment.[18]

While the Whitechapel Gallery's annual 'New Generation' exhibitions between 1964 and 1966 predictably excluded non-white artists, intercultural fringe and avant-garde groups such as Signals initiated and ran their own independent events and shows.[19] The Indian Artists Group and later, the Caribbean Artists Movement (CAM) sprang up alongside community and political organisations. Although Egonu operated largely outside these developments — he later flirted with CAM and was a founding member of a short-lived African parallel — his career gained momentum through them, especially from 1964 onwards.

In 1965 Egonu was invited by Milton Grundy, chairman of the Gemini Trust in London, to participate in the Trust's first sponsored exhibition at the Woodstock Gallery. The Trust, according to a review by Barbara Wright in *Arts Review*, was ''dedicated to showing new artists who are not necessarily 'fashionable and saleable'''.[20] Again Egonu's entries in the exhibition attracted considerable attention for their evidence of an individual, 'unfamiliar' style. The illustrator Andrew Dodd did a drawing of him which appeared alongside an article in the *Eastern Daily Press* of Norwich,[21] and introduced him to the newly opened Africa Centre on King Street in London.

Egonu also caught the attention of the sculptor Ronald Moody, who had come to Europe in 1923. Moody was moved by Egonu's use of colour which he described in a lengthy article in *Magnet News* as ''having the exuberance of a divination vessel or a chief's stool from Yoruba''.[22] Hence began a strong and intimate friendship that would involve very close creative collaboration between the two artists which would last till Moody's death twenty years later.

The same year Egonu was represented in an exhibition of 'Contemporary Nigerian Art and Crafts' in the Royal Festival Hall, alongside sculptors from McEwen's Rhodesia workshop, as part of the 1965 Commonwealth Festival. Although Egonu received good press and an audience including important political personages, the

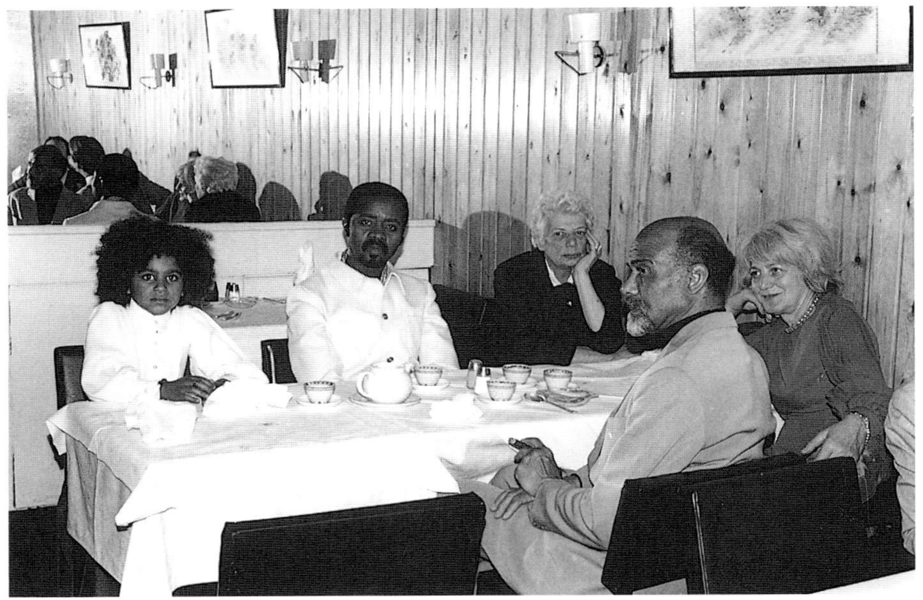

Uzo Egonu with Helen and Ronald Moody, Franka Halberstadt and youn Sheba in a restaurant in Hampstead, 20 August, 19

Royal Festival Hall exhibition was ill-conceived and poorly presented. His work also featured in the Contemporary African Art exhibition curated by Dennis Duerden for the National Museum of Wales in Cardiff, and his second one-person exhibition opened in Brighton the same year. He participated in the First World Festival of Negro Arts in Dakar, Senegal, in April the following year, together with other artists from Britain such as Ronald Moody, Frank Bowling and Aubrey Williams. Egonu exhibited *King Fighting Three Battles*, which had already been shown in the Royal Festival Hall.[23]

The Duchess of St Albans, who ran the Upper Grosvenor Gallery, visited Egonu's studio. She was taken by Egonu's work and in the summer of 1966, he showed in her gallery's summer exhibition alongside Mervyn Peake, James Fitton and Norman Gilbert, among many others.[24] In September his third one-person show opened with the gallery, commissioned by Mr Bottomley, British Minister for Overseas Development. Although some of the works in the exhibition were from 1963, the majority were drawn from what he called the 'Protection Series', a series on the theme of physical and spiritual insecurity, inspired by the political crisis in Nigeria. The exhibition was as foreboding as *Path of Thunder*, the highly apocalyptic and haunting poem which his countryman and contemporary Christopher Okigbo was working on at the same time, and which he would not finish before he was killed the following year in the Nigerian civil war.

Uzo Egonu with Mr Bottomley, Minister for Overseas Development, and Mrs Bottomley at Upper Grosvenor Galleries during Egonu's one-person show, 1966.

In Nigeria the years since 1963 had been marked by growing violence and anxiety, overshadowing the glee of independence and casting a blanket of despair over the citizens, especially those who lived abroad. As Egonu worked on his 'Protection' series, life in Nigeria was becoming more and more insecure as violence and political intolerance spread throughout the country. In January 1966 the political tension came to a head when a group of young military

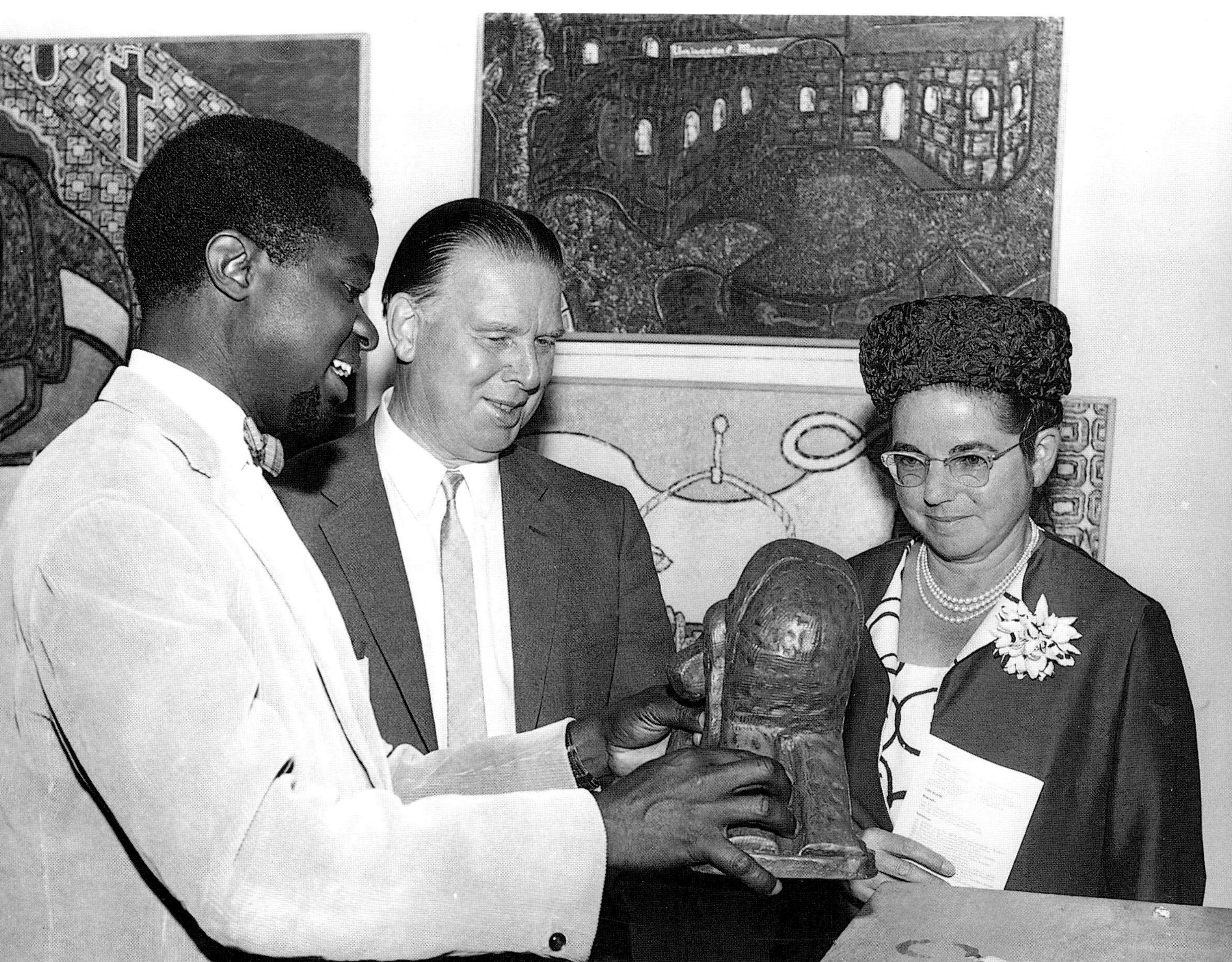

officers, led by Major Kaduna Nzeogwu, violently overthrew the elected government, resulting in the death of some of the country's leaders. Although the putsch, which was somehow inspired by that of Abdel Nasser in Egypt, was received with relief and widespread approval among many sections of the populace, it failed to install its leaders in power, and the government that took over lacked the strength to restore order quickly. A number of hasty and ill-advised policy moves at the centre, rather than reassuring the population, exacerbated the tension and ill-feelings between different sections, leading to a counter-coup and a secession bid by the larger northern section of the country which, incidentally, had lost many men in the January putsch. People in the north felt the earlier coup had been aimed at them, substantiating their position by the fact that the greater number of participants were Igbo from the eastern region of the country. What followed was a series of genocidal attacks on the Igbo population which began in the north but soon spread throughout the west. News of the slaughters reached Egonu, an Igbo, in London, and the events of the next three years would leave a deep mark not only on his life, but also on his art.

Egonu's final exhibition of 1966 was with the Hampstead Artists Council of which he was now a member. He was, however, approached by H B Frankel, secretary of the Leicester University Arts Festival whom he had met at the Africa Centre in Covent Garden, to show during the festival and to give a talk on his work.[25] His fourth solo exhibition was in Leicester in 1967, but it would be his only show that year. Events at home had taken a bleak turn with the mass exodus of Igbo people from all parts of Nigeria back to their homeland in the east, and their subsequent declaration of self-determination under the Republic of Biafra. Suddenly, Egonu's nationality had changed, and at an enormous human cost.

The agonising confusion which arose from this change is evident in the biographical detail carried in the catalogue of his next solo exhibition in 1968, where he was listed as having been born in "Onitsha, Biafra, Eastern Nigeria".[26] In September 1967 Egonu signed contracts for a second one-person show with the Upper Grosvenor Gallery from July to August, 1968. The exhibition was also conceived as a charity event to raise money for those affected by the war in Biafra. Egonu resolved to manifest his emotional and practical involvement in the crisis in his country and its consequences through his work, and was equally determined to make a material contribution towards the alleviation of suffering. In the winter of 1967 the artist had requested that the gallery channel some of the proceeds from the sale of his work to this purpose, designating ten paintings to be shown in a charity exhibition. As the conflict between Nigeria and Biafra escalated and the death tolls in Biafra began to rise, charities sprang up around the world to help where most governments chose to remain uninvolved. Some of the charities were registered, others were not. A letter from the Duchess of St Albans in October 1967 shows that the charity to which Egonu was donating ten paintings was one such unregistered effort, and the gallery's policy forbade their involvement. The 1968 exhibition was therefore carefully planned to involve registered charities, the church and recognised personalities in the aid campaign for Biafra. A short appeal written by the Reverend Robert Gibson, Dean-elect of Port Harcourt and member of the Christian Council Project, was carried in the exhibition catalogue, and the critic Laurence Bradshaw noted that not only was Egonu making his contribution to the cause of alleviating the sufferings at home, he was also making a universal protest as "death walks abroad".[27]

The title of the exhibition underlined a non-partisan, non-sectarian response to the Biafra tragedy. The exhibition was opened on July 16 by Lord Soper of the All Hallows Biafra Refugees Fund and received good press. Dennis Duerden, writing for *Arts Review*, observed that it was a surprise that with the events at home, Egonu could find the fortitude to paint at all.[28] Duerden commended the artist's ability to evoke powerful moods with his use of colour, an element which he found more effective than the explicit allegories in which the artist had indulged to best capture his feelings. The *Daily Mirror* commented that, judging from the works, "Egonu feels possibly more deeply than most about the situation".[29]

While Egonu made his contributions to the war effort, other contemporaries at home and abroad, young artists and intellectuals, some of them of international repute, headed the campaigns for the survival of Biafra. One of these was Uche Okeke who had read about Egonu especially following his participation in the 1966 Festival in Dakar in which he was also represented. When the war broke out Okeke was part of the exodus of the Igbo from other parts of Nigeria. He soon joined the war effort and headed the visual arts section of the Biafran Refugees Affairs Committee in Aba and Umuahia. In this position he put together an exhibition of Biafran art which he took on tour to Germany. From there he got in touch with Egonu, and a friendship ensued which would last long after the war. From Biafra the new nation's most well known writer Chinua Achebe undertook to present its plight to the international community in lectures and readings around the world. On the other side of the war, Nigeria's most well known writer Wole Soyinka, later winner of the Nobel Prize for Literature, was jailed for his sympathies with Biafra. The tragedy thus united the young artists even as it physically severed them from one another.

From London Egonu followed events closely as the world press scavenged them for television. His wife collected newspaper clippings. For him life hung literally on the next bit of news from behind the lines where his family lived in uncertainty, with two of his brothers fighting in the Biafran army.

Egonu held a second solo show in 1968, this time at the Commonwealth Institute Gallery in Edinburgh. He was also able to take part in a number of group shows, including one in support of Czechoslovakia following the Soviet invasion. The 'Artists for Czechoslovakia' exhibition was held at the Camden Arts Centre in London. He was represented in the 'Contemporary African Art' exhibition at the Africa Centre and in the exhibition of 'Artists of Eight Commonwealth Countries' at the City Arts Gallery in Bristol. As a mark of his status he was successfully elected to life fellowship of the Royal Society for the Arts (RSA).

In 1969, after participating in a series of group shows including the well-received 'Contemporary African Art' exhibition at the Camden Arts Centre with the collaboration of *Studio International*, Egonu was approached by Donald Bowen, curator of the Commonwealth Institute Gallery in London to show at the Stroud Festival the following year. Bowen had introduced his work to the art adviser of the Festival, Sir Oliver Heywood. Heywood expressed a willingness to meet with Egonu and to see more of his work. Early in 1970 the Chairman of the Festival confirmed their invitation for Egonu to show at the festival, and in November of the same year, a solo exhibition of his works, described by the *Stroud News and Journal* as "the most exciting and impressive one-man show seen at the George Room in Stroud",[30] opened to a warm reception. In July George Bennett, senior producer with the Africa Service of the BBC and later administrator of the Africa Centre in London, invited Egonu to participate in the BBC Morning Show competition for artists from Africa and the Middle East, at least since, as he indicated to the artist, "the

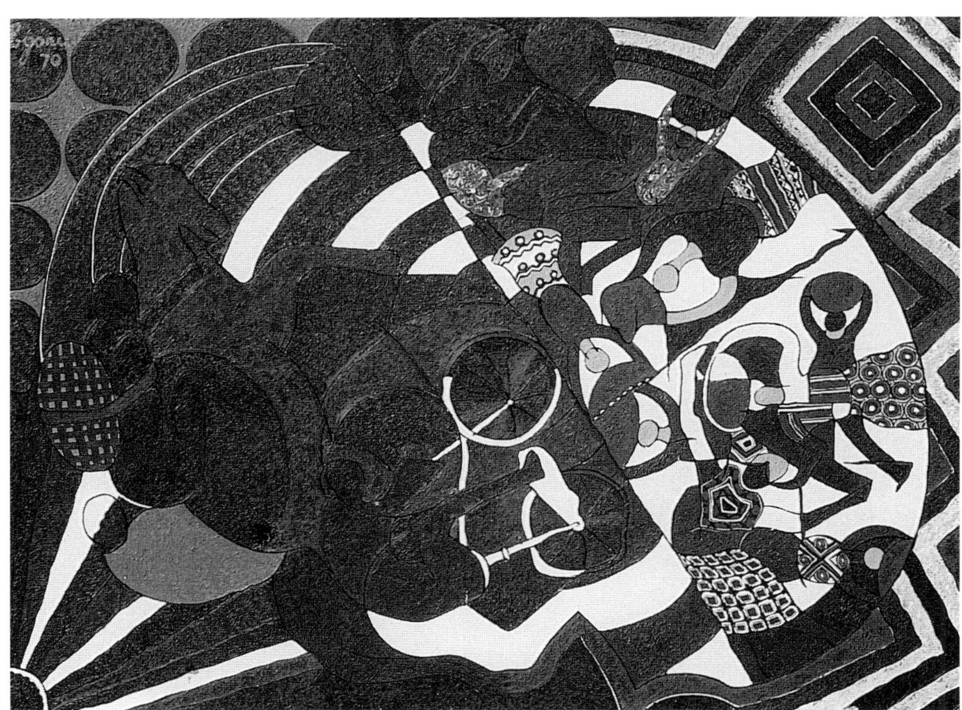

***Exodus*, 1969**
Oil on canvas
107 x 145 cm

Prizes are well worth having''. Interestingly, the first prize was £100 and, perhaps more appealingly, a solo show in Kenya. The judges were Donald Bowen of the Commonwealth Institute, the critic and art historian Edward Lucie-Smith and Dennis Duerden. The competition recorded 222 entries from 19 countries. Egonu entered one of his war paintings, *Exodus*, which won the first prize.

As part of this first prize Egonu's work was shown in a solo exhibition in Nairobi, Kenya, to excited press reception. The artist could not go to Kenya but the show, which opened on January 20, 1971, in the Gallery Africa in Nairobi, was commissioned by the Kenyan Minister for Agriculture, Jeremiah Nyaga. In attendance also was the Nigerian High Commissioner in Kenya, His Excellency I C Olisaemeka, who described the artist curiously as ''one of the most promising artists in Nigeria''. The willingness of the Nigerian government to accord Egonu this recognition so quickly after the war could easily be read as an act in the spirit of political reconciliation avowed by the government or, perhaps, a recognition of the artist's non-partisan attitude to the war and his comment that, although his winning entry in the competition was inspired by the cruelties of the war, "an artist's job is to observe, not to comment".[31] Or, perhaps, it was simply to lay claim to an artist of international reputation and to put this to the purpose of rebuilding the country's image abroad.

Before the competition Egonu had returned to serious printmaking. In 1970 he took evening classes in etching, lithography and screen-printing at the Working Men's College in Camden Town, and he and Ronald Moody built identical presses in their studios. The affinity between Egonu's oil painting and the possibilities of the classical print — flat colours, well-defined shapes, the emphasis on line — made the transition from painting to printmaking natural.

In August 1971 Egonu finally married his friend of more than ten years, the German portrait artist Hiltrud Streicher. Streicher had conducted the first detailed interview with the artist in 1966. She had not only helped Egonu with administration, establishing some sense of order in his work and dealing with buyers and collectors, she also kept house on her earnings as a private secretary, especially while Egonu was going through a period of relative obscurity in the Sixties. Soon after the marriage, the couple moved to a house in South Kenton.

The same year Egonu published a small portfolio of five lithographs illustrating an Igbo folk story, entitled *Once Upon a Time in Ibo-Land*. The prints and story, described as an "original short

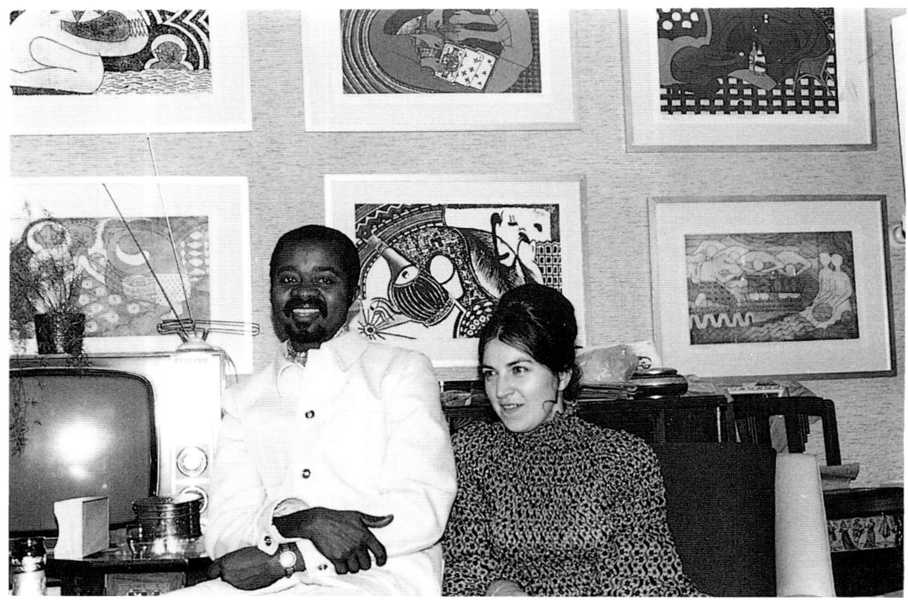

Uzo and Hiltrud Egonu, 1971

story'', were about one episode in the life of the Igbo trickster figure, the tortoise. The narrative, written by the artist himself, was plain and the language hardly exceptional, but it manifested his literary interests. In May 1970 he took the idea to Heinemann the publishers, who requested the manuscript and photographs of the prints. Heinemann declined publication on the polite grounds of production costs. However, the editor of the African section at Heinemann, James Currey, offered to arrange a cover illustration commission for the artist. In August 1971 Heinemann handed Egonu the manuscript of *Isiburu*, a novel by the Nigerian writer Elechi Amadi, for illustration. Thus began a period of serious engagement in book illustration and design that occupied the artist throughout the early Seventies and provided much needed income. During the period he designed and illustrated books for Oxford University Press, Thomas Nelson & Sons Ltd, Ginn & Co Ltd, as well as Heinemann. *Once Upon a Time in Ibo-land* eventually won him a bronze award at the 'Les Artes en Europe 1971' exhibition in Brussels.

In 1972 Egonu had a solo exhibition at the newly opened Agysimba Gallery in Berlin. Between May and June 1973 Egonu had a well-received solo show of paintings, prints and book illustrations at the Commonwealth Institute in London. Writing about the works in the *Arts Review*, Cottie Burland noted vaguely but revealingly that the artist ''is of now and makes lasting beauty which pleases even before one enters the picture''.[32] The sculptor Emmanuel Jegede coined the expression ''the vision of Egonu'' which in his words ''travels deep into human emotional problems not only of his society but the entire world''.[33] Although Egonu was moving from themes deriving mainly from the war in his country to religious themes, the exhibition featured works of the war and immediate post-war period.

From 1971 Egonu began to deal with ritual and cosmological themes from the Igbo world. In a sense this period differed from the phase of nostalgia of the late Fifties and early Sixties. This period in his work manifested a combination of the sobriety of maturity, relief from the anxieties of the war years, and confidence brought by his now established artistic identity. The work no longer expressed a search, or a feeling of loss. Instead it showed a reaffirmation and understanding of the world. In an interview with Adeyeke Adeyemo mentioned in the journal *African Arts*, Egonu spoke of his wish for an ''Ibo religious revival''[34] and though he failed to elaborate on the nature or meaning of this revival, it seems that the wish was more a projection of his more settled persona than a realistic vision. It is interesting, however, that he thought of this cultural, religious revival in narrow cultural terms rather than in a vague, pan-continental form. In a sense, despite his vacillations over nation and identity in the Sixties, he was settling for a more precise cultural identity undoubtedly sharpened by the Nigeria-Biafra war. The war, after all, had thrust the Igbo nation into the international spotlight, and the inscription of Biafra in the Igbo psyche had transformed it finally into a nation, a political unit of visible form in a manner unprecedented in the people's history. Just as the anti-colonial struggle and the rise of nationalism had created a Yoruba nation out of a diversity of hitherto antagonistic groups, the events of the mid and late Sixties and most especially the war, had cohered a particularly loose group and created a semblance of cultural unity. It was this unity that formed the basis of Egonu's religious vision together with its political sub-text.

Egonu was invited to serve on the panel of judges for British entries for the World Black Festival of Arts and Culture (FESTAC) in 1977; he also received an invitation from home to be part of the Nigerian representation. The letter of invitation described him with characteristic official vagueness as "one of Nigeria's important artists", recalling the description by the Nigerian diplomat in Nairobi five years earlier. In both cases this official description betrayed a vague familiarity, a feeling that although the artist was known in his country, this was only by a handful of people, and official circles only knew him by reputation rather than through direct contact with his work.

And yet, not only was the invitation and recognition from home dear to Egonu, he also looked forward with great excitement to the opportunity to visit Nigeria. The period was one of general excitement as artists, cultural practitioners and politicians prepared for the great get-together. The United Kingdom contingent pledged their determination to "make a major contribution to the festival and one which reflects the life-style and artistic activities of black people in the UK".[35]

Egonu finally travelled to Nigeria for FESTAC, his first visit in thirty-one years. For him it was a particularly significant experience, like returning from exile. "When I arrived in Nigeria", he recalled in a conversation in 1990, "for the two days I was in Lagos, believe me, it felt like setting a bird free from a cage." For him the return was also the fulfilment of a long-held dream, and the reception accorded him in Nigeria gave him a feeling of rehabilitation. However, this moment of glory was to be rather shorter than he had planned. On the second day of his trip he went down with flu, a very rare ailment in tropical weather, and had to be flown back to Europe before the festival got under way. And if he thought of returning to Nigeria soon afterwards, events and incidents in his life in the next few years would make the chances rather very slim.

The 1970s came to an end with Egonu's name firmly established in international art circles. From the BBC Morning Show prize in 1970 to invitations to participate in the world's most prestigious graphic art events, he had worked his way to prominence. A rather uniquely worded letter from Rudolph Mayer, organiser of the Internationale Buchkunst-Ausstellung, Leipzig, in 1976, invited him to participate in the exhibition, designed to ''show which are the means in graphics and printing nowadays existing and how they can be employed with distinguished and various results by prominent artists''. But the letter noted further that the show could not be representative enough should the organisers ''renounce to your giving a contribution''.[36] As a printmaker Egonu had, after all, won some of the important prizes in cross-cultural, international competitions within and outside Europe. Logically one could claim that with these his reputation was established on the scene of international contemporary art.

The 1970s had been Egonu's printmaking decade, just as the 1960s were given almost completely to oil painting. And although he and Moody had built woodcut and etching presses, his preference in the 1970s was for etching, a medium whose appeal was profoundly influenced by his exposure to the etchings of Dürer and Rembrandt. For him the etchings of the two European masters were unassailable in their impressionable vigour and ''the sensibility and simplicity of lines''. Also, etching, more than any other printmaking technique, yielded most easily and effectively to his own love for the simple statement, and gave him room to explore what he described in 1966 as ''the poetry of lines''. The possibility of direct drawing on the plate and of achieving the most interesting textures are the strengths of etching, and Egonu's move towards textures and monochrome from the 1970s made this the perfect medium.

But etching has its hazards. Without the correct equipment, the technique could indeed be fatal. Not only are the acid baths dangerous upon contact with the skin, but fumes from oxidation in the etching process are dangerous both through inhalation and to the eyes.

Apparently, Egonu was not sufficiently protected against the latter, and gradually throughout the 1970s the fumes began to damage his eyes. By 1979 cataracts had developed in both eyes, and with impaired vision he began his period of "Painting in Darkness".[37]

So severely impaired was his vision that he could no longer see his own work or palette, and had to mix colours by memory. To get an idea of the arrangement of elements on a painting he would roll up a black tube through which he would peer at the work in progress. Preliminary drawings on canvas would gradually fade away before he could apply colour. Interestingly, it was during this period of 'darkness' that he created some of his most colourful and memorable works: the celebrated and multiple prize-winning screenprints, his socio-philosophical series, 'Stateless People', and the cycle of nature studies, 'The Four Seasons'. And it was in this difficult state that he moved into a new decade.

In March 1981 Egonu represented Africa on a jury for the UNESCO Poster competition for that year. He visited Paris for the assignment and his contributions are recorded in the minutes of the jury meeting in Paris on March 16, 1981. What is interesting is how the artist could have carried out this assignment with his failing sight. A portion of the minutes of the jury notes: "Mr Egonu felt that... since a calender performs twelve months of service, it must be worthy of a long look."[38] A bitter irony since the artist could no longer sustain a long look at any work without it fading into greyness.[39]

Egonu nonetheless continued to work and in 1981 took part in a number of group exhibitions and international competitions including the International Biennial of Graphic Art in Yugoslavia, the Seoul International Print Biennial at the National Museum of Modern Art, Seoul, and the second National Exhibition of Modern British Prints in Blackpool. He produced sketches of ideas for paintings and a few paintings, but the meaning of painting had changed for him. Not only did the personal significance of creative work deepen for him, he also found that working was not a luxury but a necessity for both his material and spiritual survival in the circumstances. Painting in this "period of darkness", he wrote later, "lifted [his] morals".[40]

In April and May 1982, Egonu's screenprints were shown in a group exhibition to mark the tenth anniversary of *Okike*, the literary journal and cultural foundation which the novelist Chinua Achebe founded in Nsukka, Nigeria. The exhibition featured original works of artists who had contributed illustrations to the journal in the past, among them prominent African artists such as Skunder Borghossian, Malagantana Valente, Nja Madoui, and Bruce Onobrakpeya. Although Egonu's works had not previously appeared in the journal, four of his new colour screenprints were exhibited as a celebration and homage. The *Okike* exhibition was put together by the journal's art editor, the poet and painter Obiora Udechukwu, a friend and great admirer of the artist who described him in the exhibition brochure as "the doyen of African artists in London and perhaps the finest African painter".[41]

Early in 1985, a prospect that Egonu had always looked forward to in his career, that of having a show in Nigeria, materialised if only in a modest form. An exhibition of 22 original etchings, screenprints and lithographs, his first ever solo show in Nigeria, was curated by the painter Obiora Udechukwu for the Ana Gallery in Nsukka, and was opened by Nigerian publishing tycoon Abdulaziz Ude, a collector of the artist's work. Although Egonu was not present for the opening, the exhibition was a homecoming of sorts. Ude called on the University of Nigeria to "make it possible for Uzo Egonu to return home by establishing a new chair in this department [of Fine and Applied Arts] and appointing him a Visiting Professor of Arts."[42] Although this was not followed up, it renewed Egonu's enthusiasm to visit home, and his hopes for a bigger show in Nigeria soon after.

In July a second exhibition of his work opened at the Galerie Neue Horizonte in Frankfurt. While in Germany for the exhibition, he had a severe heart attack. As he was convalescing, he had a repeat attack in London the next year, and was given a few months to live. Although he speaks very little about this period, he has described it as his "traumatic experience",[43] one that changed his lifestyle and further deepened his attitude to life. He began to put his papers and estate together, organise his works and sketches, and to reorder his life and habits. He spent more time indoors except on the mandatory walks recommended by doctors and, although he took the medical prediction on his fate seriously, he had some conviction that with proper attention to his health he could beat it. During the period he continued to work on his cycle of philosophical paintings, 'Will Knowledge Safeguard Freedom?', and out of the experience would later come another cycle of work aptly titled 'A New Lease of Life'.

On New Year's Day, 1986, the Greater London Council set up an omnibus exhibition of Egonu's work, 'Uzo Egonu Now 1986', in three venues. 'Stateless People' from the period of his sight problem, went on show at the Royal Festival Hall in London. A retrospective of his entire printmaking *oeuvre* was organised at the Black Art Gallery, moving afterwards to the People's Gallery. Although this celebratory exhibition did not arouse the interest of the mainstream art press and establishment in Britain, as indeed Egonu's work had ceased to since the beginning of the Seventies despite his successes and international acclaim, it was embraced by a new audience relatively unfamiliar with the artist's work. The Black Art Gallery show gave the black community in London an opportunity to see Egonu's work, and though slightly bewildered, a growing black press took warmly to it. Rave, if somewhat superficial, reviews appeared in *The Voice, Chic, The Weekly Gleaner, African Concord, Westindian Digest, West Indian World*, and many others. Most of the journalists were young and had no knowledge of the artist's existence, and in the atmosphere of the growing Black Arts movement in Britain in the early Eighties, they found the artist and his reputation a significant source of affirmation. Particular attention was paid to Egonu's affinities with African art and the strong sense of home in his work, elements with which his new audience easily identified. Despite his prominence in the art world, especially in the graphic arts, Egonu was a discovery, and though he had identified and seen himself as an artist for his community for two decades, this audience was only beginning to identify with him. In the next few years Egonu aligned himself more closely to the black art community, becoming more involved with black and younger artists. In 1987 he took part in 'Double Vision', an exhibition of ten black artists at Christchurch Mansion in Ipswich.

In 1989 he participated in *The Other Story*, the exhibition curated by the artist and writer Rasheed Araeen with the aim "to examine historically the contributions of Afro-Asian artists to the mainstream development in the post-war period in Britain, and to show that their achievement is part of the history of modern art".[44] Although a few artists abstained from the exhibition, Egonu was only too knowledgeable in its significance. Despite his health he was at the opening with his wife, holding a copy of a particularly inflammatory and dismissive preview of the exhibition by the British critic Brian Sewell. Sewell's scornful review only underlined the point of the exhibition. In a conversation on the exhibition in 1990 Egonu recalled the fate of his friend Francis Souza who rose to the top of the British art scene in the late 1950s and early 1960s. "Then," said Egonu, "after some years, that's full stop. No one wanted to know him. Yes. Because he was non-European. When the media start ignoring the artist, they don't want to know, it ends. That's the thing. Everyone comes to the same boat.'' That was his own fate.

Egonu's experiences in Europe, what he describes as his ''metaphorical journey'', are not easily summarised. He sold his work mainly through private agents, especially after the galleries began to lose enthusiasm. He worked regularly even in poor health, striving strenuously to live by his art. Although he describes himself as ''more or less invisible'', he knew visibility at a stage in his career, and that visibility may have suffered less from his failing health than from the intransigence of the British art establishment.

Egonu continues to work in his South Kenton house where he lives with his wife and two cats. As for his place as an artist, he is quite satisfied with his efforts. In a press interview in 1990 he said:

> As a non-European artist in Europe, it has not been easy at all. But I feel I've achieved something. In this society there's a time one can't be denied what one has achieved. And I have achieved something.[45]

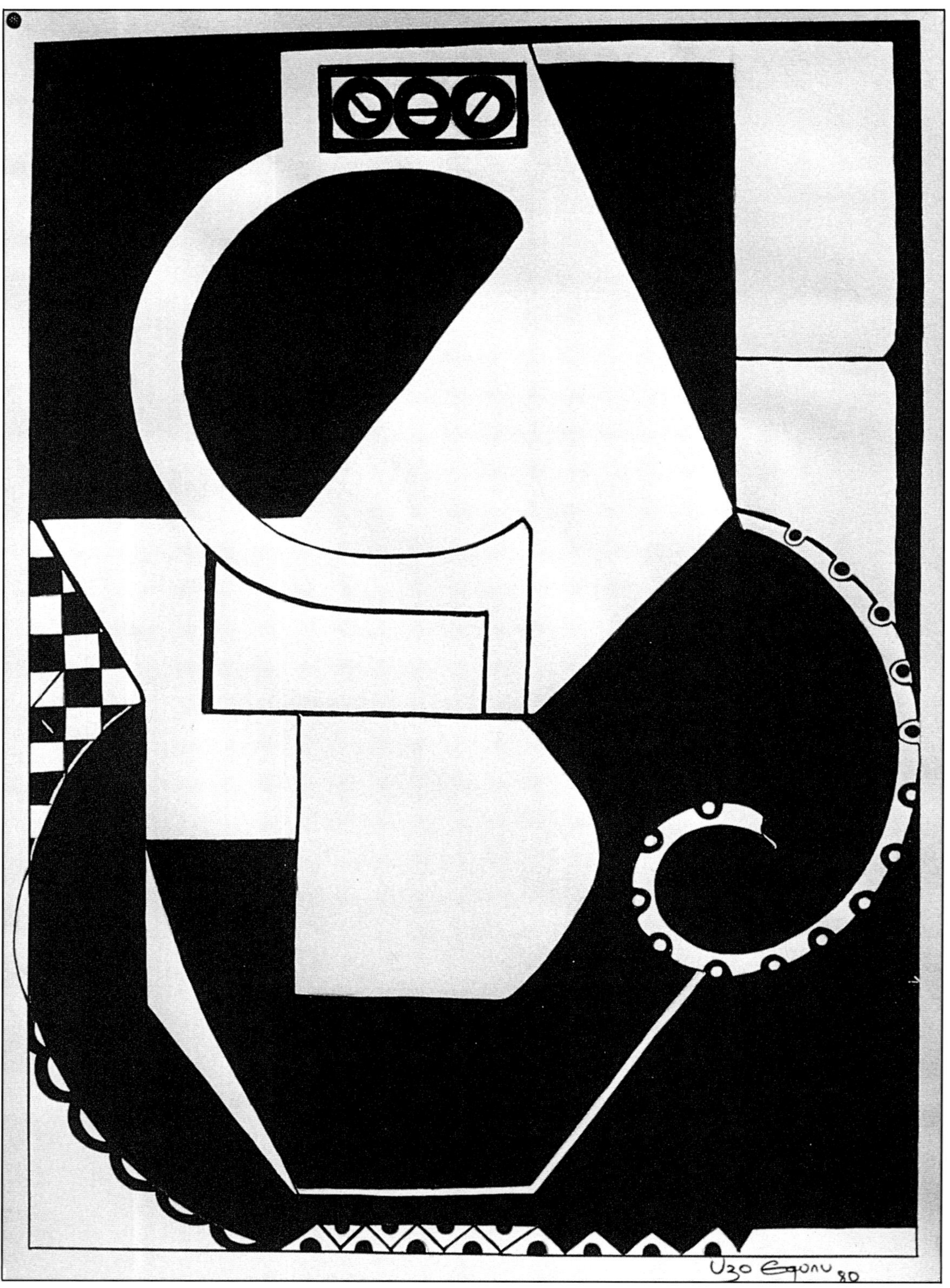
Uzo Egonu 80

The Egonu Aesthetic

Egonu's search for a personal aesthetic began shortly after Camberwell and reached a watershed in the mid-1960s, and this is especially noticeable in the painting, *Nude Woman Combing Her Hair.*[1]

Nude Woman Combing Her Hair belongs to a group of works done by the artist after his 1963 painting, *Mask with Musical Instruments,* which he described as his 'Bridge' to a new phase. This phase began early in 1964.[2] *Mask*, according to the artist, revealed to him "different possibilities in the art of painting" and changed his artistic vision. It was the effective milestone in his transition from what may be termed his 'naivist' period. Egonu has noted that his work prior to 1963 was influenced by his student days.[3] To come into his own, however, he had to invert the hold of that influence and, with it, much of the western academic tradition. In order to do this Egonu first rearmed himself with an even deeper knowledge and understanding of that tradition, after which he proceeded most calculatedly to subject it to his own needs. For the rest of his career he would maintain his claims to that tradition, quoting and subverting it at will, and eventually synthesising it with the canons of his African heritage and the demands of his own personal vision, acknowledging it and yet dismissing it. In this way he defined his place in the metropolis and in history as not so much that of the impure and ambiguous, the 'mongrel' of Derek Walcott's reading inescapably abandoned at the crossroads of modernity, but as one of the pioneers of a different modernism based on the recontextualisation of the western tradition.

***Vase in Interior*, 1980**
Gouache on paper
76 x 56 cm

The Restless Years

Although he identifies 1964 as his "period of restlessness",[4] Egonu's effort to fashion a personal aesthetic began before 1963. His stylistic development can be divided into specific chronological phases. After his tour of Europe, visiting galleries and museums and studying works of the great masters, western and African, he returned spiritually saturated from what was an invaluable and most enthralling experience. For Egonu, however, his tours in Europe were only an extension of the academy, an adventure into secrets which were only accessible through a first hand, visual and mental confrontation with the masters and their works, and a dialogue with their methods. Such experience fills a young artist with confidence as well as a redefined sense of discipline, but not always a new vision. On the contrary, new discoveries may arouse self-doubt and dissatisfaction, leading to possible frustration, or to a determined subversion of the newly acquired knowledge.

Egonu's study tours resulted in the latter, for although he continued to work in a style akin to that of his immediate post-Camberwell paintings until the end of the 1950s, there was evidence of growing dissatisfaction with his work. Egonu destroyed about thirty works in 1959 so he could re-use the canvas. According to Hiltrud Streicher, he would load them into the huge bath at the Goldhurst Terrace flat, and soak them in water, then she would scrub off the paint and hang the canvas to dry. Although this process could be attributed to hardship, it seems nevertheless very extreme. There is a greater likelihood that Egonu had rather little faith in certain works to want to overpaint them, and the rather drastic measure suggests a general dissatisfaction rather than the usual inclination of artists once in a while to destroy a work they consider unsuccessful.

It is safe to suggest therefore that the destruction of the paintings may not be completely unrelated to the frustrating experience of discovering in them a hitherto unrevealed handicap, namely, the inability to arrest the overwhelming experience of the artist's contact with both European and African art traditions, and fashion out of this a new and satisfactory aesthetic. Conscious syncretism does present a challenge which is not only technical but also psychological as the artist struggles to create a sense of consistency and clarity amid a barrage of references. Confrontation with masterpieces is in itself an essentially frustrating experience for the ambitious young artist since it poses a challenge to match their technical virtuosity.

One very interesting development here is that of contact with Paris as a result of the confrontation which Egonu had with the European masters, including Picasso and Miró, and masterpieces of African art, as well as with Paris itself, a confrontation with which Picasso himself had to deal. Arianna Huffington has described Picasso's mood in Paris in 1901 as that of ''existential nothingness'',[5] one of ''not knowing what other road to try''. It is also interesting that Huffington observes a connection between the growing darkness and torment in Picasso and the advent of Père Manyac, the art dealer, into his life. According to her, the artist was in a process of rebellion against the orderliness which Manyac had brought into his work and life. It is unclear whether Hiltrud's entry into Egonu's life at the period of the destroyed paintings could have contributed to his unconfessed frustration deriving, perhaps, from an unconscious striving to satisfy a scrutinising presence, a process which is both human and aesthetic.

The Period of Nostalgia

From 1960 Egonu moved into what might be called his years of nostalgia. As if marooned and rootless, he began to clutch at strands of memory from his childhood in Africa. Egonu had been in London for approximately eleven years, and in Britain for sixteen, enough time for someone to find a remarkable wall between him and home. In that period he had not visited home, and his links with it were considerably damaged. The contact which Camden Town and the West African Students Union had provided during his years at Camberwell was no longer there, and the community which was available for him then was no more within reach, thus accentuating his natural disposition as a loner. There seems to be a vital connection between the frustrations of aesthetic development within an overwhelming foreign culture, and the desperation to return home, to escape. The moment of awakening to the reality of difference and awareness of the self could be likened to that of a swimmer's awareness of drowning when they must clutch at every lean straw within reach to avoid sinking.

Egonu's awareness of his own loneliness and vulnerability within not only his physical environs but even more so the cultural landscape underlined his sense of difference. Coming into contact with classical African art prompted him to conduct a silent comparison between it and the western tradition as he sought validation and indeed salvation in the strength of his own heritage. By concluding through

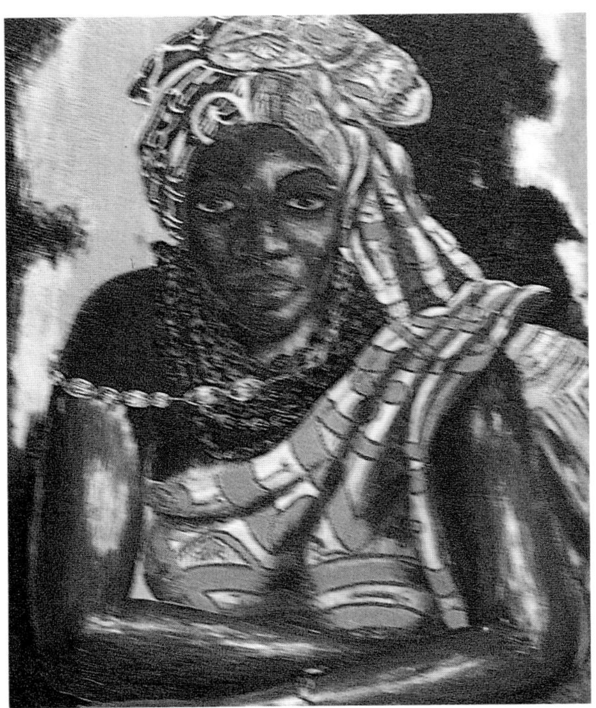

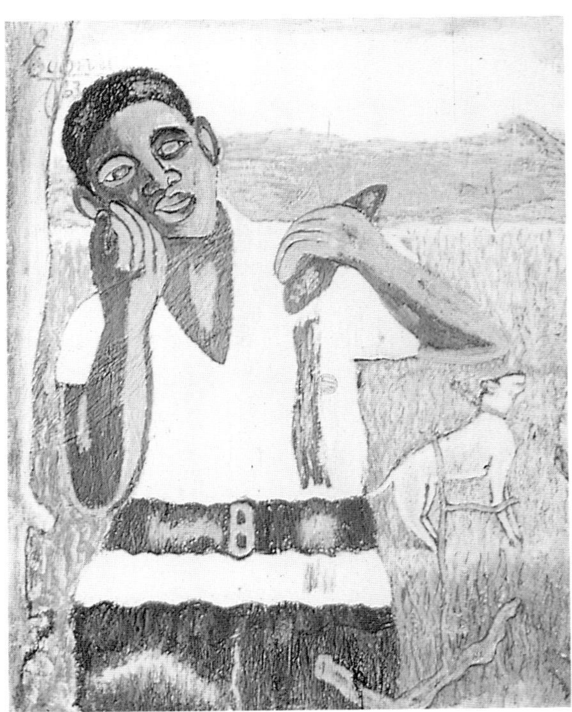

***Portrait of a Nigerian Girl*, 1962**
Oil on canvas
124 x 99 cm

***Boy Eating Sweetcorn*, 1963**
Oil on canvas
75 x 56 cm

his observations that this heritage was just as accomplished as any other, he found reason also to believe in his own abilities to reach levels of artistic accomplishment equal to his contemporaries in the West without necessarily sharing their visions. He realised that each culture and artistic tradition derives its fulfilment, greatness and vision mainly from within even as it references the outside. He also concluded that alongside this essential ethnocentrism, whether thematic or formalistic, lies a discriminate eclecticism, what one might term the syncretist imperative without which a culture is bound to atrophy. With these conclusions Egonu fashioned an appropriate framework for relating both to modernism and the West, and to his own traditions.

The socio-political ambience of the late Fifties and early Sixties, often referred to as the period of the African dawn, played an equally crucial role in this process. The political and aesthetic philosophy of Negritude, founded earlier in the century and championed by notable African scholars and artists, was beginning to wane amid controversy and critical interrogation.[6] The nationalist struggles in Africa were beginning to reconfigure the history of the 20th century. The emergence of the independent state of Ghana, for instance, coincided with a global consciousness which soon manifested in the civil rights movement in the United States.

The growth of nationalist fervour, characterised by nostalgia among expatriate populations, coincided with Egonu's efforts to reconstruct himself within the West, and inevitably influenced his strategies. One of the earliest paintings from the period, *A Boy with a Budgerigar*, 1960, was inspired by memories of his father and brothers. In the painting the budgerigar represents his father's parrot which was much loved by the boys, while the boy represents his brothers. Of another painting from 1960, *A Boy Eating Sweetcorn*, he says: "I chose the subject because of nostalgic feelings for my country; the feeling of being far away from home evoked these images in my mind."[7] These were followed by a series of genre pictures which found their subjects in Africa, like the 1961 *Village Blacksmith in Iboland*, *Portrait of a Nigerian Girl*, 1961, *Portrait of a Guinea Girl*, 1962, and versions of *Boy with a Budgerigar*, 1963, and *A Boy Eating Sweetcorn*, 1963.

Although realism was not his greatest strength, Egonu worked

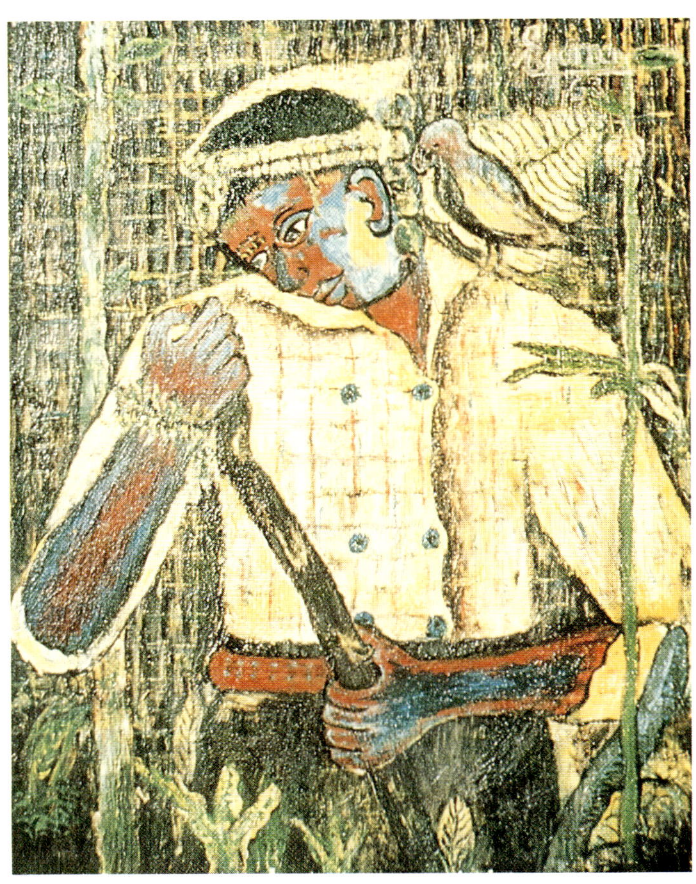

***Boy with a Budgerigar*, 1963**
Oil on canvas
94 x 71 cm

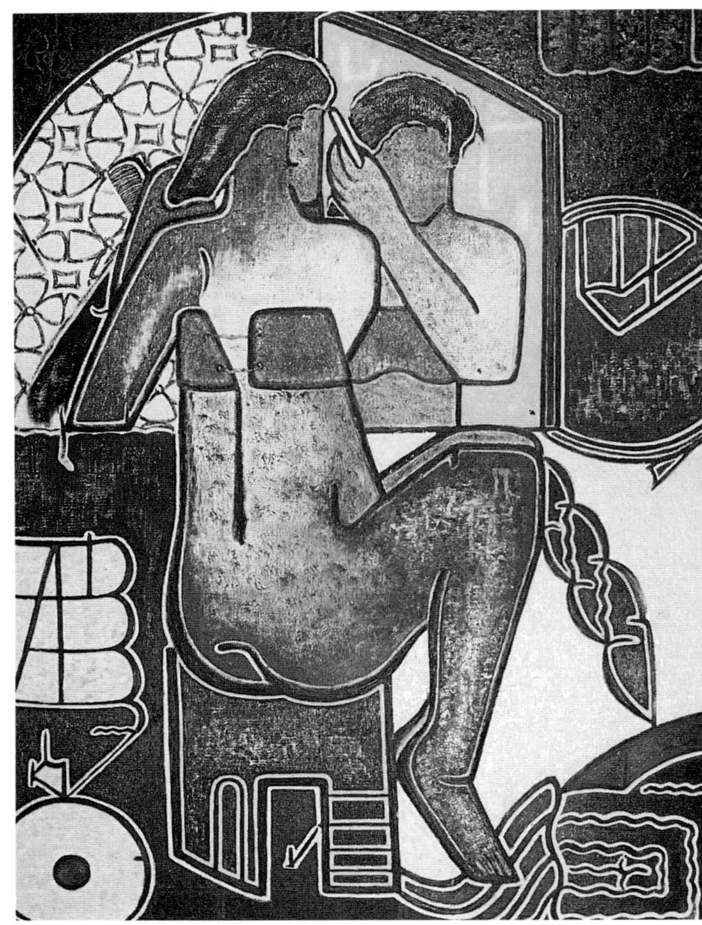

***Woman Before a Mirror*, 1965**
Oil on canvas
104 x 103 cm

to improve his life drawing around this period. At the same time, the paintings show an effort to subvert the very canons he was taught and show him seeking greater freedom of imagination. In *A Boy Eating Sweetcorn* the dog in the background is merely outlined without any concern for naturalistic depth, modelling or colour, whilst in *Boy with a Budgerigar* local colour is disregarded in favour of a polychromy guided more by design instinct than by objective observation. According to Egonu he had little regard for 'aesthetics' at this stage, aesthetics in this case meaning western canons of representation. The aim was to discard once and for all whatever inhibitions and restrictions the academy imposed, and thus clear the way for a true self-discovery and definition. For him the mimetic traditions of the academy had to be disobeyed, ignored, twisted and ridiculed. Reflecting on this in 1989 he said rather mockingly, "Twenty years ago the Royal Academy here... would insist [on looking] at things in a particular way, as if you were competing with 2nd century art. And you wonder, why don't they engage a photographer and be done with it?''[8]

It is interesting, however, that, while Egonu fervidly defied academic tendencies, he nevertheless continually quoted aspects of western art, thus locating himself squarely within its modernist tendencies. Not only were his attitudes to mimesis truly modernist, but several paintings of this period made clear reference to specific masters.

In *Nude Combing Her Hair* of 1964, Egonu quotes Degas. Speaking about the painting in 1965 he points to Degas's *toilette* paintings as his 'direct' source. Furthermore, he insists that it is inconceivable that an artist should paint the nude ''just for the sake of following the artistic tradition'' or ''because it is just like painting a book or a table''. And yet, according to him, the appeal of the nude lies in its ''many possibilities... possibilities that the male nude lacks''.[9] The grounds for this argument, which are that ''there are more interesting lines in the female figure than in the male...'', also give him away as a victim of tradition. Egonu's argument, we discover,

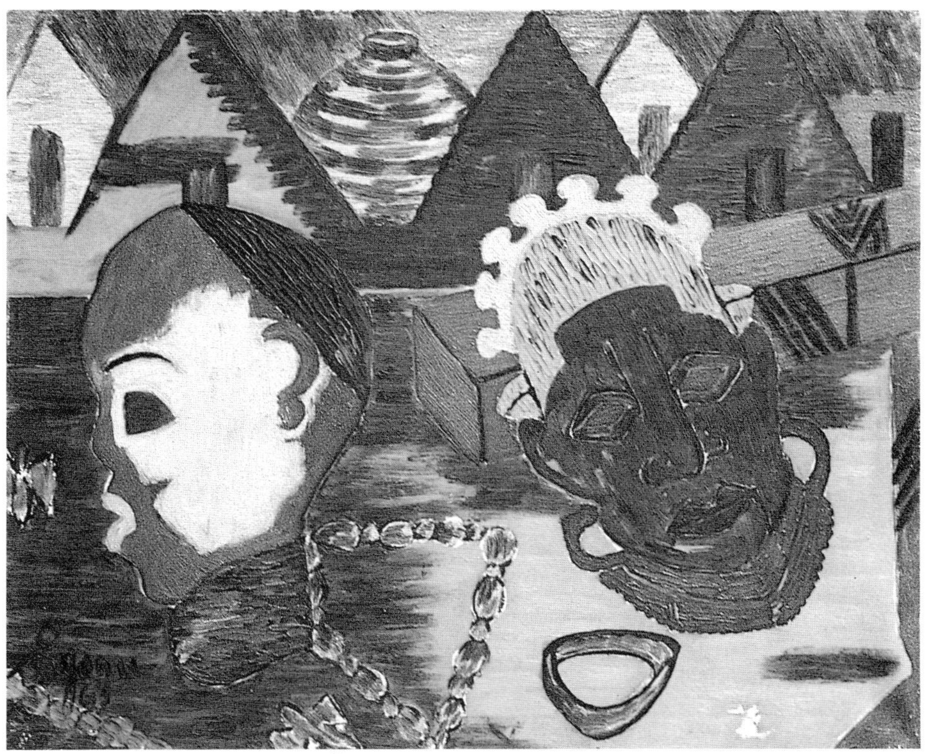

African Masks, 1963
Oil on canvas
51 x 61 cm

derives directly from Hogarth's theory of the 'Line of Beauty', proposed in the *Analysis of Beauty* of 1753, which contended that, with the help of stays, the female figure exhibits "such a perfect, precise, serpentine line", a line of beauty the like of which cannot be found in the male form, naked or clothed.[10]

In *Woman before a Mirror*, 1965, we see that the woman's dress is a cross between a nightgown and a corset with visible draws on the back. It is clear that the painting was not modelled from life, but derived from earlier interpretations of the subject by other artists, the corset revealing the artist's sources as clearly western. By employing recognisably modernist strategies of representation such as polychromatism, conceptual rather than mimetic detail, and an

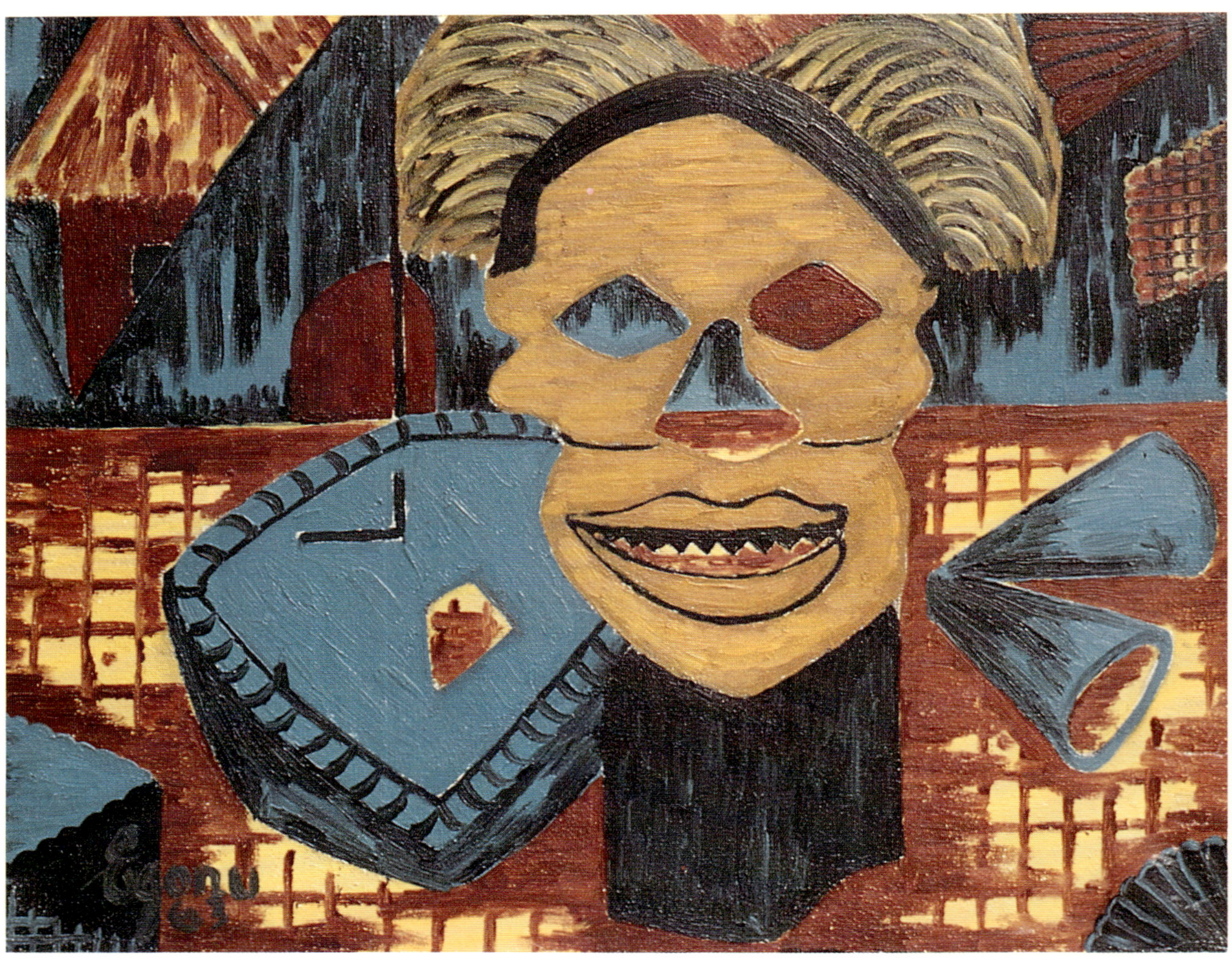

***Mask with Musical Instruments*, 1963**
Oil on canvas
51 x 61 cm

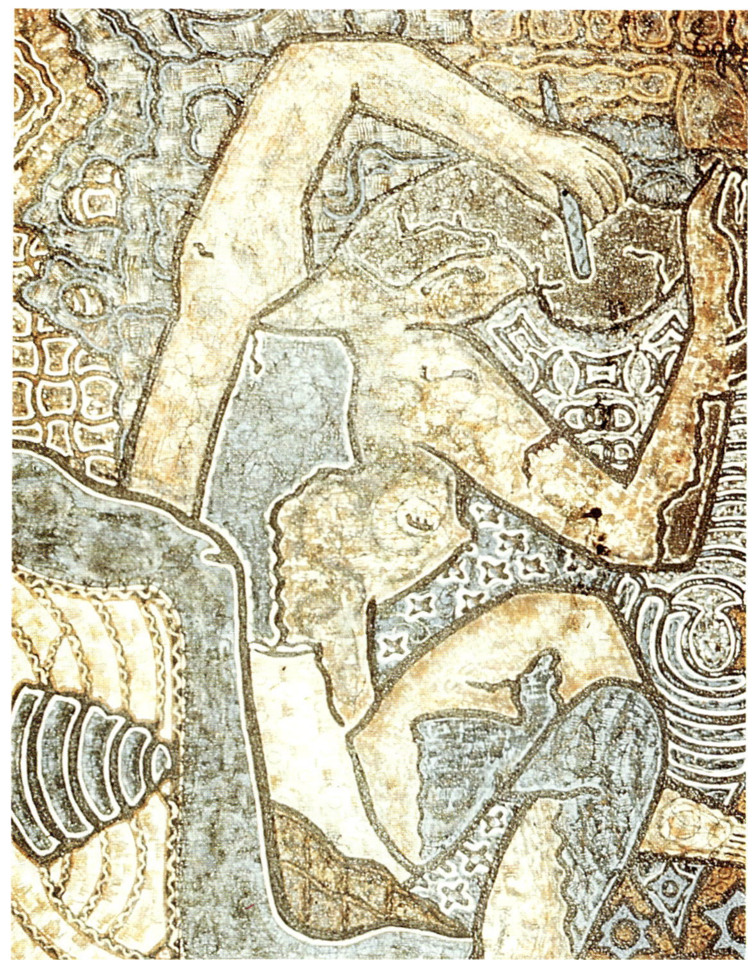

***Nude Combing Her Hair*, 1964**
Oil on canvas
122 x 92 cm

increasing regard for texture, Egonu located himself at the centre of modernism even as he sought through his thematic particularity to broaden the borders of the western modernist space; indeed, he sought to emphasise that modernism is the rightful heritage of the African artist.

In the paintings from this period, therefore, Egonu is able to appease his nationalist cravings while also contributing to the redefinition of modernism. With time only certain elements of the work from this period would remain as he transcended the demands of self-definition and, having clearly established his place within the epoch, moved on to other concerns.

The late Nostalgia period in Egonu's work is characterised by a logical relocation of the tropes of cultural difference. Beginning with

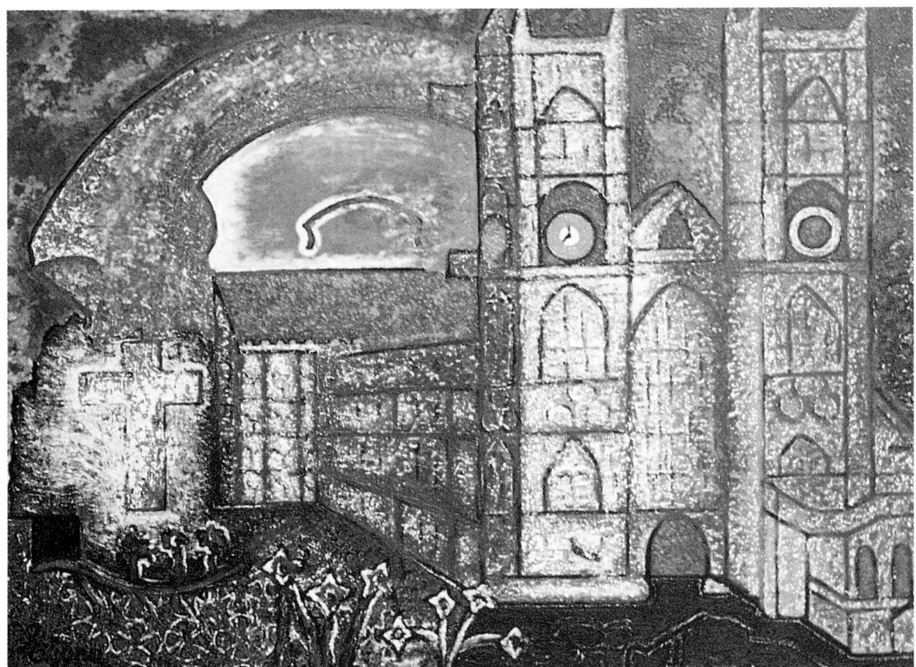

***Westminster Abbey*, 1966**
Oil on canvas
71 x 92 cm

the painting *African Masks* in 1963, he moved on from genre to work with more symbolic content, replacing the narrative strategy of the earlier paintings. In these later works Egonu began to figure cultural symbols, especially masks, which he describes as "metaphors".[11] In *African Masks* he sets the central motif against a background of huts. The composition is bolder, more carefree and loose than in earlier work. Dimension, perspective and modelling are almost completely done away with. Form is represented not by modelling but through crudely blocked-in positive shapes hedged in with thick line. One mask, alluding to a well-known Bini ivory mask, is stained with arbitrary patches of colour, whilst in another, more of a head with a skull cap than a mask, form is only suggested through a few definitive lines and darker stains.

Closely scrutinised, this painting and subsequent ones from the same period reveal a deliberately limited palette of very basic, often earth colours, defined by a broad symbolic essence: blue, yellow and rock burnt sienna, all of which are related to the specific environment they evoke, but more importantly belong to the palette of wall painters from the artist's Igbo culture.[12] We find the same reference in *Boy with a Budgerigar* and *Boy Eating Sweetcorn,* both of 1963.

In *Still-Life with Mask in Landscape*, 1963, the principle of free organisation of design elements recurs and the artist chooses his objects without regard for formal homogeneity. There is spontaneity and no attempt at verisimilitude. The central and unifying element in the painting is the provenance of the objects depicted, frames of reference which seem to derive directly from the artist's Igbo origins. Each object is chosen as an allusive sign, deposited in place of a whole corpus of anecdotes, rituals and contexts. And yet, these are presented under titles which allude to the artist's immediate environment and his knowledge of the western tradition; a sort of merger with the evoked cultural heritage as the core and the western element signified in the title as the frame, the 'take-away' wrap.

There is another related connection which Egonu points out in his interview of 1966 with Streicher. According to him, not only did he choose the mask in this series as a "symbol of the African past" and an inseparable part of African art, but also because he was "thinking of the influence African masks had on modern art, especially on Cubism".[13] By approaching modernism as only one of several heritages and locating it within his space, Egonu had already justified whatever elements of eclecticism may be found in his work. This was his claim on modernism. In defining his place and identity he had moved from the extremist and naive to the affirmative, from the sentimental to the intellectual.

Egonu has described the late Nostalgia period in his work as his 'window' period. It opened up his vision and he was finally able to

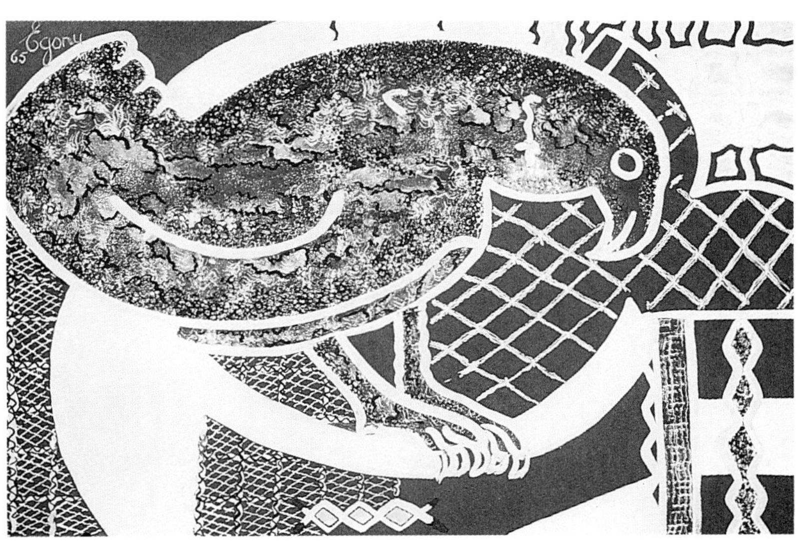

***Goldie in Captivity*, 1965**
Gouache on paper
52 x 78 cm

Collage — Cuttings from Magazines, 1965
Gouache on paper
51 x 61 cm

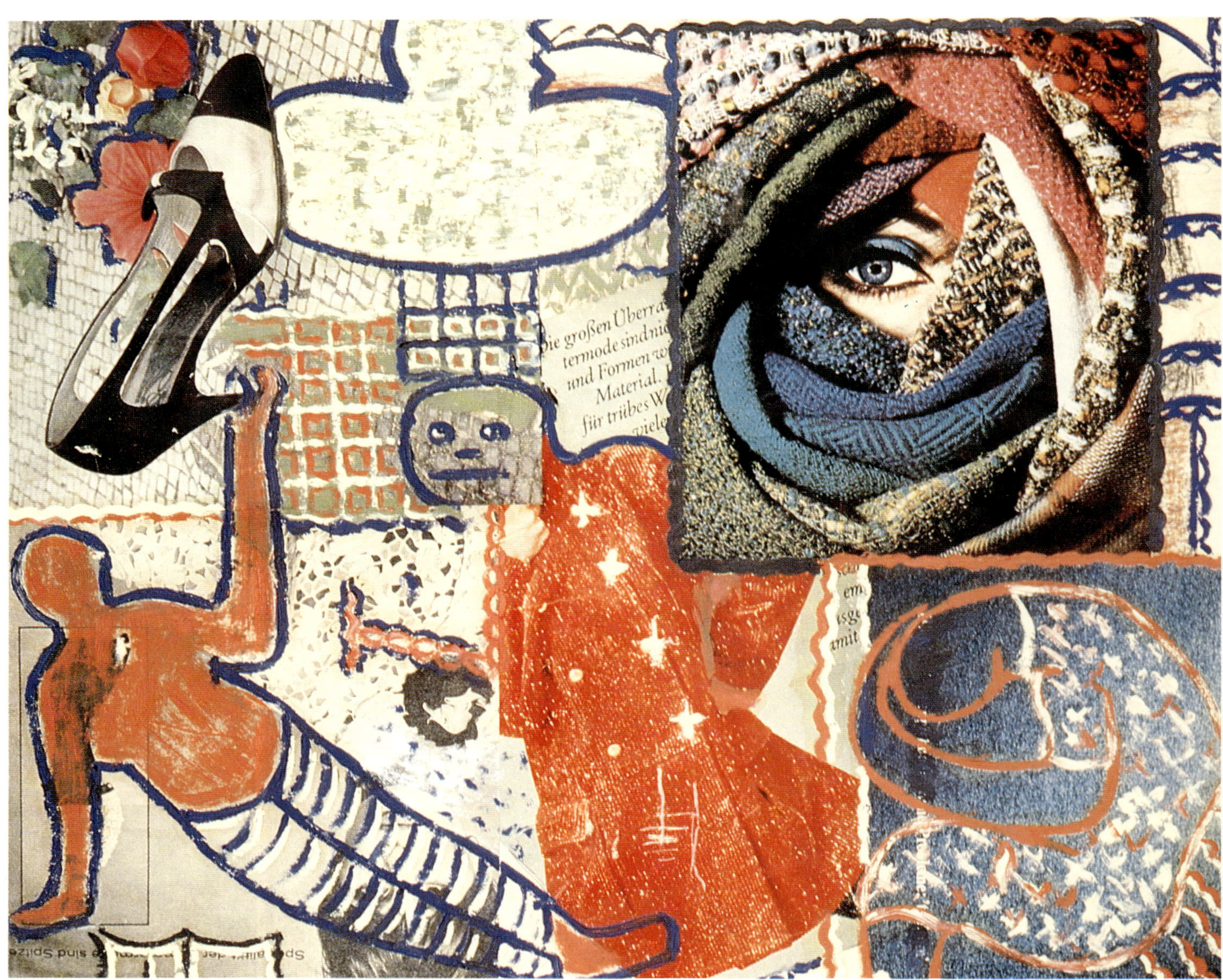

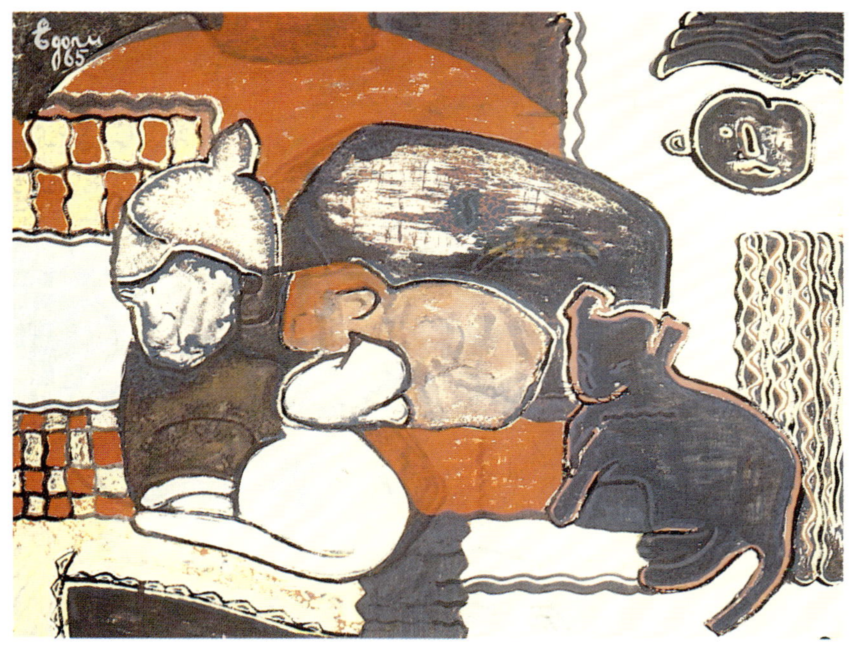

***Cat and Her Kittens*, 1965**
Gouache on paper
52 x 63 cm

see his way through to an aesthetic persona. His frames of reference became clearer and these, rather than impose restraint, legitimised and encouraged experimentation and exploration. As soon as he established that defining his place was not a process of choice between Africa and Europe, but rather one of recognising modernism as a mongrel and locating himself within it, the window was open.

The Bridge

Still-Life with Mask led to *Mask with Musical Instruments*, the last painting in the series and a landmark at the end of the Nostalgia period. Egonu identifies *Mask with Musical Instruments* as one of the 'bridges' in his development, one that served him "not only for crossing in order to explore, but also as a basis for experiment".[14] It led to the group of paintings of 1964 which belong to another phase in his work. In purely technical terms, the painting does not differ from his other work of 1963. The limited palette of *Still-Life with Mask* is retained, for instance. To the right of the composition a landscape is rotated 90 degrees so that it stands on its side. The immediate background in what is in fact a flat plane, is worked into grids to echo the bodywork of a thumb piano in the top right corner. The mask in the painting is a deliberate cross between the ugly and the beautiful, perhaps copied from a photograph but completely reinterpreted, its form reduced to cones and the suggestion of planes. The mask is garish, yet it seems to be smiling.

Egonu has said that his interest in working with masks lies in the observation that the countenance of every mask in African art is deliberate and symbolic, and not at all simply mimetic, or a mere representation of beauty or the beast. As a little boy borne on his father's shoulders to masking events, he was intrigued by the 'aesthetic' diversity of the masks on display. According to him the masks' 'artistic beauty' resides in their design and the interplay of formal elements. With this as a point of reference Egonu began to prioritise design in his paintings and this formal strategy has remained fundamental to his work.

In addition to masks, Egonu began a closer study of specific styles and objects of African art, especially the 9th century BC terracotta images from Nok in Northern Nigeria, and his observations led to a momentary shift towards a purely formal aesthetic. His fascination for the intricate syntheses of form in Nok terracotta pieces resulted in an element of analytical formalism in his work from 1965. In an unpublished, undated essay titled 'The Reproductions of Nok Culture Terracottas Showing: Spherical Shape, Cylindrical Shape, & Conical Shape', Egonu extols the formal sensibility of the Nok, their ability to deconstruct natural forms into shapes and geometric units, eventually resynthesising them into a new whole. For him "the creators of these works were keen observers of nature, and very much influenced by her".

Through his studies of African masks Egonu concluded that there was an invariable connectedness between art and religion. He saw African masks as essentially religious images, a position probably deeply influenced by salvage anthropology, postulations with which he was very familiar. Thus in the interview with Streicher, we find Egonu asserting that "religious images are the base of African Culture".[15] Henceforth much of his work would fall within the conceptualist, even functionalist stream. The fascination with religion would likewise be at the centre of a series of works in the early 1970s.

In masks the artist saw a strong link with the African past; beyond representing a moment or experience in the individual memory, a mask also serves as a repository of history and a symbol for the culture of its provenance. Although he had concluded that beauty resides in the resolution of design elements, form for him was now not mere design but also a vehicle of history, ideas and the individual or group experience.

After the Bridge

As he crossed his 'Bridge' into 1964, further significant changes took place in Egonu's representational strategies. First, he brought into his repertoire of 'metaphors' motifs without figural reference. In moving to the sign he advanced the process of his own abstraction of the self, the process of his personal transition from nostalgia to a defined place in the metropolis. Having attained a level of clarity and confidence in his sense of place, Egonu no longer encoded himself and his culture in the pictorial and the prosaic, but in the concise body of the sign.

Also, this advance was registered not merely in the specific motifs which we see in the paintings from 1965 but, perhaps more importantly, in the fact that Egonu had identified abstraction as a central distinguishing element of the culture within which he elected to locate himself. The artist could lift the motifs from identifiable sources or create anew, and in doing so see himself as working within a tradition.

It is safe to conclude at this point that while Egonu formulated his personal aesthetic within an identifiably modernist framework,

Northern Nigerian Landscape (A), 1964
Oil on canvas
97 x 152 cm

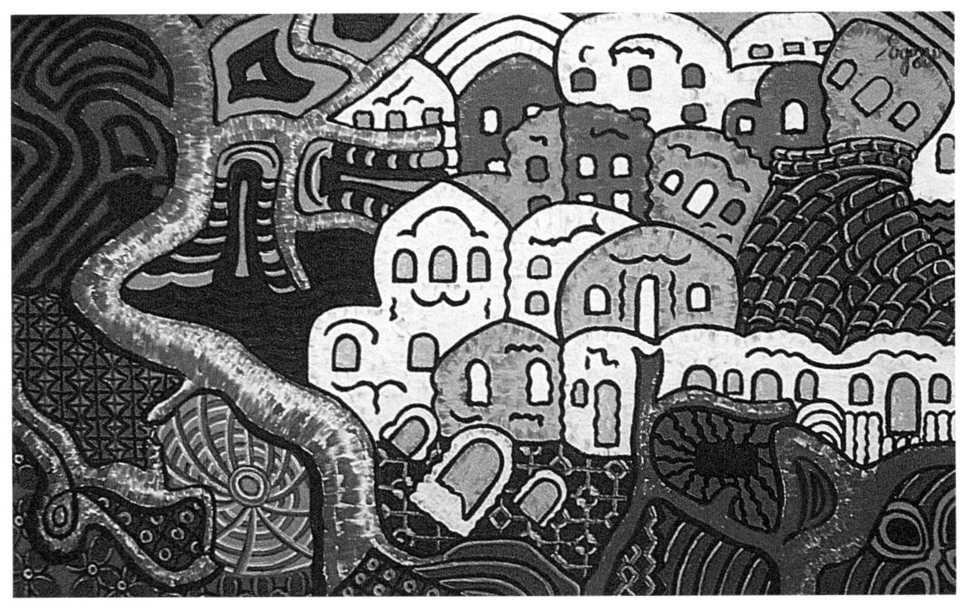

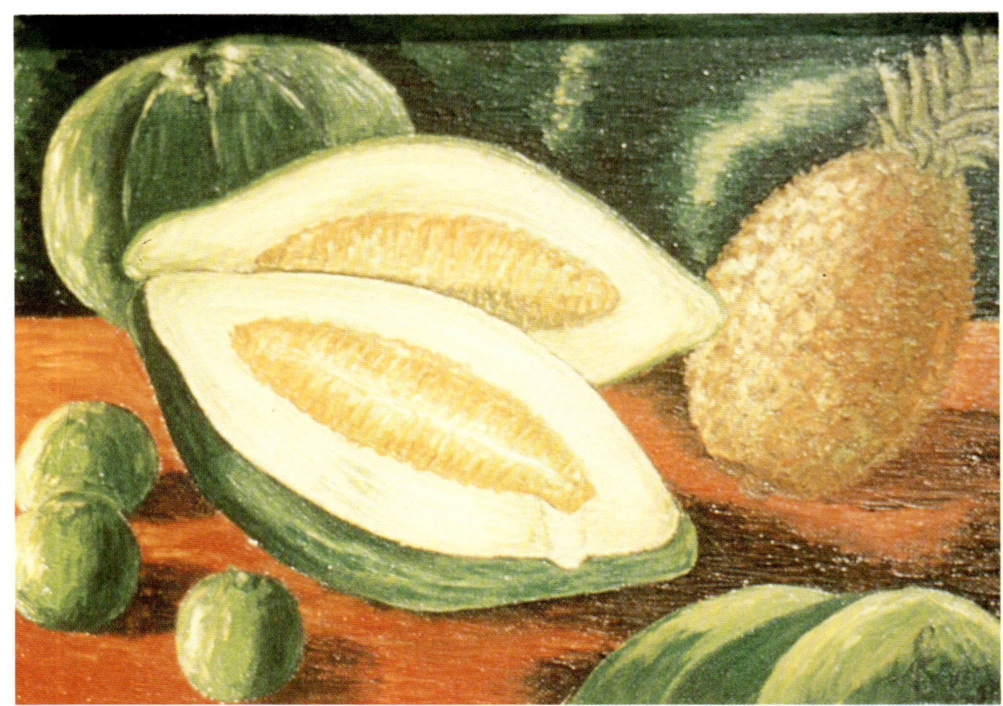

***Still- Life with Melon and Pineapple*, 1958**
Oil on canvas
94 x 131 cm

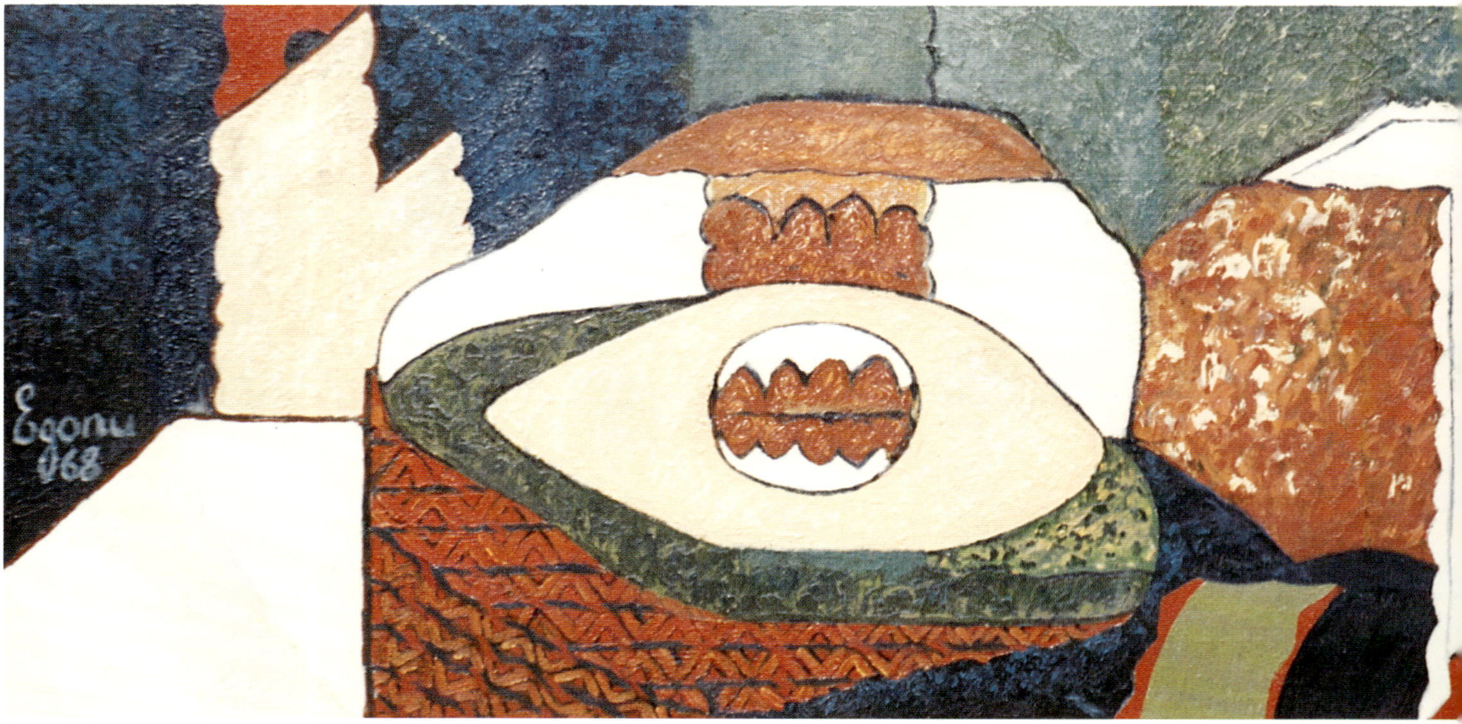

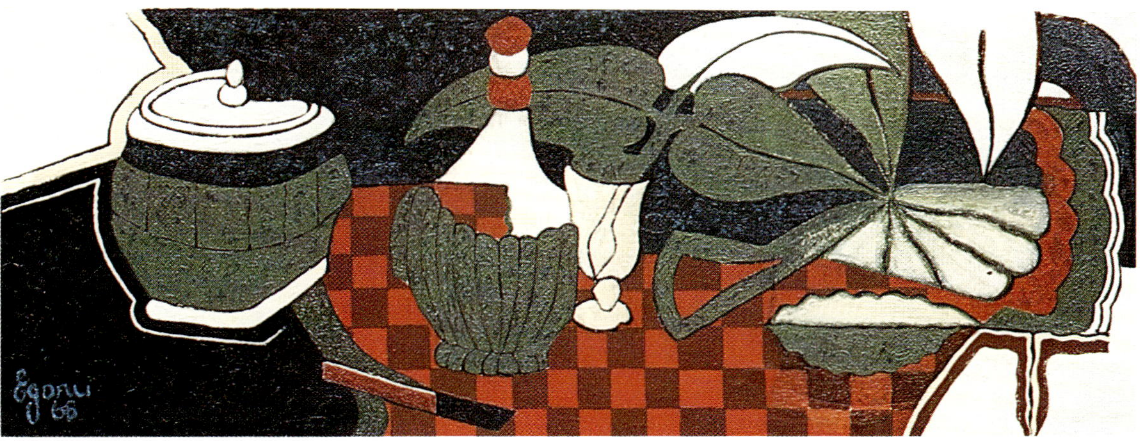

***Still-life in Tropical Garden*, 1968**
Oil on canvas
48 x 122 cm

***Still-life with Melon and Pineapple*, 1968**
Oil on canvas
48 x 122 cm

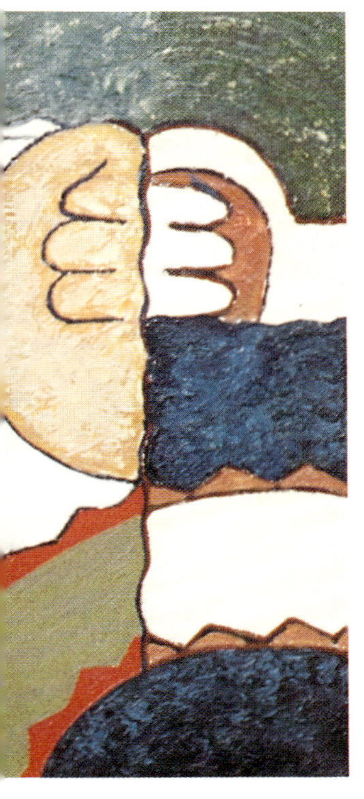

the subversion of mimesis and other received canons of representation, he also did so with a persistent intention to move beyond the confines of European modernism by establishing a special link with his own traditions. In a conversation in 1989, he mentioned that while he searched for sources and frames of reference, he knew that African cultures are ''as rich and engaging as any other'' for this purpose. In making reference to Gauguin and the fact that in all his rebellion and his subsequent adventures in the South Seas, the artist observed that Gauguin never completely departed from the academy and its canons: easel painting, received definitions of the picture plane, prevailing patterns of patronage and thematic preoccupation, materials and techniques. In all of these the western tradition remained Gauguin's frame of reference. For Egonu it was only proper that African artists should not lose themselves in the fiction of a universalist modernism. Instead, they should define a place for themselves within modernism whilst also registering the specificities of their origins.

Egonu's self-formulation in this direction is strikingly discernible in two paintings of the same subject: *Still-Life with Melon and Pineapple* of 1958 and another version of 1964. While the 1958 oil painting is a conventional still life painting in the naturalist tradition, complete with divisions of dimension and depth, perspective and strict observation of the rules of chiaroscuro and colour harmony in green and red, a faultless segmentation of the picture frame into the golden section, the diagonals carefully arranged and echoed, the 1964 painting is remarkably different. Although the range of the palette does not change much, its relatedness to the objects in the painting does so quite significantly. While in the 1958 painting the local colour of green is dominant, naturally complemented with red in the tablecloth and the yellow and ochre of the pineapple, the colours in the 1964 work have absolutely nothing to do with local colour or realist objectivity. The centre of the pineapple is painted in sienna, the body in black and the flesh in ochre. The primary concern is the mood. Even more remarkable is the way in which the objects are embedded in what is basically a complex of decorative patterns in sienna, black and ochre, more reminiscent of textile design than painting from life. There is no mimetic intent, and no narrative. The moment is everything.

Another shift in his use and interpretation of form could be seen in his prioritisation of line from the late Nostalgia period. While until 1963 Egonu's line was crude and tentative, more evident of a rebellious arbitrariness and bravura, it subsequently became more emphatic and assured, not only defining form but being form itself. In the paintings from 1964 onwards there is calculation in the manner in which line is carefully introduced, thick and rough as it is, laid down in determined paths that interweave more to create design than merely outline shapes. Thus, in *Still-Life with Melon and Pineapple*, 1964, line is the primary element: all form is interpreted as line, subordinated to and subsumed in it. Even the shapes are variations on the form of line, each one being a collection of thick marks brought together to form a shape.

In *Northern Nigerian Landscape,* one of the transitional works from the same period, the artist makes both imagistic and formalistic reference to his country but, strictly speaking, transfers elements from the still life. His palette is the same though there is a more obvious relationship between the colours and the subject. This relationship, however, is only with the subject and not individual objects in the picture: the palette is chosen to evoke a particular atmosphere rather than make a faithful representation of objects. The architecture in the landscape is plain and largely uniform, defined by apertures which again do not necessarily reflect objective reality. In the middle right side a section of patterns occurs which seems to have been lifted straight from the *Still-Life with Melon and Pineapple*. While in the earlier painting it represented the pineapple, in *Northern Nigerian Landscape* it becomes vegetation. What in the left side appears like a road is also a tree with bare branches. Each element invokes and reinforces ambiguity, thus subverting the tendency towards direct interpretation.

Depth is subdued and only its possibility is suggested. In this way neither depth nor flatness is firmly established. The purpose, it seems, is not to remove three-dimensionality entirely, but to unseat it. As in the still life, line holds the magic. With it the artist is able to deform and re-interpret without inhibition. The key is the bold line, the scrawl.

Another prominent element in Egonu's paintings from this moment onwards is texturality. In addition to the evocation of texturality through patterning, we find him making a deliberate effort to imbue his paintings with tactility by such techniques as stippling or by using crude scrawls. In *Northern Nigerian Landscape* the road/path/form is stippled to suggest texturality and volume. In *Man with Pipe* this is more extensive, but while this texturality tends to evoke volume and depth, such reference is countered through the use of lines. All other identifiable references to mimetic reality are subjugated to plain geometric shapes.

By 1965 Egonu's aesthetic of selective syncretism was fairly clearly defined. It was characterised formally by ambiguity, the preeminence of line, pattern and texturality and the use of decorative motifs. From 1966 he introduced even more unique devices such as cyclical and bird's eye views in his work. This we find most conspicuously in the

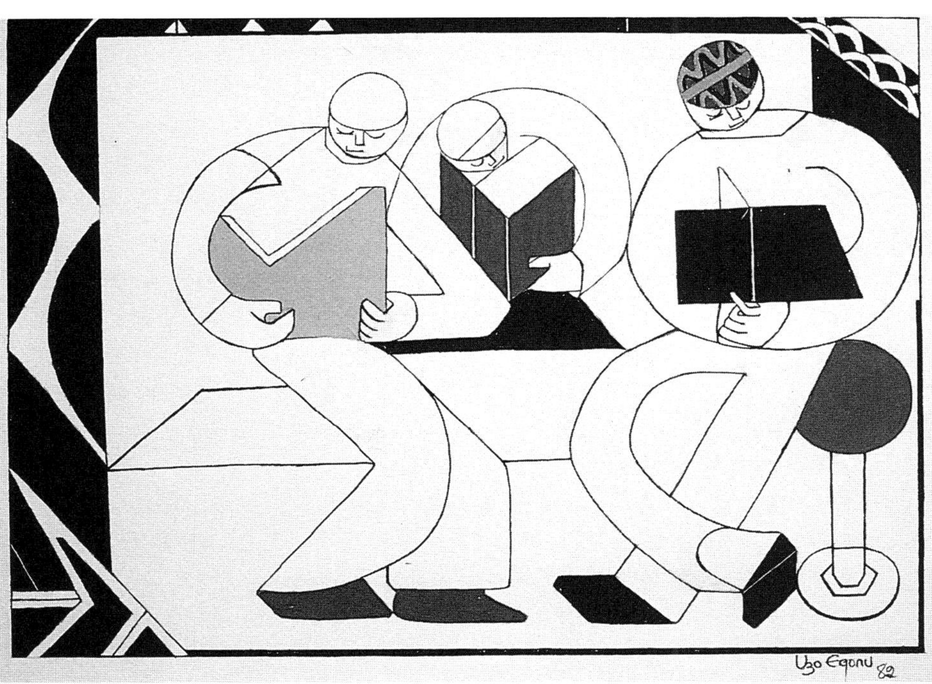

Men Reading, 1981
Gouache on paper
56 x 67 cm

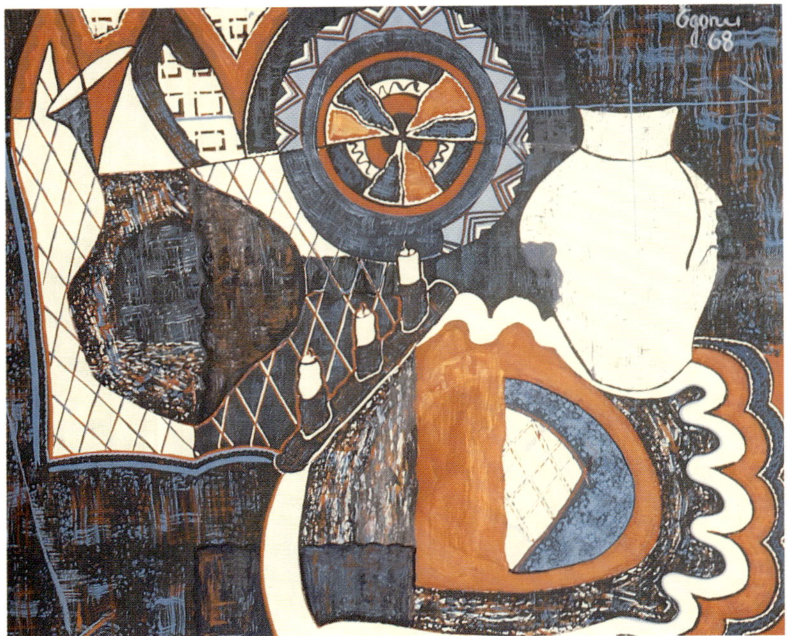

***Still-life with Candle Holder*, 1968**
Gouache on paper
56 x 67 cm

'Protection' series and especially in the painting, *Exodus* from 1970. By the 1970s the austere palette of the 1960s had given way to a more relaxed attitude to colour, especially in the prints. The contrapuntal juxtaposition of positive and negative space, the delicate balancing of the occupied and the fallow, which we see most remarkably for the first time in *Woman before a Mirror*, became a trademark of his work.

While these devices establish Egonu within the modernist tradition, it is important to note that most of them are also found in the art of the Igbo. The preeminence of line, for instance, is found in Igbo mural painting and door sculpture, with which Egonu was familiar as a little boy. But line in Igbo art is not simply a graphic element but a sign which links art to the pattern of existence. The thick border line which segments and divides the picture and outlines shape derives from the role of borders for a sedentary people. For an essentially agricultural people, land is sacred. In the case of the Igbo, who are reputed to have the highest population density in Africa, it becomes even more important because it is scarce. People exist and operate within physical and social borders which are usually reinforced and often strictly adhered to.[16] In his foreword to *Igbo Arts: Community and Cosmos*[17] the novelist Chinua Achebe brings to mind a popular verbal formulation of this idea of fragmentation and

Man with Pipe, 1978
Oil on canvas
91 x 80 cm

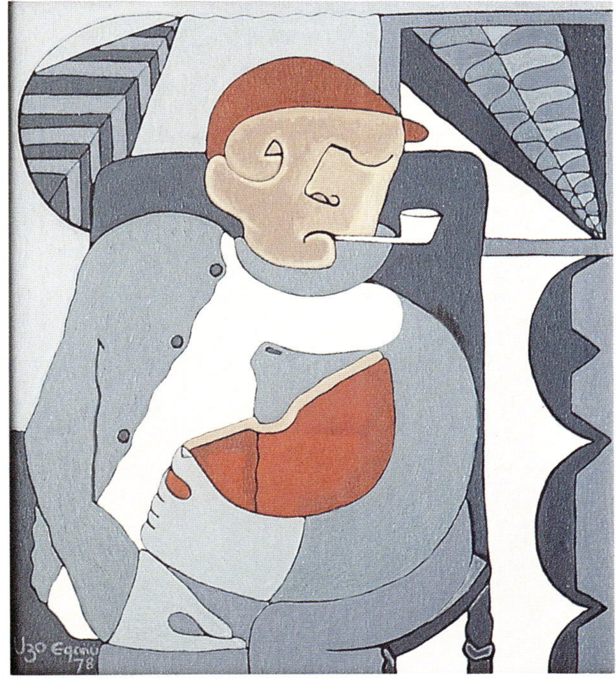

Exodus, 1961
Oil on canvas
107 x 145 cm

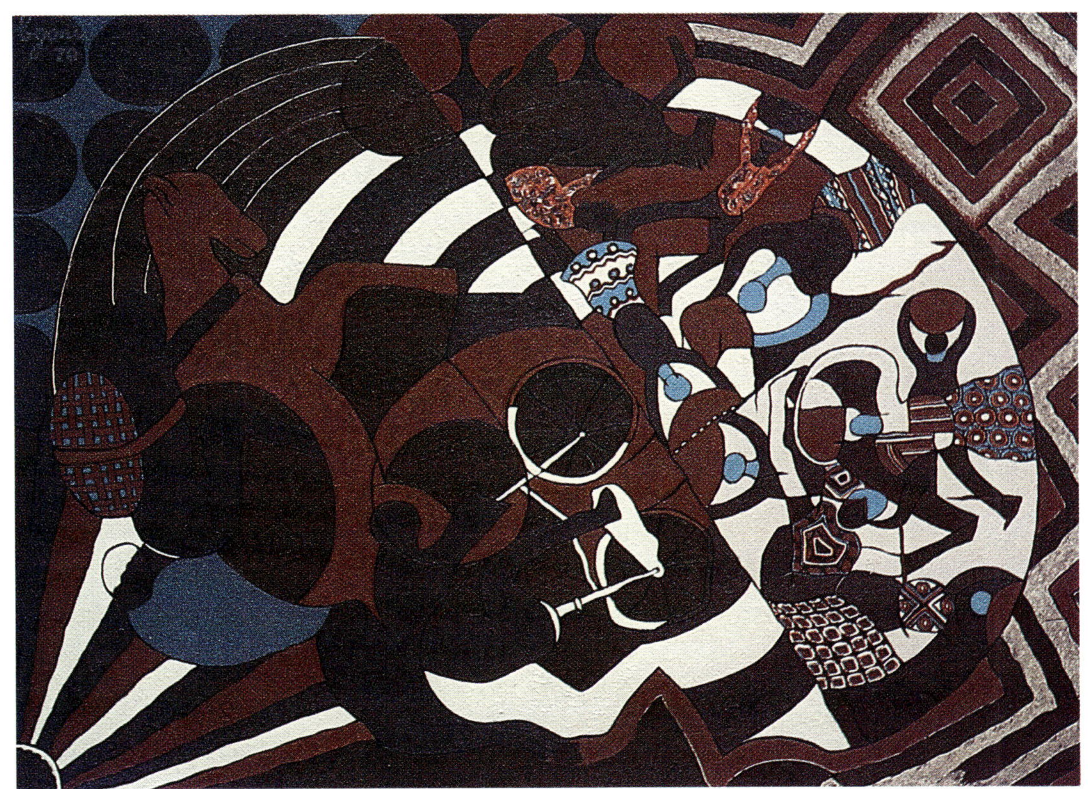

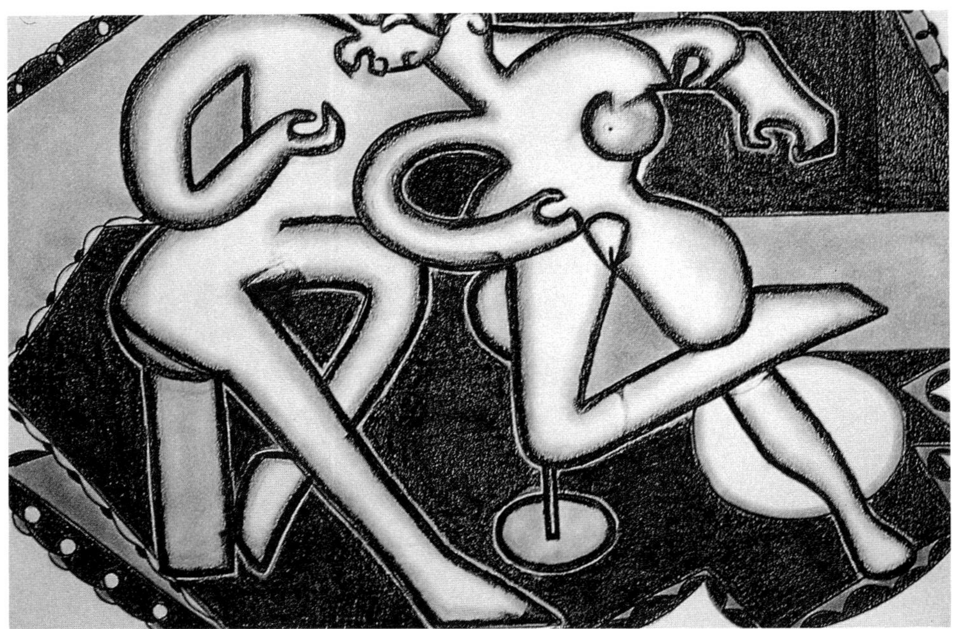

Two Friends, **1979**
Charcoal and crayon
56 x 76 cm

borderisation — the public exultation, *Onye na nkie, onye na nkie*, which, though he translates it as ''everyone *and* his own'', actually stands for ''everyone *in* his or her own place'', the word *na* being both a preposition and conjunction. Both translations underline the concept of individual space. It can indeed be observed, even in an era of growing industrialisation and urbanisation, how, among the Igbo, property owners spend more on erecting reinforced boundaries than they spend on developing their property. The late 1980s and in the 1990s saw a growing art of sculptured walls around private dwellings. Borderisation remains a living part of the Igbo sensibility.

Another manifestation of this is in the Igbo tradition of uncompromising individualism within an essentially communal structure. Achebe makes reference to the Igbo verbalisation of this phenomenon in which they insist that, though two people may be born of the same mother, no two people are created by the same *chi* or creator. According to Achebe, ''this is individualism taken to its utmost''.[18] Not only does each person, each family, hold inviolable right to a portion which must not be trespassed, each individual also holds title to a separate identity which is clearly demarked and cannot be compromised. And this is encoded in the line between.

The form of the line in Igbo art indeed differs as one moves from among the rain forest Igbo, who have a higher demographic density and greater attachment to the land, towards the north-eastern Igbo with a sparse population and poor, savannah vegetation. The line is thick in the Mbari mural painting of the southern Igbo which is strictly patterned and structural, while it thins and floats in the *uli* paintings of the central and northern Igbo where there are more open borders.

Line has yet another major symbolism in the Igbo world: as a route, a channel, a road. First, Achebe identifies the concept of channels of power or energy, borne in the expression, *Ike di na awaja na awaja* (power/energy runs in channels).[19] As he rightly notes, ''energy is the essence of all things human, spiritual, animate, and inanimate''. The universe is thus constituted of lines of energy, line rather than shape being the theatre of energy and essence. Reality is not diffused in patches but striated into lines of essence. Above shape and wholeness, then, is line, the path of power.

Second, the Igbo prioritise the road or path as the channel of other principles less abstract than energy.[20] Communication between the different 'worlds' or layers of the cosmos is conducted along routes. The dead and the unborn need paths between them and the living, and these thoroughfares are crucial for balance and peace. It would not be overstretching our references to Achebe to cite yet another

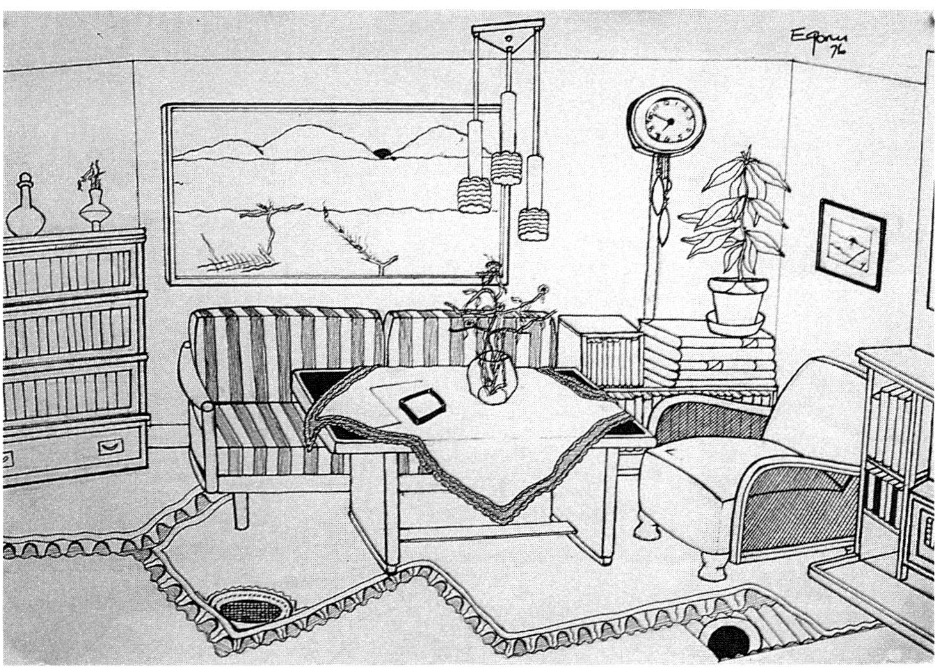

***Living Room*, 1976**
Indian ink on paper
42 x 59 cm

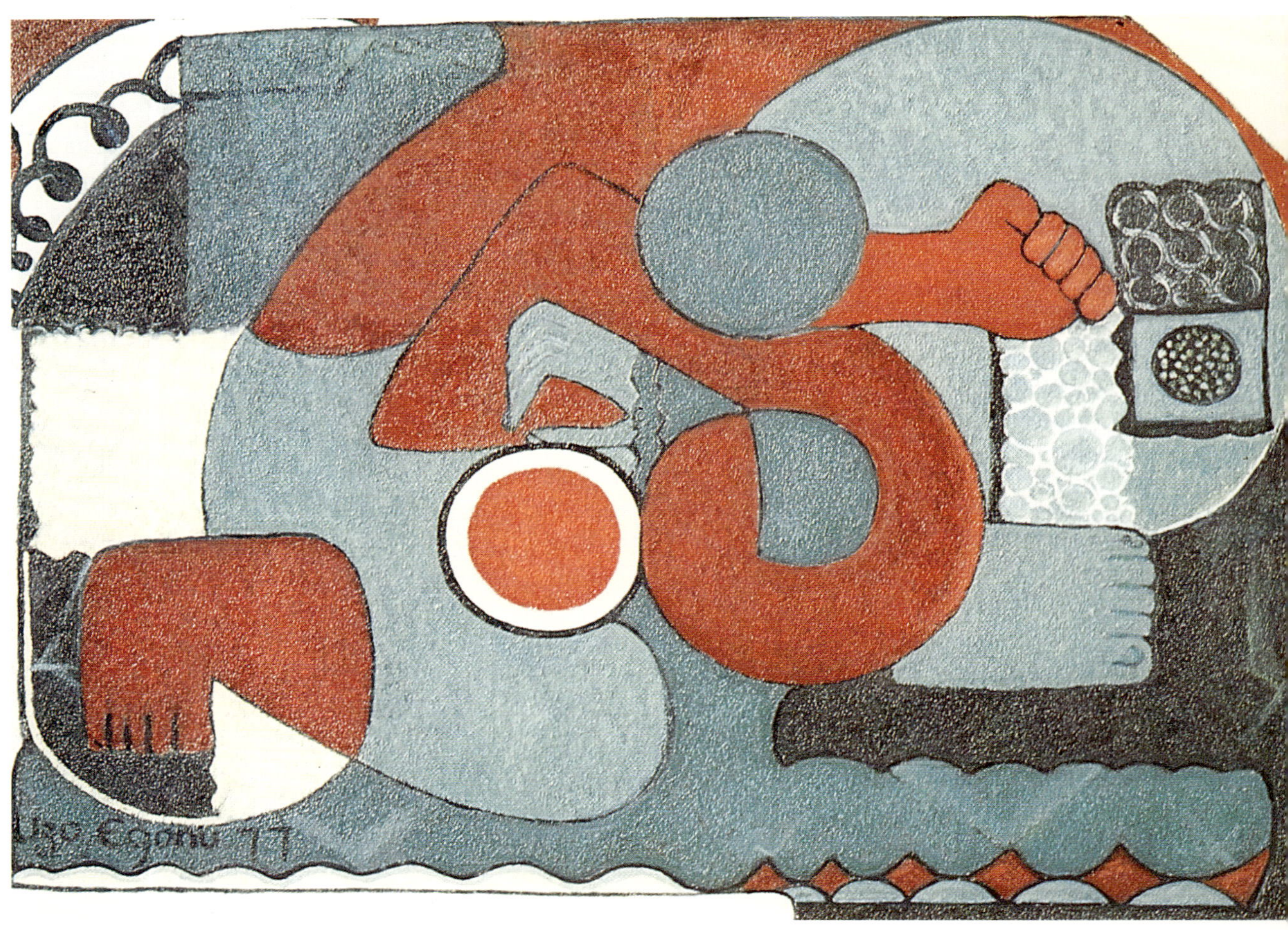

Mother and Child
***Before a Shrine*, 1977**
Oil on canvas
80 x 144 cm

***War and Peace #5*, 1969**
Gouache on paper
51 x 66 cm

articulation of this principle from his work since he demonstrates in his writings an unrivalled understanding of the Igbo world. In one of his earliest stories,[21] a young and overzealous village head teacher instructs his pupils to landscape a portion of the school property. In the process the pupils cover an ancient path which, according to the villagers, is used by spirits. Soon after this, strange happenings begin to occur in the village and there is anxiety since it is feared the dead would be held up on their way out, and women would no longer conceive since the unborn could no longer make their entry. Such is the strength of the belief that when the Christian head teacher refuses to re-open the path, forces in the village take matters into their hands

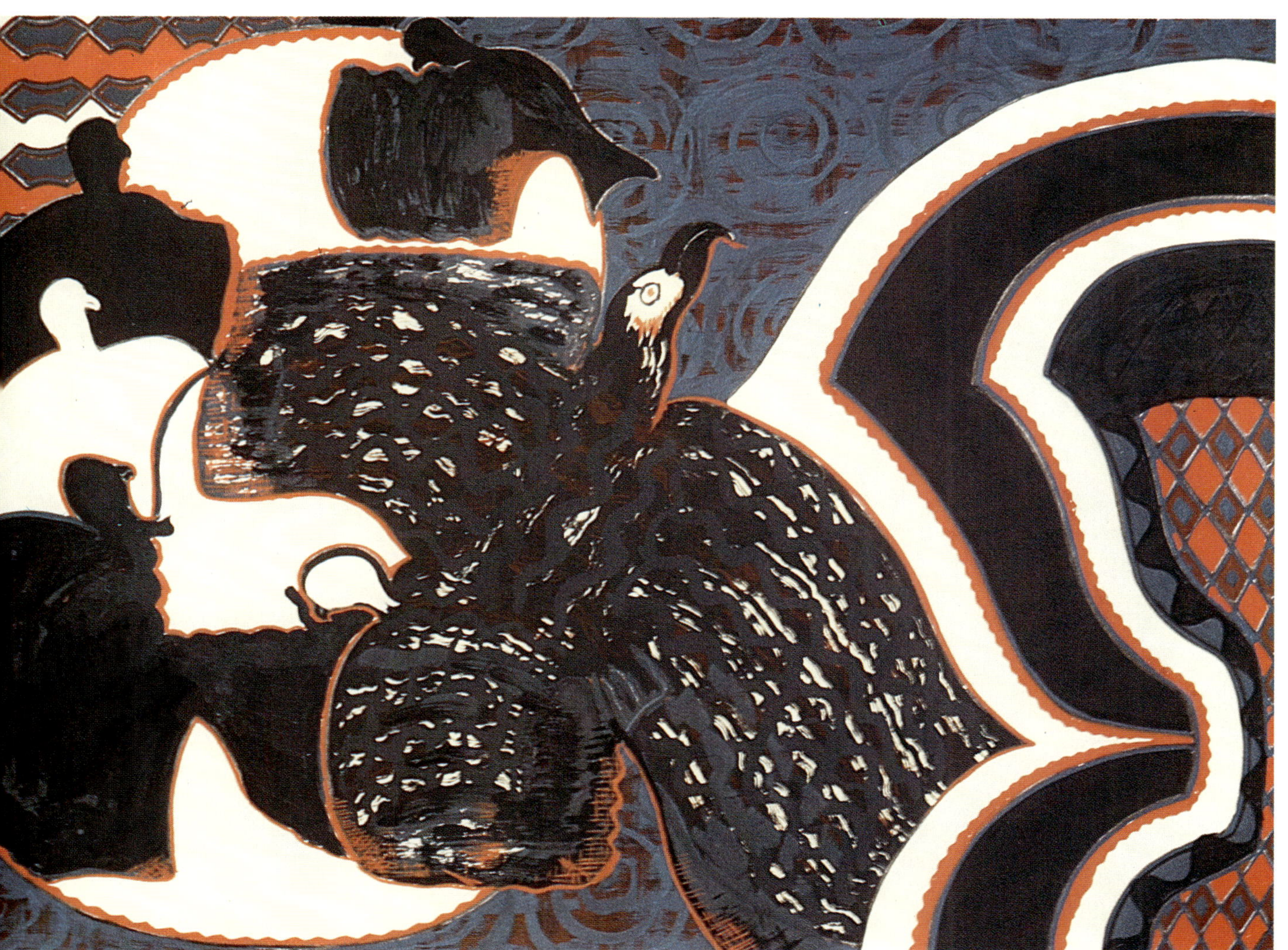

and under the cover of darkness ruin the entire landscape.

The line, the road, is not only crucial for necessary communication between symbiotic layers of reality, it is also a symbol of opportunity and endless possibilities, a prerequisite for the mobility which human beings crave in order to fully act out their destinies. This concept is borne in a common formulation, *E liwe uzo, liwe ehi, m aghara uzo toro ehi: ẹhi wu anu e riwe e riche ye, uzo wu a gawa a gacha agacha* — if a cow and a road are tethered and I am called upon to choose, I would pick the road, for the meat of a cow finishes; the road has no end. The concept of the endless road embodies the extremism of Igbo optimism, the idea that there is no limit to individual achievement and mobility as long as there is a thoroughfare. The thoroughfare signifies fate, the path of destiny and social advancement which opens up to the daring and the venturesome, and guarantees success and progress to the hard-working. With the road the lowliest have the opportunity to reach the heights of nobility. The line or track, the road, is thus not only the path of energy but also of destiny, the two

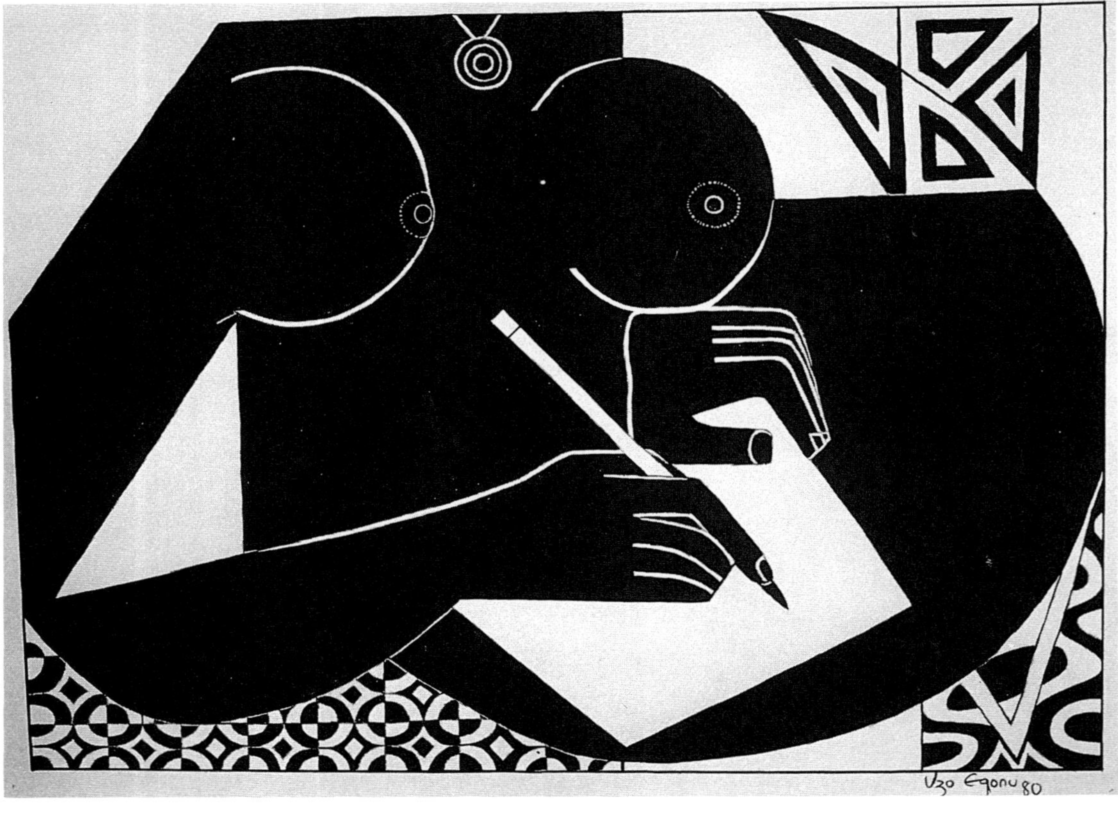

A *Letter*, 1980
Gouache on paper
57 x 76 cm

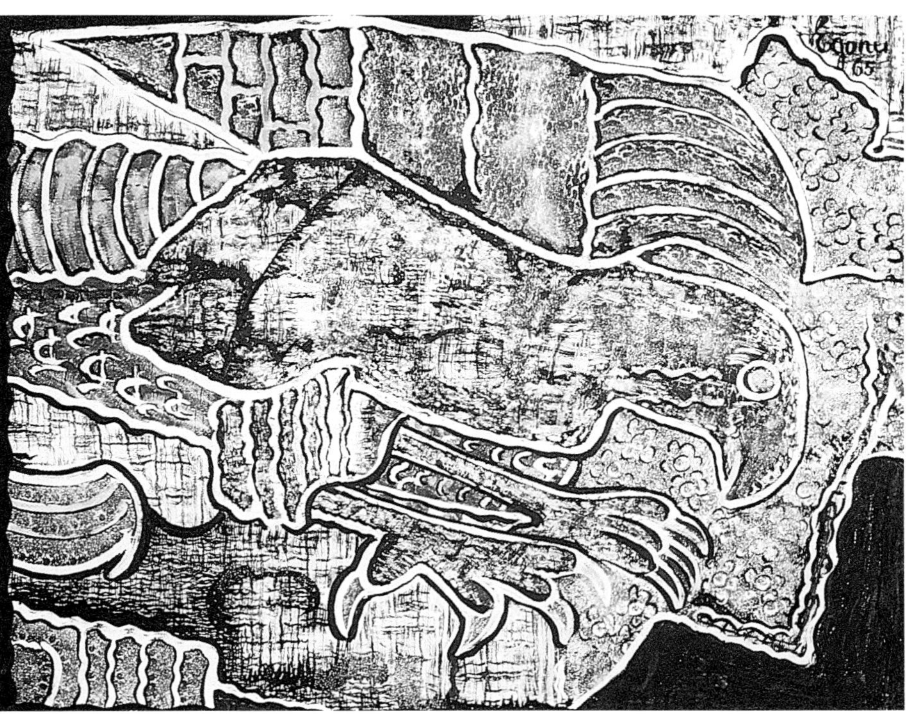

Eagle (Goldie), 1965
Gouache on paper
52 x 65 cm

most important complementary principles in the Igbo world.

The peculiar use of space and delicate balancing of positive and negative shapes referred to earlier on, which occur first in *Northern Nigerian Landscape* and *Woman before a Mirror* and would become a defining device in much of Egonu's work in the 1970s and 1980s especially the prints such as *A Cup of Coffee in Solitude* and *Lone Eater*, may be found in much Igbo art as a figuration of Igbo social structures. The tight structure of southern Igbo painting, with little negative space and close-knit patterning, relates directly to village planning, organisation and architecture, as well as to the social and political structures which, though they form borders, also de-emphasise hierarchies. What has come to be known as Igbo republicanism, the complex structure of family and lineage units with evenly distributed power, is most pronounced in this Igbo region. And this is projected in both the dwelling patterns and in art. Among the monarchical central Igbo, however, this rigid structurality gives way to patterns of positive-negative dichotomy. Areas of emphasis are countered by those of absence or de-emphasis. Negative space is given as much importance as the positive. Also, only a limited number of elements can go into a composition for it to maintain this balance between negative and positive, between the powerful upper classes of King, men of title and priests, and the lower classes. Even within such hierarchical arrangements, the Igbo still insist that the individual is his or her own ultimate monarch and, irrespective of the position in the socio-political strata, s/he must be accorded both visual and symbolic recognition. This balance between the noble and the plebeian, so to speak, is necessary for the survival of the group.[22] And parity of negative and positive space, which we find in Egonu's work from 1965, may be regarded

***War and Peace #2*, 1969**
Gouache on paper
51 x 63 cm

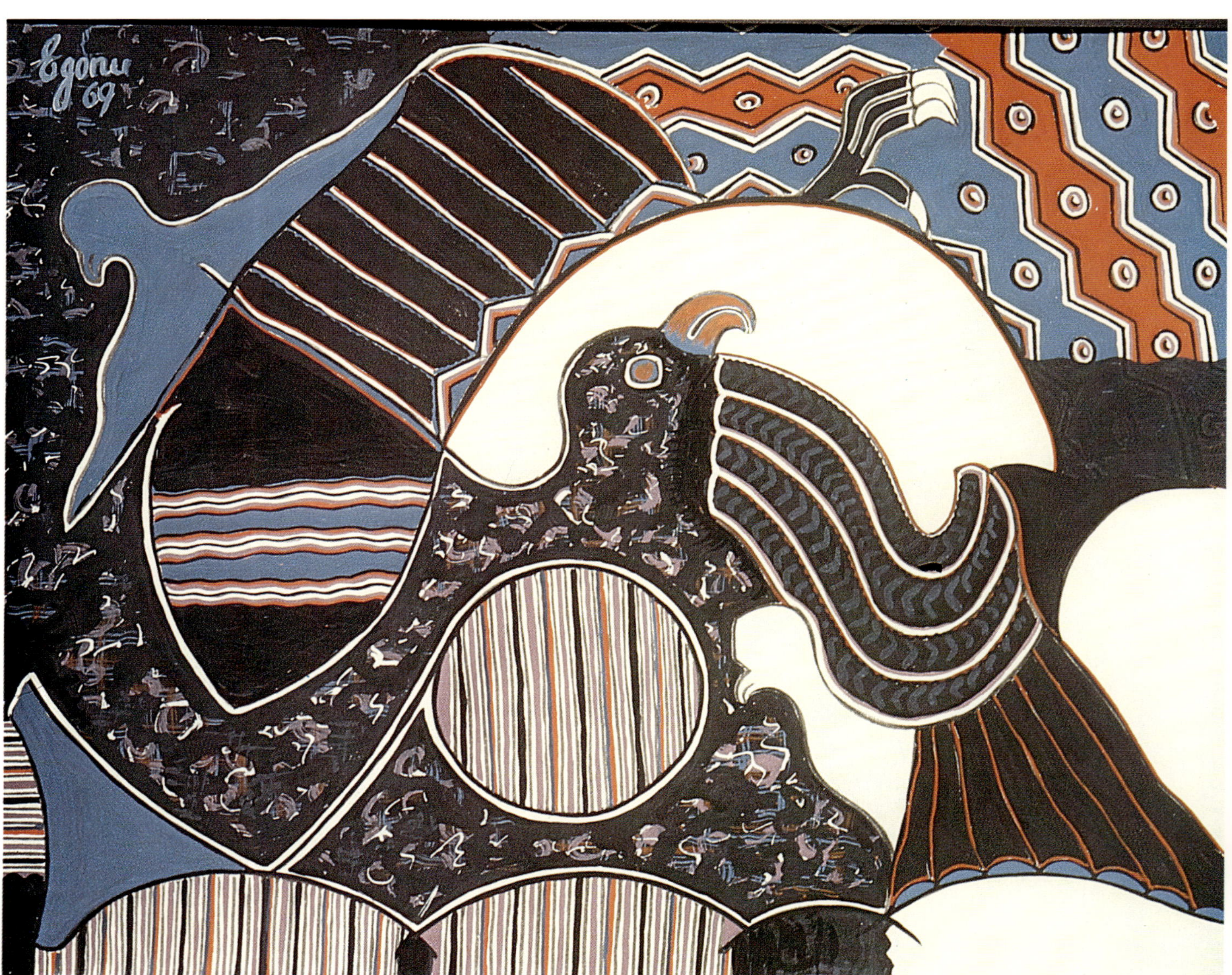

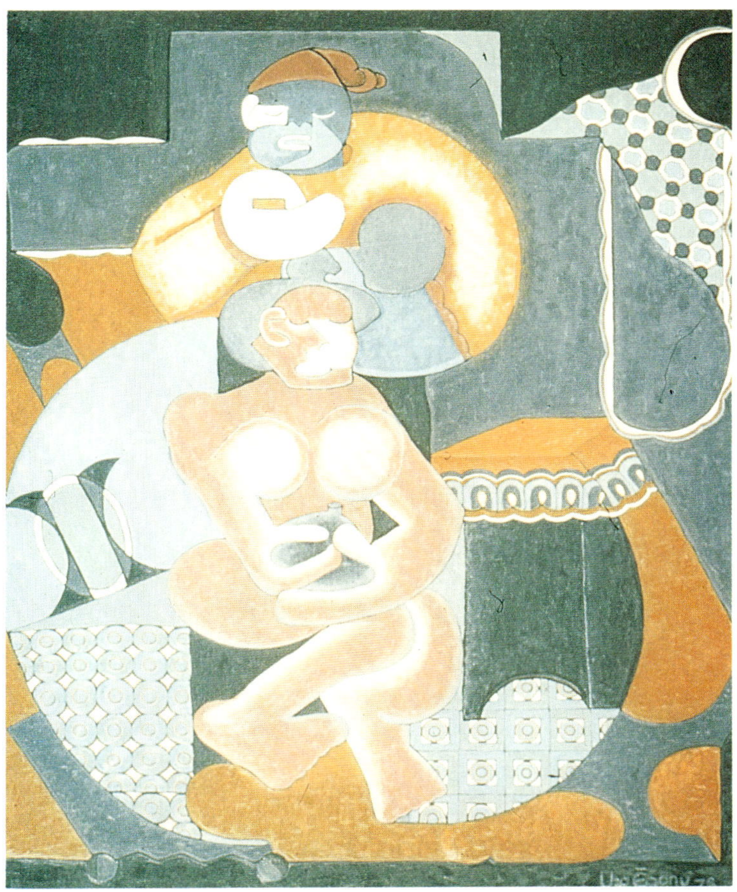

***Hair Plaiting*, 1978**
Oil on canvas
154 x 126 cm

as a conceptual construction alluding to the social structures of his origins in Onitsha, the major surviving monarchy among the Igbo.

In the parity between the open space or fallow land, and inhabited space among the Igbo, both in physical and symbolic terms, the inhabited space is for the living, while the uninhabited is the reserve of spirits and the wild. While the homestead is space for safety and survival, the open is precarious and threatening which, nevertheless, for a sedentary people, is the source of living and sustenance. The frontier must be confronted and engaged daily, as well as endlessly solicited and appeased. Not only must both the open and the occupied spaces be attended to, there must also be a healthy relationship between them, for the safety of humans depends as much on their own actions as on the whims of inhabitants of the spirit world who occupy the open spaces and act invisibly. There is permanent tension, therefore, between these domains on which the well-being of the community rests. And, just as the relationship between humans and spirits must be one of mutual sustenance, a symbiosis,[23] so must that between the different spaces they occupy and govern.

Also, while the centre of the family unit is in the homestead, it is usually in the central and open space that the group comes together, in the uninhabited arena where such symbols of group cohesion as the communal shrine and the men's houses are located. While each family may propitiate its own ancestors at the family shrine, the collectivity of ancestors can only be attended to in the centre, the open space, which is not only the geographical focus of the village group but also the political and spiritual nerve centre.[24] It is noteworthy that even after the arrival of Christianity, believers were allotted portions in the centre of the communal dwelling for their new shrines. According to Herbert Cole and Aniakor, "whatever the local traditions, a village centre is spatially and ideologically dominant".[25] The centre is not only dominant, it is in fact indispensable; it is the centre which holds the group together, especially when there are no unifying figure-heads.

Not only must these spaces be venerated, then, they must also not be infringed upon or crowded. It is in line with this principle that the Uli painter refrains from introducing an additional motif or stroke to a drawing or painting when it reaches 'saturation', even if negative spaces still abound.[26] In Egonu's work, beginning with *Northern Nigerian Landscape* and the 1965 paintings, and more prominently in the 'War and Peace' series and the prints of the 1970s and 1980s, one notices a parity of the negative and positive spaces which is not formalistically logical, but symbolically very much so, and this parallels the parity in the Igbo spacial sensibility, and its figuration in Igbo painting.

The principles of dualism and complementarity, the belief that nothing is complete of itself and all existence manifests in association, are very central to Igbo life and philosophy. Cole and Aniakor identify in the Igbo world such dualities as the human and spirit worlds, the male and the female, the white and the black. Between these binaries, however, these scholars also identify a 'complementarity' which, for instance, is the underlying "visual structural principle of much Igbo masking". The principle that "wherever one thing stands, another will stand by it",[27] translated in visual terms, requires that the positive be complemented by the negative, that black have a white by it, that a fine line is juxtaposed to a broad one or by a shape, making counterpoint a central device in Igbo art. While the choice of decorative motifs may be arbitrary, their composition and colour is governed by a strict principle of balance and counterpoint.

There is a certain element of harmony in these works, one which finds its reference in the conceptual connection between visual, social and cosmic harmony among the Igbo, and their ability to recreate the latter in the former. Harmony, perhaps, may not be the most apt description for the social and cosmic configuration of the Igbo world, the perpetual state of tension requiring constant resolution, rather than the fluidity and sedate agreeability of elements which harmony evokes.

The music theorist and historiographer Akin Euba, though writing generally about Nigerian music, has observed that it is dissonant and contains little harmony. According to him, ''the few harmonies that occur from time to time are an outcome, not of a pre-conceived harmonic basis, but of contrapuntal movement, and are dissonant''.[28] The music is also characterised, he observes, by what he calls '''fragmentation' in the extreme'' which, in visual terms, would denote multiple segmentation *contrapunto*. This pre-eminence of the contrapuntal is confirmed by the leading Igbo musicologist W W Echezona who posits that the central element of Igbo drumming is ''a conflict of rhythms in a highly organised rhythmic contrapuntal development''.[29] According to him, Igbo drummers actively subvert harmony by constantly departing from the basic rhythm. Each rhythm line is pitched against the other to draw it out, this act deriving from and underlying the individualism within community. A level of non-uniformity complements the conformity which communal existence demands. The result is balance, and not wholesome harmony. This principle one finds in Egonu's replication of design elements in an essentially contrapuntal manner and not necessarily for reasons of visual harmony. The elements are not meant to flow into each other or produce rhythmic fluidity but to exist each by itself while checking and at the same time complementing one the other.

Ulli Beier has interpreted the contrapuntal in Igbo philosophy as evidence of a belief in ''the possibility of simultaneous truth''; and Achebe notes that beyond this, it also implies a concept of ''*movement* in the metaphysical sense! We are not fixed in a particular idea of truth''.[30] In another context, another Igbo scholar Ossie Enekwe has related this to what he calls the ''dynamism of context'' in Igbo theatre.[31] In most Igbo theatre, which is usually outdoors and in the

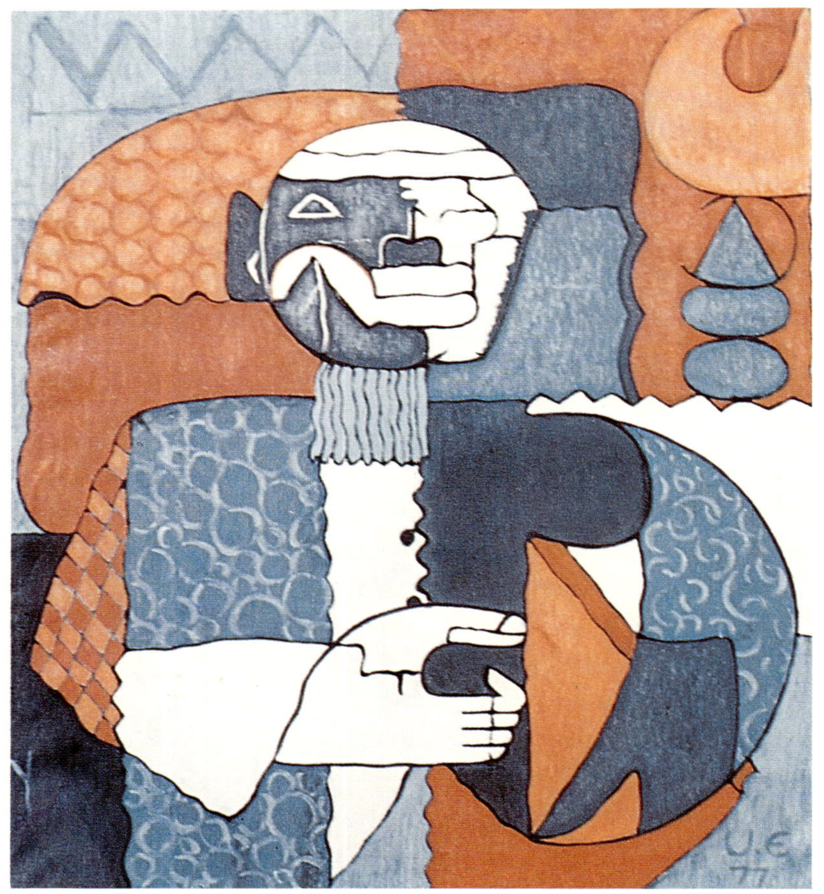

Flamboyant Poet, 1977
Oil on canvas
91 x 80 cm

round, almost every element is figured in a structure of constant tension and flux. The stage shifts just as do the 'actors'. The audience acts as a counterpoint and occasionally the stage expands to incorporate it, transforming it into the centre. Focus moves from one location to another, from one section to its opposite. And this echoes Achebe's theory of metaphysical mobility and multiple truths; in other words, the absence of absolutes. Achebe concludes that, " 'I am the way, the truth, and the life' must have struck the first Igbo people as heresy".[32] Within the Igbo world there is no room for grand narratives.

All of these the critic Donatus Nwoga has summarised as "texturalism" - the syncopated and contrapuntal juxtaposition of clearly defined fragments, held in delicate balance and resting on what might be called the 'hanging note'. On one level, this reflects the balance of acute individualism and republican communalism, and on another,

Coffee House at Bad Orb, 1980
Oil on canvas
154 x 126 cm

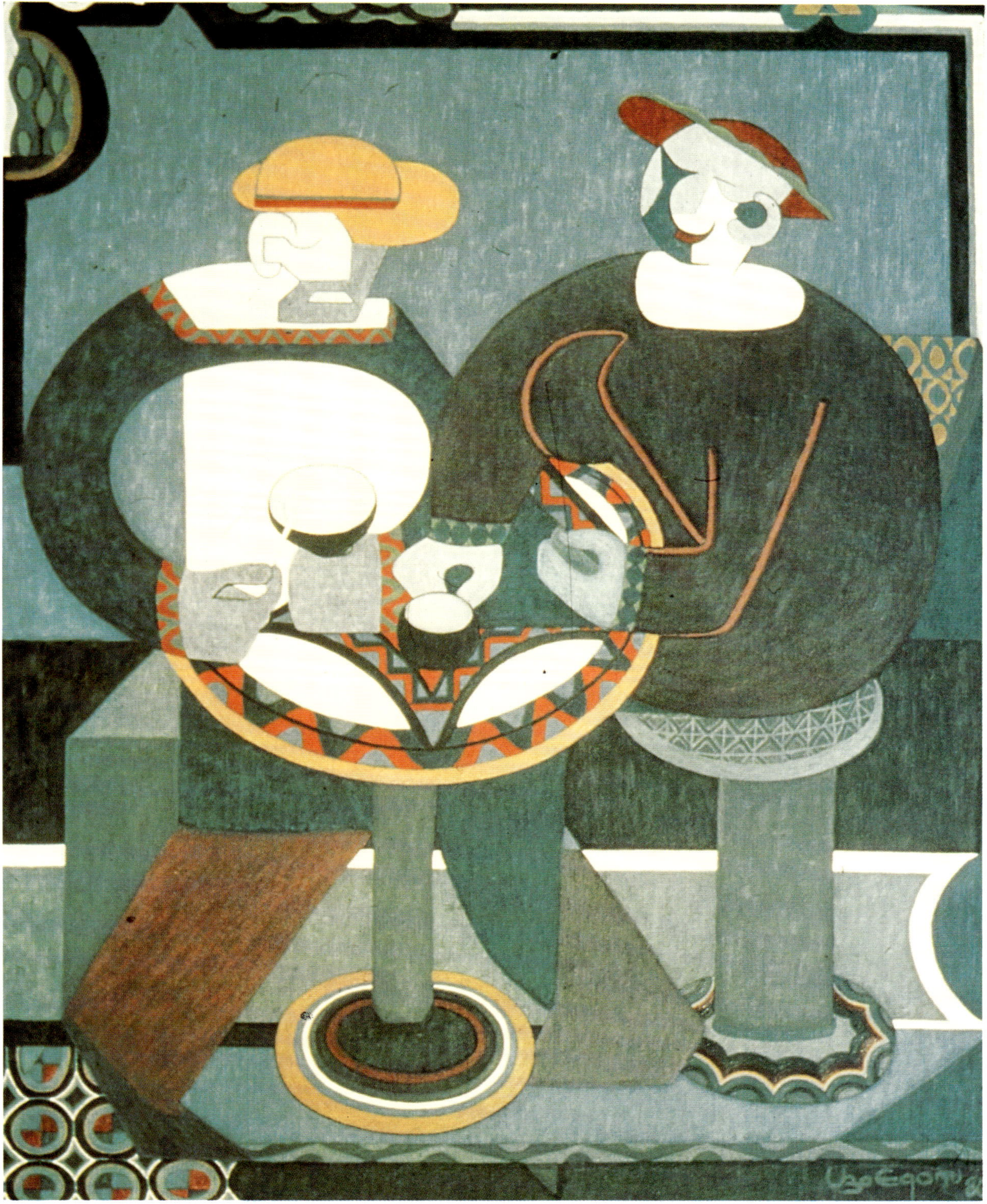
Uzo Egonu

the duality of reality, the pluralism of phenomena in nature, and the absence of dominant absolutes.

Form for Egonu is a projection not only of physical but also metaphysical and social reality, a kind of systemic rather than formal mimesis. From this point one could indeed ascribe to his work a semiotic aesthetic, in the sense of that which formulates the structure of feeling, feeling being not entirely subjective but also projectively objective, that is, communal by inference. Whatever their subject matter, Egonu's work can be seen as translations, as a system or *doxa* which derives from and fits within a tradition beyond the individualism of modernism.

In the 1970 essay 'On Myself and my work' he states:

> My aim was to utilise the decorative symbols which I was used to as a child in Igbo-land, to express myself and to communicate my thoughts to others.[33]

There could be no better summary of Egonu's vision as an artist and the manner in which this manifests through form. The Egonu aesthetic is as private and subjective as it is 'visionary' or social, and in both cases it is rooted in his Africanity. From his flower paintings to his war paintings, from the wit and subtle sarcasm of *Flamboyant Poet* to the melancholia of the series, 'Stateless People', Egonu sustains this duality of the private and the public. The result is a thematic pluralism that excludes little: nature, wildlife, hunger, the vanities and vagaries of human nature, pain, anguish, loneliness, alienation and disability, the whole range of human experience and emotions.

Community and Commitment

Another essential parameter for understanding Egonu's work, and one which locates it only within a certain stream of modernism, is that of social relevance. His development and the evolution of his work exhibits, on the surface, a single-minded individualism which is as remarkable as it is important in understanding certain aspects of his work and convictions. Yet, broadly speaking, there is a discernible if slightly obscure connection between the form and content of his work, and those of some of the more significant artists in his homeland. We note, without insinuating or confirming any derivative inferences, a similarity to the pseudo-naivist work of Ben Enwonwu's middle period. We have also noted parallels between Egonu's work and aspects of Igbo art. It is significant that some of these details can also be identified in the work of other modern Igbo artists like Obiora Udechukwu and Uche Okeke where we find the same privilege given to line and borders, and a similar predilection for contrapuntal orchestration of colour and space. Furthermore, Egonu has maintained a practice of consciously relating to his background, past and contemporary, both formally and thematically. He has remained emotionally attached to events in his home country, this attachment becoming more concrete and realistic with time, especially after his dreams of an early return vanished and it became apparent that his career and life were inevitably located in Europe.

If his contact with home was largely emotional at the beginning of his career in Europe, defined more by a personal vision and determination, this was later reinforced by contact not only with his kin

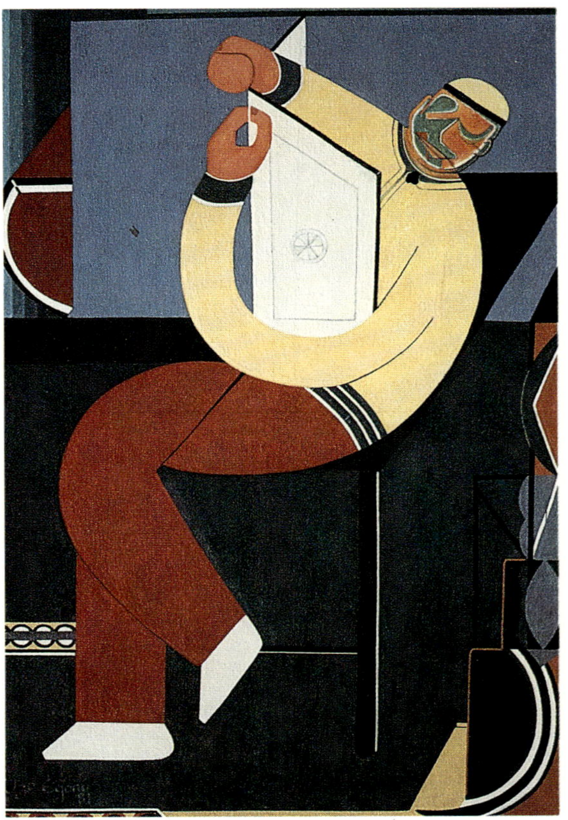

***Poet Reading*, 1981**
'Poets & Philosophers' series
Oil on canvas
173 x 119 cm

in Nigeria but perhaps more so with the Nigerian artists and intellectuals emerging after colonial disengagement. Some of these contacts and meetings were on a personal and intimate level, like his friendship with the painter Uche Okeke and later with the painter and poet Obiora Udechukwu. Many others were through reading, as with the writers Chinua Achebe, an enthusiastic collector of Egonu's prints, and the Nobel laureate Wole Soyinka, neither of whom the artist has yet had the opportunity to meet.

It is useful to consider parallels between Egonu's vision, the nature and form of his work and those of some of these artists and writers not only within the frame suggested in the previous chapter, but also on the grounds of an awareness of events and developments in the new art and literature in Africa, much of which is broadly informed by the same background and perception of reality. The question of the relationship between the artist and his community, and the role of art in society, or what has come to be known as commitment, has been one of great significance for African writers and artists

***Restaurant at Bad Orb*, 1980**
Oil on canvas
124 x 178 cm

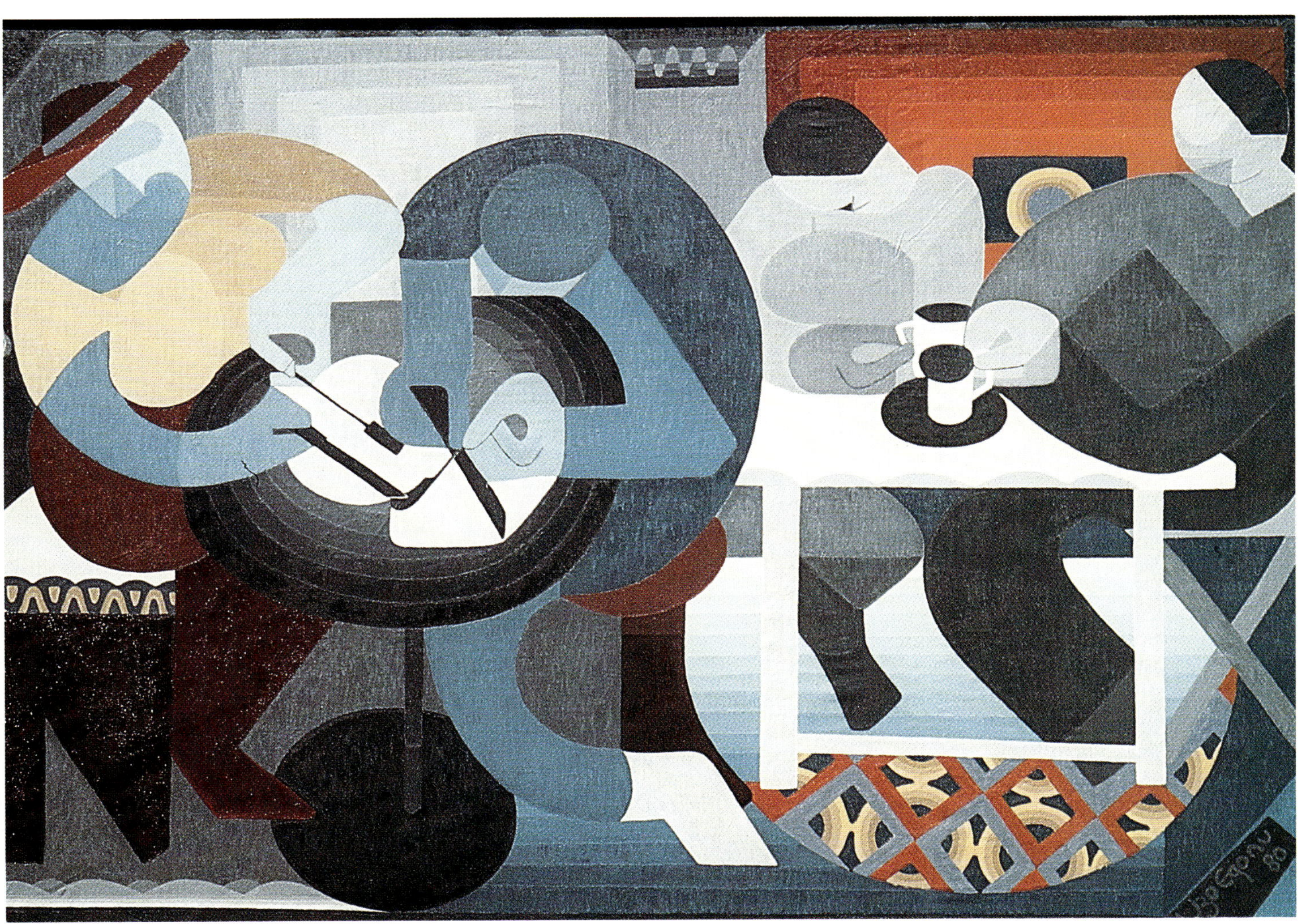

for the past thirty years. Since the ascent of a new literary and artistic epoch, signified most notably in the publication in 1958 of Achebe's anti-colonialist novel, *Things Fall Apart*, this enjoyed a centrality in discourse which quickly fell victim to hasty architects of categories and typologies.[1]

The philosopher and nationalist Leopold Sedar Senghor had prefigured the subsequent debates over commitment in his 1956 essay, 'L'esprit de la civilisation ou les lois de la culture negro-africaine' in which he first posited that artist and community are inseparable in Africa. In his polemic style, Senghor asserted that "in Africa, art for art's sake does not exist. All art is social,"[2] a position which Achebe would echo years later by asserting that "Art for art's sake is a piece of deodorised dog shit."[3] One might remark that Senghor was not, in the particular event, writing with reference to post-colonial, industrialised Africa with its new values and social structures, but was formulating his theories of art and society in Africa under the strong influence of the French Surrealist and socialist circles, pioneers of the philosophy of commitment in Europe. Achebe's declaration sought to theorise not only the art of contemporary African societies but, seemingly, all art.

Achebe has subsequently qualified his position in elaborate explanations. In 'The Writer and His Community' he goes beyond the formalistic positions which we identified in the last chapter as defining the Igbo sensibility or world, and details the relationship between that world and the life, practice and preoccupation of its artists. He redefines the position of the artist in his society by re-emphasising the essential and extreme individualism of the Igbo personality which guarantees that the artist and his community "do not have to agree on how to make the best mask. But they are all interested in the process of making and the final outcome."[4] This definition differs markedly from the conventional understanding of commitment whereby society either dictates to the artist or severely delimits his or her creative and thematic space. Taking time to disclaim the notions of absolute dichotomy between the West and Africa which Senghor verges on, Achebe qualifies commitment as a sense of identification with community which offers both artist and community a grip on reality, whether through an attempt to comprehend, or through an effort to reveal and, consequently, apprehend the forces of that reality.

Wole Soyinka has stated that "for poet, novelist, or sculptor, the artist labours from an in-built, intuitive responsibility, not only to himself, but to his roots''.[5] By this Soyinka implies that responsibility need not be conscious, and that the artist's responsibility to his roots is inevitable and non-negotiable except at great cost, implicitly contractual yet irrevocable, since it is intuitive and its negation is against the nature of the artist.

Soyinka further clarifies the meaning of commitment by drawing a line between ''ideology'' and ''social vision'',[6] and this is a distinction which is very relevant in understanding Egonu's work. While granting that ''concepts of an ideological nature'' are central to much creative production in contemporary Africa, Soyinka asserts that a social vision concerns itself primarily with observations on and projections of society, rather than with philosophical deliberations on the nature of either society or creativity. To extend reflections on reality ''beyond the purely narrative'' and to posit specific failings of the social arrangement is quite different from speculating on an alternative world view which, quite often, remains more intellectual and theoretical than practical. Social vision therefore qualifies not necessarily an ideological debate in either the creative or political sense but a practical position on experience. And because experience, even at the most internalised and personal level, is human and thus social, reflections on experience, whether individual or collective, inevitably assume a social significance. When such reflections relate not only to the personal experience but also to the communal or group experience, their social relevance is enlarged and the relationship between artist and community is re-emphasised. The essential responsibility to the artist's roots to which Soyinka refers becomes easily discernible and one may talk of commitment. In other words commitment does not necessarily imply a position of a politically ideological nature, as is naturally assumed in arguments against committed art or for a ''free'', autonomous art, and indeed in some arguments for art of a ''committed'' or '' 'properly' political'' nature.[7]

Commitment in Egonu's work can be seen in this light, for, while most of his contemporaries in Africa have at one point or another declared positions of an explicit ideological nature, that is to say, positions on the left-right political axis, Egonu subscribes to no such stated position. Despite a clear disenchantment with the structures of western politics and society,[8] the artist has so far steered clear of any specific political avowals.

In Egonu's work commitment involves a strong and unmistakeable identification with his community, with an emphasis

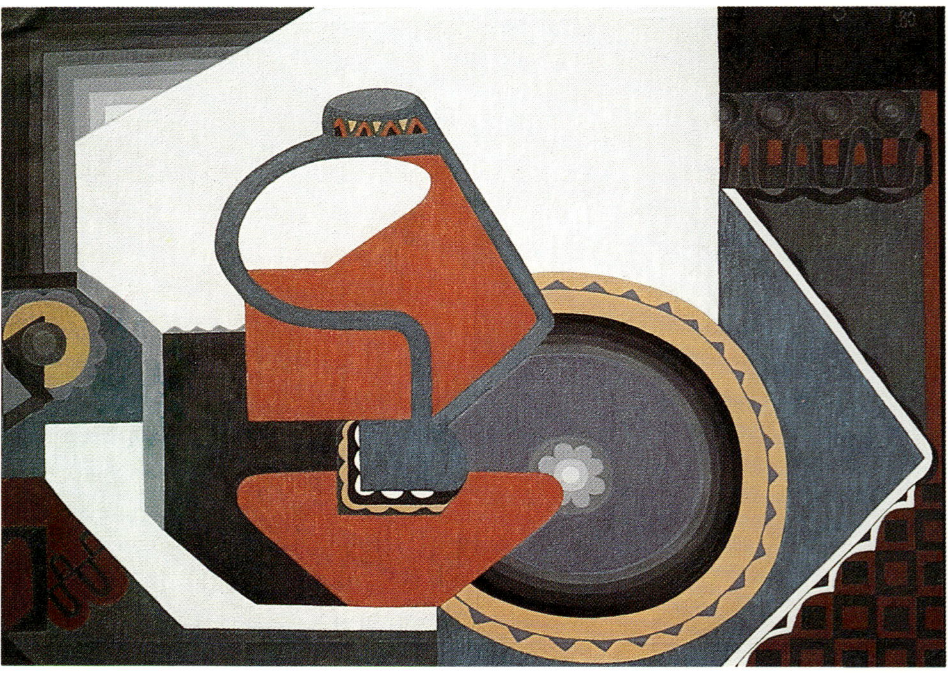

***Vase with Wall Plate*, 1980**
Oil on canvas
106 x 145 cm

which in a sense transcends political partisanship or radicalism and resides in what we might call the discerning concern, the propensity to celebrate or lament as the situation or mood demands, but at all times in participation. Achebe concludes that in Africa artists ''lived and moved and had their being in society, and created their works for the good of that society''.[9] It is this role which Egonu plays through his work.

One might wonder how an artist could fulfil this imperative while being geographically distant from his or her community. The necessary condition for this, however, is not physical proximity but the active, inferential location of the individual persona within a particular symbolic context or space. Conventional definitions of 'community arts' are often unacceptably narrow and banal in their literalness since they restrict relationships between the artist and his or her community to physical location and even communal production. Within the confines of this definition, art for the community is reduced to a residency in the local school or hospital, or the collective production of sculpture for the village park. Without contesting the value of this concept of art to community, it is necessary to acknowledge a triteness which derives from an essentially semantic misconception, the confusion of 'communal arts' with 'art for community'. While the former implies a collectivity of experience and an interactive, incestuous artistic relation of such experience, the latter entertains the possibility of deputation or individual assumption of responsibility outside the immediate reaches of the collective, the legitimacy of representation, of the individual burden, and indeed, penance. The former precludes the possibility and historical validity of the artist as visionary and as self-appointed representative of his or her community who assumes the duty of projecting that community beyond its physical or material reaches.

Although the publication of Achebe's *Things Fall Apart* in 1958 has been described as "a landmark in the cultural and political development of Africa",[10] and his writing in general hailed as a

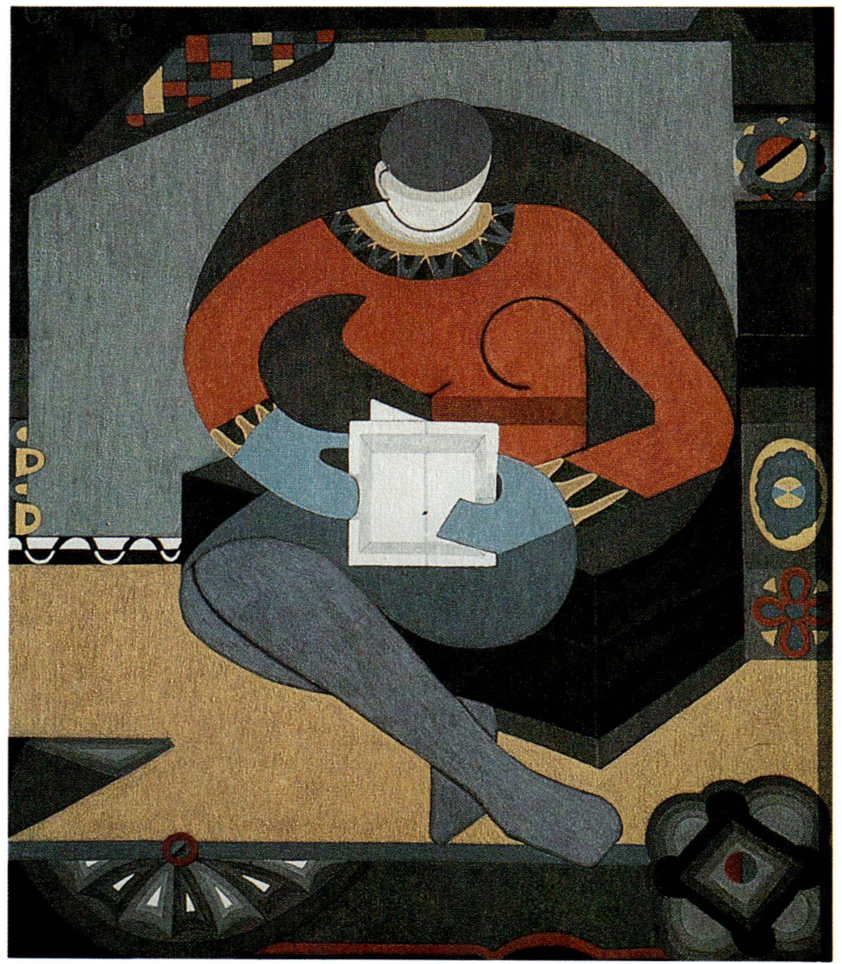

Poetess, **1980**
'Poets & Philosophers' series
Oil on canvas
152 x 124 cm

most significant contribution not only to an understanding of his own culture but of the entirety of colonial Africa, it is remarkable that his works are not directly accessible to a great portion of his community.[11] Nevertheless, this has not affected the very high regard in which he is held by that community, manifest not only in the recognition he has received from the section which has access to his work but also in titular honours and positions of a more provincial nature which he holds in his home town and elsewhere. Even the non-literate members of his community are able to recognise his contribution in projecting to his audience the humanism of his people and their heroism before the colonial onslaught, efforts which have inevitably portrayed them in a different and more realistic light before the world.

In this context then, community is clearly desynonymised with audience, and commitment is projected not in the mundane sense of availability for direct consumption but in service, albeit self-appointed, through representation before an audience fairly distinct from the artist's own community.

On a different level, it could be argued that physical distance from the community does not constitute automatic or perpetual alienation from it and that indeed some distancing from the community is essential for a proper articulation of its experience and a successful fulfilment of its creative expectations. Such argument could equally be made with regard to Egonu's work and his relationship with his homeland. Drawing from Achebe's studies of the arts and community among the Igbo, Simon Gikandi has argued that "the artist in the Igbo aesthetic achieves creativity when he or she is isolated 'from the larger community in a ritual with more than a passing resemblance to their own death or funeral'".[12] Here Achebe and Gikandi refer to the production of Mbari installations during which the artists are mandatorily removed from the rest of the community, sometimes for several years. This severe alienation or disengagement is considered necessary, on one level, for the degree of sanctity required for the production of an artistic sacrifice to the goddess of sanctity, and on another, equally significant level, for the solitude which the creative process demands. In a different essay Achebe observes that the Igbo observed and respected the solitary nature of the creative individual and considered him or her essentially removed, by their calling, from the rest of community.[13] In other words, the artist was conceived as deserving, by the demands of the creative preoccupation, of a distance, an individual space not only spiritual but also physical.

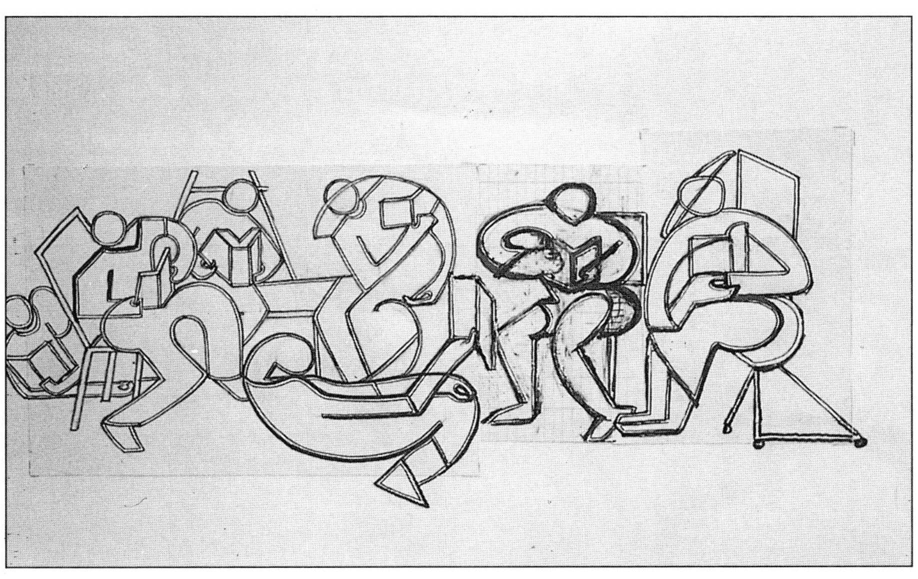

***Library in Autumn (study)*, 1983**
ink and pencil

It would not be wrong, therefore, to venture a theory of 'essential alienation' as fundamental to the relocation of a modern artist like Egonu. The symbolic, ritual removal of the artist from the rest of society equates, within the loose structures of modernity, the spiritual and physical distance between the exile and his or her community.

Even beyond the concept of physical distance as a creative prerequisite, an exile's conscious re-appropriation of his or her perceived heritage and community, or construction and assumption of an identity located within this heritage, constitutes in itself a restitution or rehabilitation, a return, and logically relocates him or her within that community. While the community itself may not be aware of, or indeed recognise, this reunion, its symbolic validity is not in the least diminished. The process of defining and adopting — of 'identifying with' — establishes a link, no matter how ambivalent, between the artist and a community, physical distance becoming only an incidental equivalent to that original, creative distance which Igbo artists required, for instance.

In his essay, 'George Lamming and the Colonial Situation',[14] Ngugi wa Thiong' shows that Lamming posits the necessity of exile for a true understanding of one's homeland or community. Lamming's characters insist that, for a proper understanding of the homeland

***Vase in Interior*, 1980**
Oil on canvas
106 x 152 cm

***Will Knowledge Safeguard Freedom #8*, 1988**
Oil on canvas
168 x 244 cm

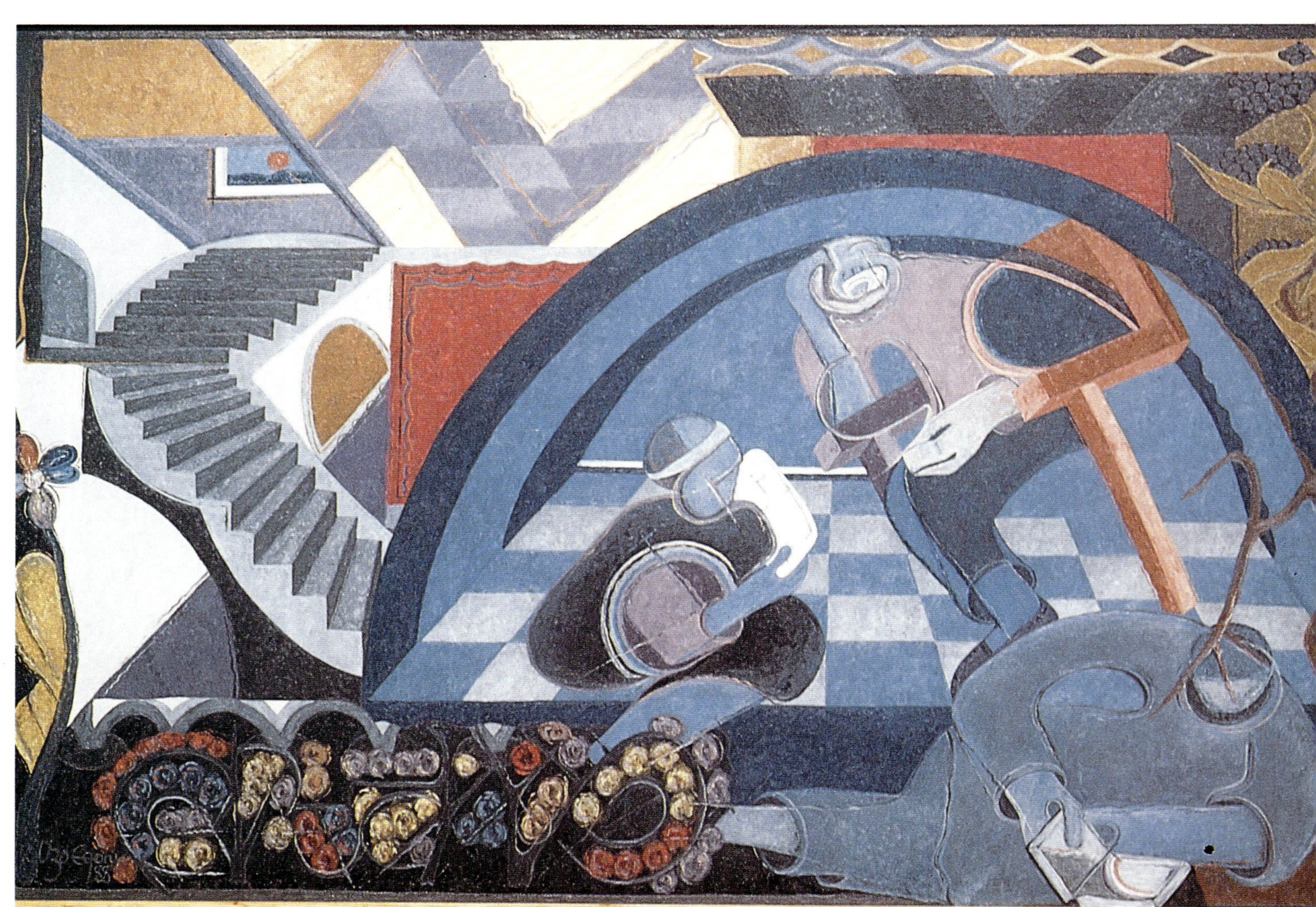

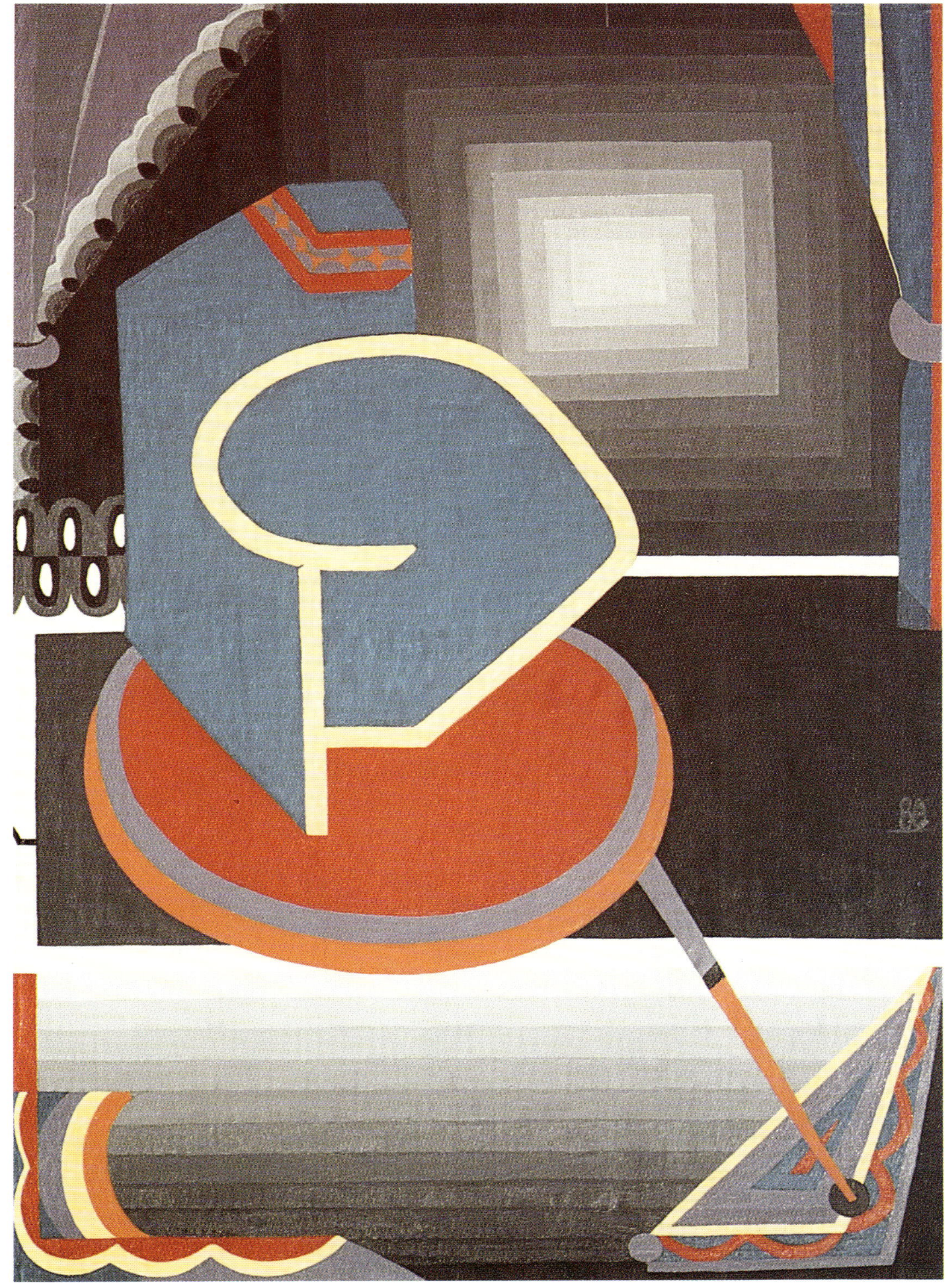

or original community, one must first be removed from it and, in experiencing the outside, come to see it in a different, more endearing light. One of the characters from the novel, *The Emigrants*, insists that:

> If there is one thing England going to teach all o' we is that there ain't no place like home no matter how bad home is... those comin' after goin' make better West Indian men for coming up here and seein' for themselves what is what.[15]

In other words to become a proper or 'better' part of one's homeland, to know it and believe in it, one needs to escape it and, by acquiring an alternative experience, come to appreciate and identify with it, to truly claim it. This is confirmed by Egonu when he states that, after settling in England, "it dawned on me that I am a Nigerian, an African. It dawned on me that in the culture in which I live I would never be accepted."[16]

It is this context of a community apart from the society of residence which frames content and commitment in Egonu's art. Having come to the above conclusion on his relationship with England, and recognising at the same time that, as he put it, "if you are living here [in Europe], you cannot say, no, I am African, I have to be in Africa",[17] Egonu strove to be relevant to his original community by apprehending its diverse complexities and experiences at different social and historical moments and projecting these before his, albeit limited, and distinct audience. This he did, not passively, but with intent to elicit reaction, to engage and provoke response calculated and anticipated to benefit that community in the long run.

The War Years

Few things have affected Egonu more personally and strongly, with the exception perhaps of his illness in the 1980s, than the tragedy of the Nigerian nation in the long half decade from the middle to the end of the 1960s. The liberation movement in Africa, and the wave of new nations, beginning with the independence of Ghana in 1958, was, as we indicated earlier, a historical development of enormous significance for most Africans, especially for the émigré in the heart of Empire. The emergence of new nation-states from the colonies was not only a geo-political process but also had psychological implications for citizens of those states. It signified an alteration in relations among peoples as well as individuals. The emergence of 'nation' and 'nationhood' not only involved separation from the imperial centre and the fabrication of new parameters of freedom and vision, it also entailed the creation of new individuals. The eventual humiliation of Empire — which was the way most colonial subjects perceived the demise of imperialism — symbolised their rehabilitation as fully-fledged individuals with dignity. They were no longer subjects but citizens of nations, 'foreigners' as opposed to faceless, second-class members of a vast, vague sea of imperial vassalage. They were automatically relocated from the peripheries of an amorphous commonality to the centres of new, autonomous spaces. Peoples hitherto struggling to enter the 'centre' found a plurality of emergent centres which signalled new visions and possibilities.

But independence posed its own challenges. To invalidate finally the ideological premises of the colonising mission, it was now the duty

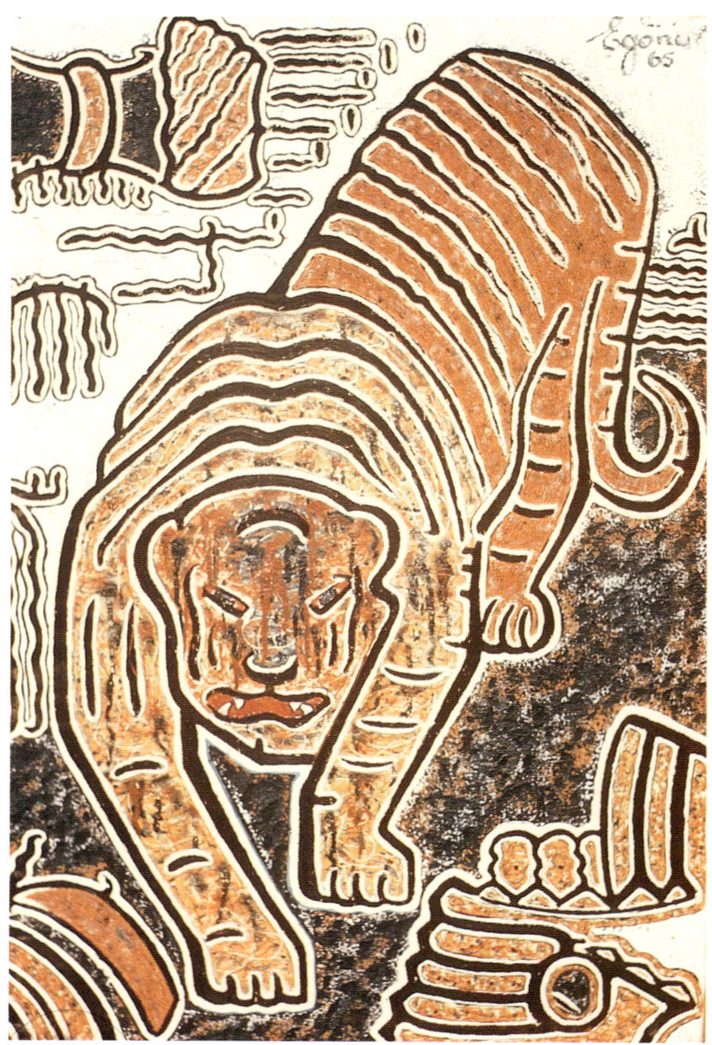

Tiger, **1965**
Oil on canvas
130 x 94 cm
Coll: Mrs D Low, London

of the newly independent nations to exhibit the abilities of self-governance and efficient modernisation without recourse to outside intervention. The euphoria of independence was thus mixed with brash optimism and genuine anxiety. For former colonial subjects living in the metropolis their status hung in the balance and pride was checked by the frightening possibility that the new nations might indeed collapse. Such collapse would bring dishonour, and a resumption of the uncertainty and precariousness of their existence within the insecure holds of Empire. If colonial emigrants suffered mildly as the lower caste of Empire, the decolonising process actively transformed them into permanent enemies and detractors, and into perpetual outsiders. Only success with the project of independent nationhood in their own countries could guarantee them the most minimal physical and psychological security in the West.

Throughout the period of agitation for independence attitudes in Europe towards immigrants from the emerging nations was characterised by unprecedented levels of hostility and violence. In France, Algerians were murdered in the streets just as they were murdered back in their homeland by French forces. In Britain the spin-off of the disengagement of former colonies from the imperial stranglehold was the enactment of hostile, anti-immigrant laws in the early 1960s, as well as the inflammation of public hostilities by political leaders. If such was the cost of colonial disengagement, the failure of the nationalist undertaking threatened even higher prices.

Just as the emergence of Nigeria as an independent nation helped shape and strengthen Egonu's nationalist predilections as well as define his artistic persona, so the uncertainties that gradually appeared in the new nation like cracks in the wall inescapably replicated themselves on this persona. The emergence of the post-colonial nation signified the advent of the new 'native' — for nation, as Raymond Williams reminds us, is, after all, "radically connected to 'native'".[1] The nation comes to symbolise this new personality, and should the former collapse so will also the latter. In such an event the new 'native' returns

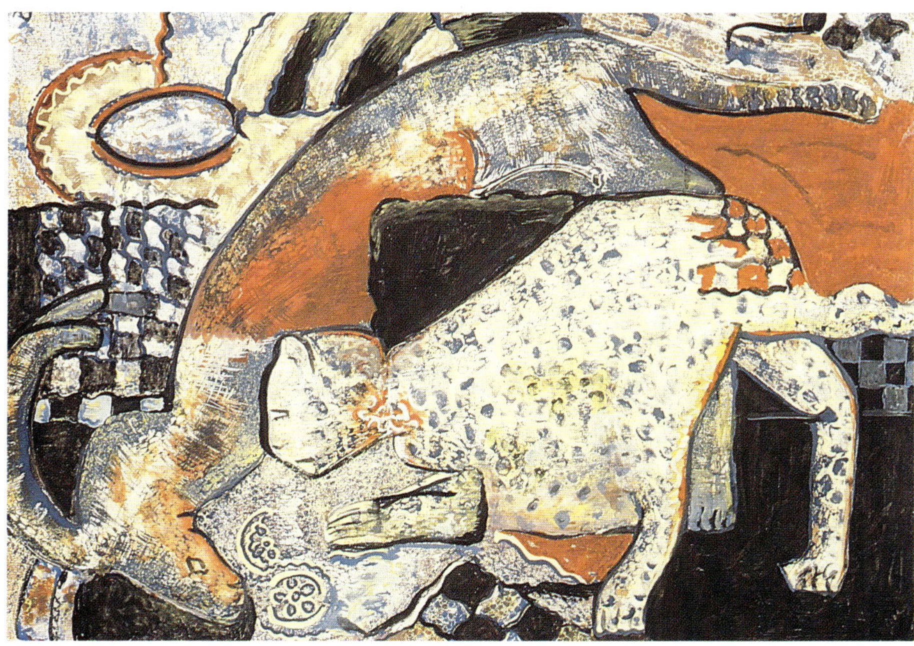

***Cheetah Attacking Its Prey*, 1965**
Gouache on paper
52 x 76 cm

to the state of vassalage. The prospects of such a fall initiate a crisis, especially in the émigré who is often unable to make an accurate assessment of the situation and is therefore liable to greater anxiety and desperation.[2] By 1966, just as he was consolidating the grounds of his artistic persona, the anxieties of this precarious historical moment began to show in Egonu's work. As the boat of self-governance rocked in Nigeria, slowly sinking under escalating violence, disappointment turned into genuine apprehension and the initial glow of hope turned into fear. Chaos had taken over and tragedy was inevitable.

Chinua Achebe predicted the events in Nigeria in his novel, *A Man of the People,* which was published almost to the day of the eventual termination of Nigeria's First Republic. Unlike Achebe, Egonu had access to a less accurate picture of the situation gleaned from the British press. However, as the world media closely followed the political upheavals, daring to predict the disintegration of the country — the historian Basil Davidson had noted in the *Daily Mirror* of London as early as December 1964 that a real danger of disintegration existed in Nigeria[3] — Egonu responded in a number of paintings which not only reflected his anxiety but also bore an element of the apocalyptic.

Among these are *Tiger* and *Cheetah attacking its Prey*, both painted in 1965 before the coup of 1966. The two paintings introduced a new symbolism to the series of paintings of animals which Egonu made that year. In these and subsequent paintings such as *Leopard*, 1966, *End of a Sheep* and *Two Fighting Cocks*, both painted in 1967, and *Death of an Elephant* from 1968, Egonu deals with anxiety, uncertainty, danger, insecurity and strife on a magnified level. Unlike other paintings from the same period, these were allegories in which the artist crafted an apocalyptic fiction employing animal imagery.

Tiger is a bold painting whose composition is dominated by the centrally placed image of a reclining tiger. The animal is set against a dark background of sparse vegetation and lattice-work, suggesting a cage or other metal enclosure. Above it are broad stripes which resemble ringside ropes, descending into a central, circular aperture very much like a barred shutter. A few leaves resembling ears of wheat represent vegetation. We notice that the tiger is not in an entirely reclining position, but rather leans anxiously on its forelegs, like the crouch before a defensive strike. The atmosphere of bondage or restraint in the painting is further emphasised by the animal's encasement in the rope work, as well as its proportion and location in the picture, which makes it struggle almost physically across the composition. Dark spaces press down on it, leaving no breathing space. Its crouch projects the unsettling feeling of a silent struggle between its body and the enclosing space, as well as evoking a sense of imminent unwinding, a moment of unleashing. The animal's eyes are tiny, diamond shaped and blank, set in the middle of the face with a blind and cold unease.

One possible reading of this picture is the recreation of a moment of uncertainty in the history of a society. Egonu's allegorical strategies are of immense importance. By figuring the tiger, the artist seems to imply a certain viciousness not necessarily in the character of the society which this painting narrates, but in the nature of the moment. The viciousness is epochal. Encaging the animal indicates that this viciousness, as far as the artist can perceive it or is willing to grant, is more latent than already manifest. The blank stare of the tiger qualifies this potential, locating it outside the realm of the contemplative or rational. The animal may be caged, but it is also lurking, crouching, held down by the strictures of institutional order. Restraint is only suggested and not defined; it is present, but not foolproof.

The interplay of elements and metaphors in the picture reflects a certain precariousness presaging possible anarchy and/or tragedy. The animal represents the latent violence of all societies, held in check by structures and institutions of governance. Unleashed from such confines all societies are beastly. In other words the painting seems to suggest, much like William Golding's *Lord of the Flies*, that disorder is intrinsic to human nature; without law and order, humanity is at the mercy of its own instinct. In this case Egonu seems to suggest, as his contemporary the poet Christopher Okigbo put it in his own apocalyptic poem from the same period, that "the smell of blood hangs/ in the lavender mist of the afternoon".[4] *Tiger* was both prophecy and plea.

Leopard, which was painted the following year, realises what *Tiger* anticipated. It is unclear at what precise moment in 1966 this picture was painted but indications are that it was after the bloody events in Nigeria that January. *Leopard* is in contrast to the earlier painting both in form and intent. For one, it is conceived on a perpendicular axis; the animal is centrally positioned as in the earlier work, but this time falls on a slight diagonal rather than a horizontal. The picture is divided into three horizontal sections. The head of the animal is placed slightly above the line of the lower segment, its bared teeth and red tongue located on the line itself. The mouth is dead centre of the perpendicular axis. Also, except for a dull red portion in the top left of the painting and a foreground stippled in pale cobalt and burnt sienna, the red of the bared mouth, the purest red in the picture, marks the optical centre of the painting, and by extension, the focus of signification.

As already noted, the animal in *Leopard*, bulky and emphatic, falls on a diagonal,. creating the unsettling image of an arrow in descent. The animal is on the prowl, and the spatial arrangement in the picture creates room for this. A background set under a form of canopy casts the leopard out from the picture plane, and creates the impression of a doorway, implying an act of emergence, a leap forward.

***No Place for the Weak*, 1968**
Oil on canvas
81 x 112 cm

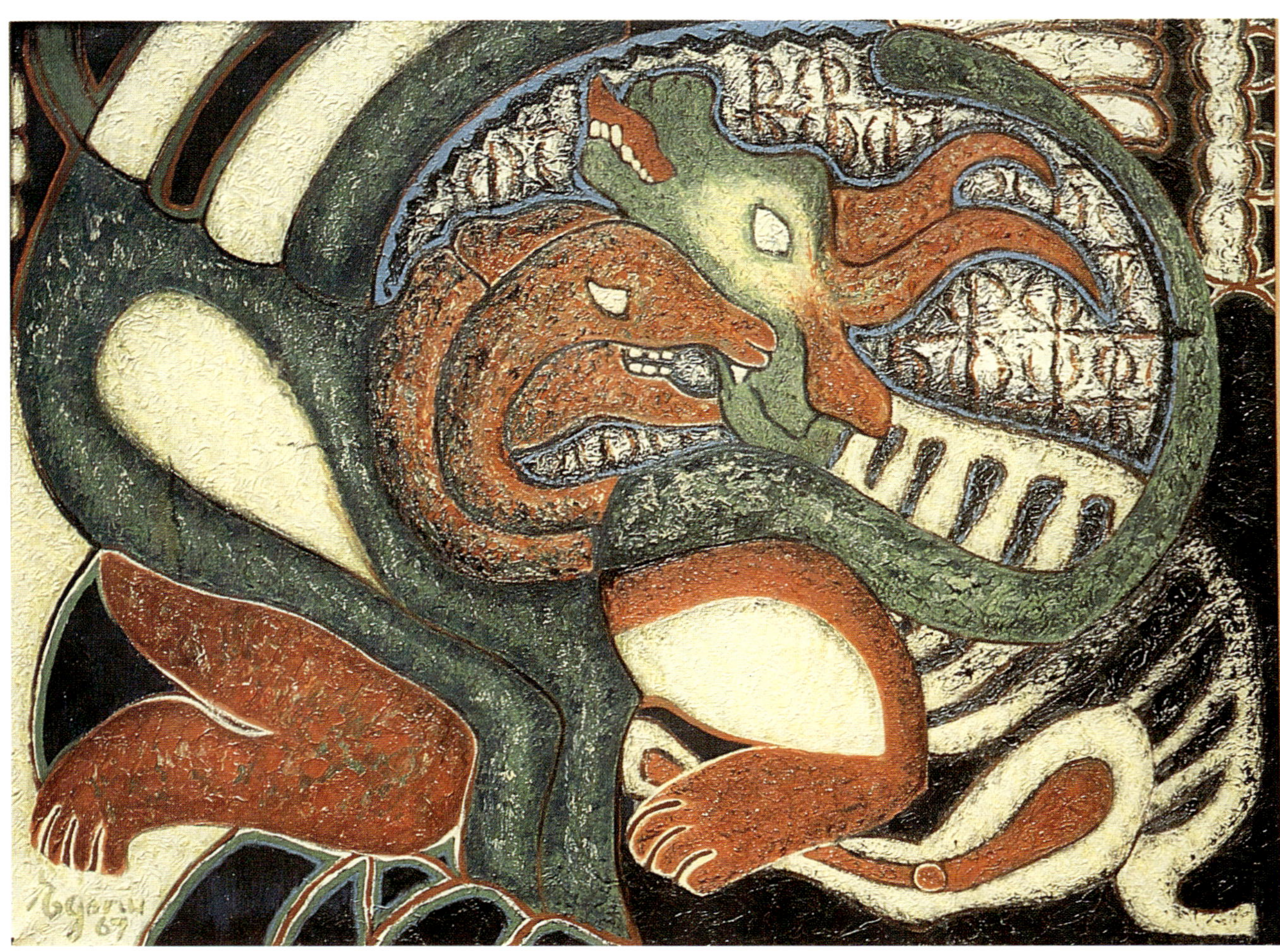

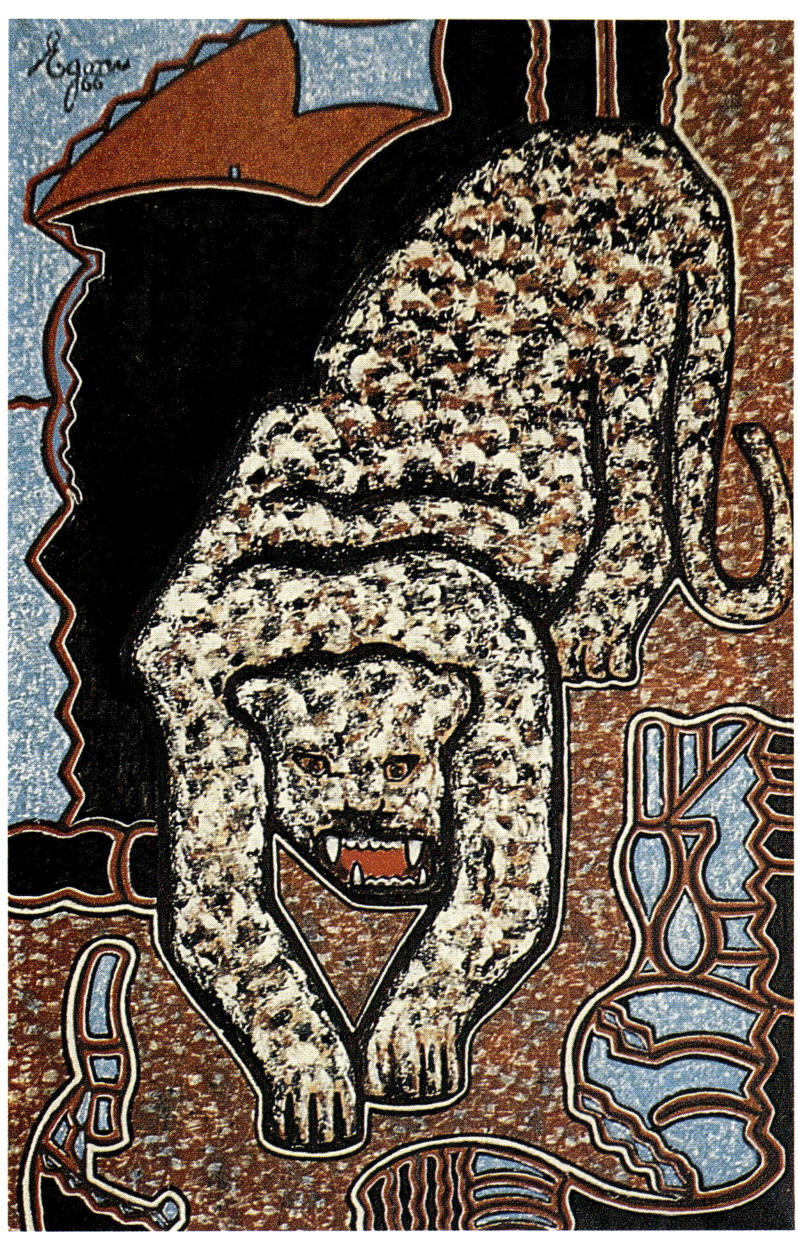

***Leopard*, 1966**
Oil on canvas
128 x 81 cm

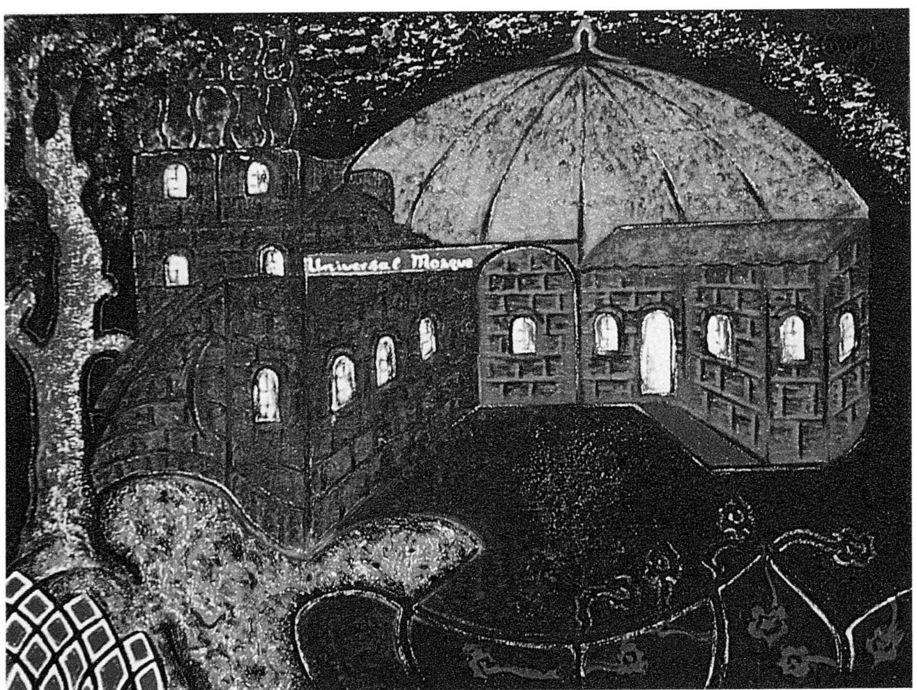

Universal Mosque, 1966
Oil on canvas
71 x 91 cm

While in the earlier painting the animal is reclining and restrained, the leopard in this painting is loose and in the act of charging. There is no clear indication of vegetation, and the animal emerges into what seems like a barren arena. A few decorative elements occur in the painting but purely as design. Notable as well are the eyes of the beast, which are not diamond and blank as in the other work, but beady and bloodshot; the leopard is fierce, its stare intense. The scenario recalls W B Yeats's *The Second Coming* with its graphic depiction of anarchy and inevitable disaster. The forces of anarchy, the restrained viciousness figured in the caged, reclining tiger, are unleashed in the charging leopard, and "mere anarchy is loosed upon the world". In 1968 Lawrence Bradshaw summarised the significance of Egonu's allegory of the prowling leopard in his appreciation of the painting and the historical moment which produced it in the following, succinct words: "Today Death walks abroad."[5] In *Cheetah attacking its Prey*, and perhaps even more clearly in *No Place for the Weak*, 1968, we see the ultimate unfolding of the apocalypse as the beast devours its victim, signifying the momentary triumph of the strong over the weak.

In Egonu's subsequent paintings, the series 'Spiritual Protection' which he began in 1966, there is a move from apocalypse to entreaty as the artist addresses the themes of dislocation, flight, refuge and protection. The 'ecumenicals', as we may call this series of pictures, especially since a common theme is a plea for religious tolerance, employ religious architecture as a central metaphor. These works are at once appeals for protection for the threatened and persecuted, as well as entreaties for sanity and reason. They posit, on one level, the common kin of peoples and the equality, if not sameness, of faiths. The context to this vision of religious harmony and the primacy of spirit over religious dichotomy, at once desperate and frustrated, is that religious acrimony, real and invented, between the 'Muslim North' and the 'Christian South', was offered as an explanation for the events in Nigeria in 1966 and after, although from a closer perspective the fallacy of this theory was obvious even at the time.

The central motif of *Universal Mosque*, 1966, is a mosque which, architecturally, suggests little that is Islamic. It is built on what appears

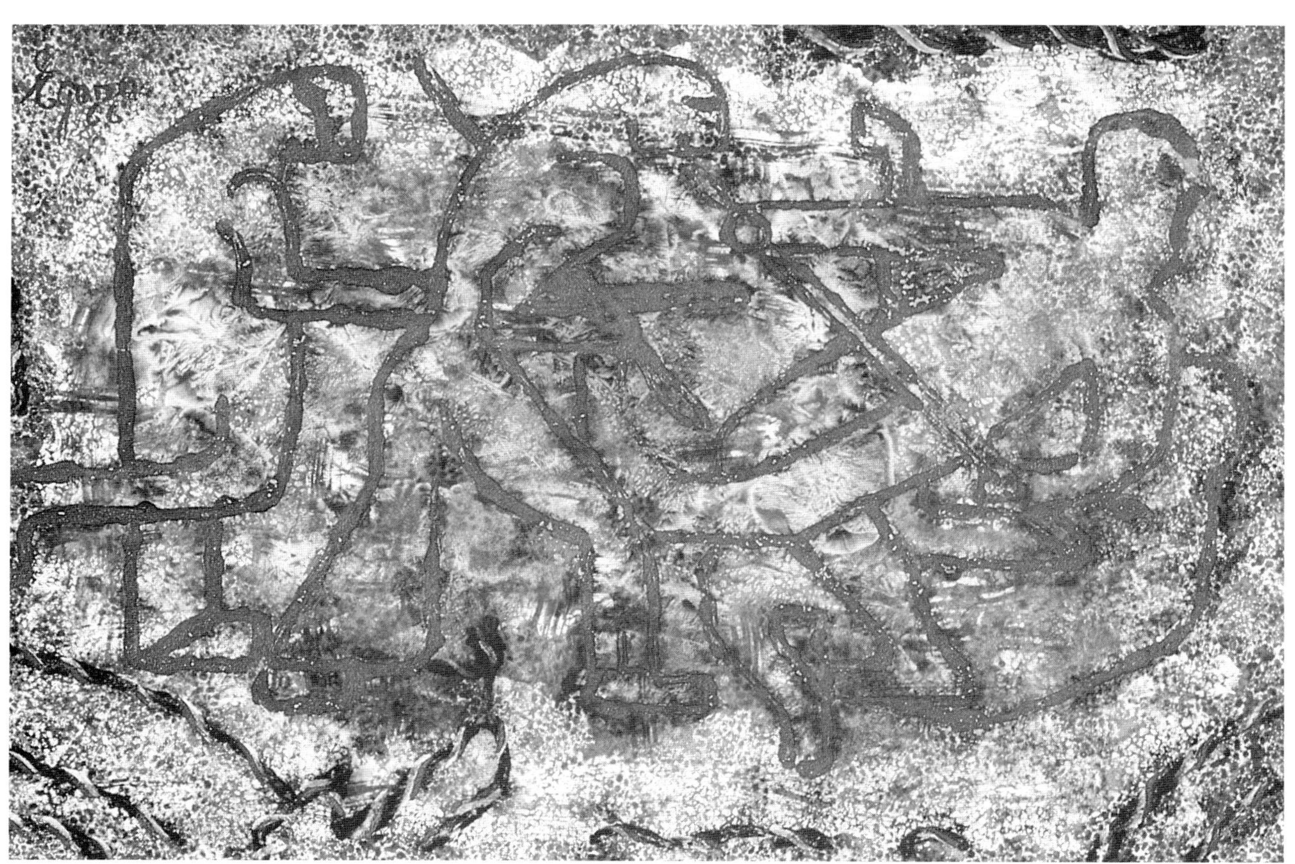

***Battle*, 1966**
Gouache on paper
51 x 61 cm

to be a rectangular floor plan, yet it is discernibly circular, cut into like an apple to provide a space which serves both as courtyard and entrance and yields a narrow corridor to the right of the building. This section presents an angular sphere with a ribbed dome suggesting brick or cast copper. The dome bears a greater resemblance to that of St Peter's in Rome or St Paul's in London than to the more ornamental versions of Islamic architecture. The left section of the building is a long hall with what appears to be a small tower and an exterior flight of stairs in weathered stone. The door and windows are arched, and in the foreground is a scrawled inscription which reads

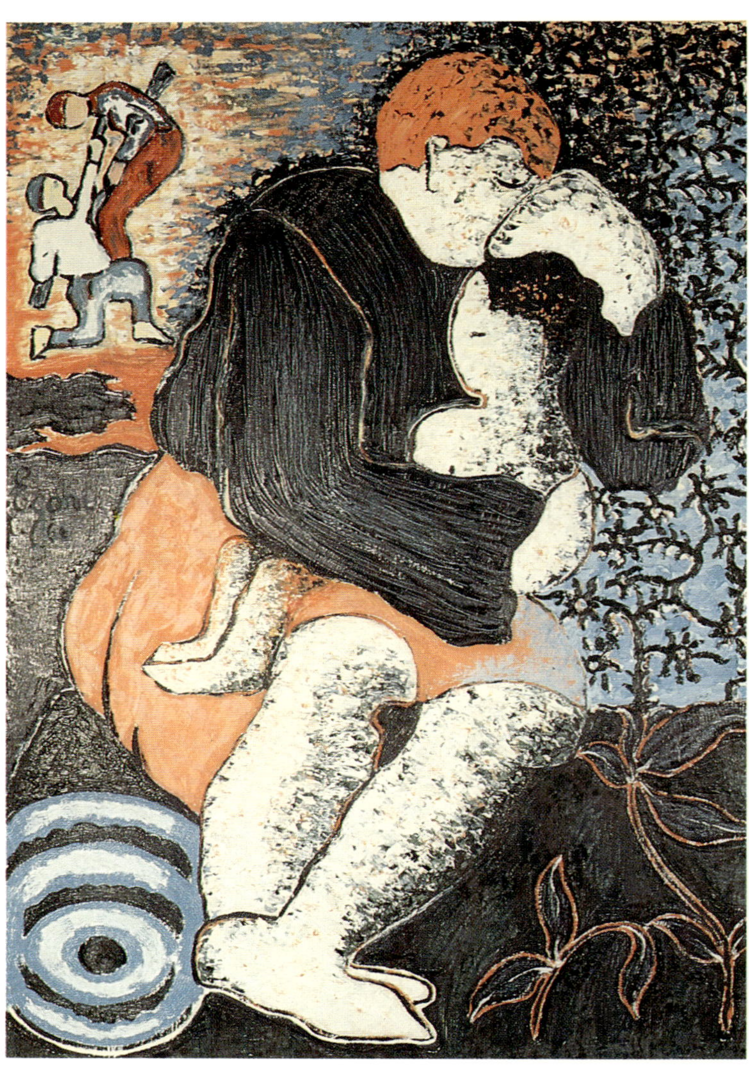

***Mother and Child*, 1966**
Oil on canvas
81 x 122 cm

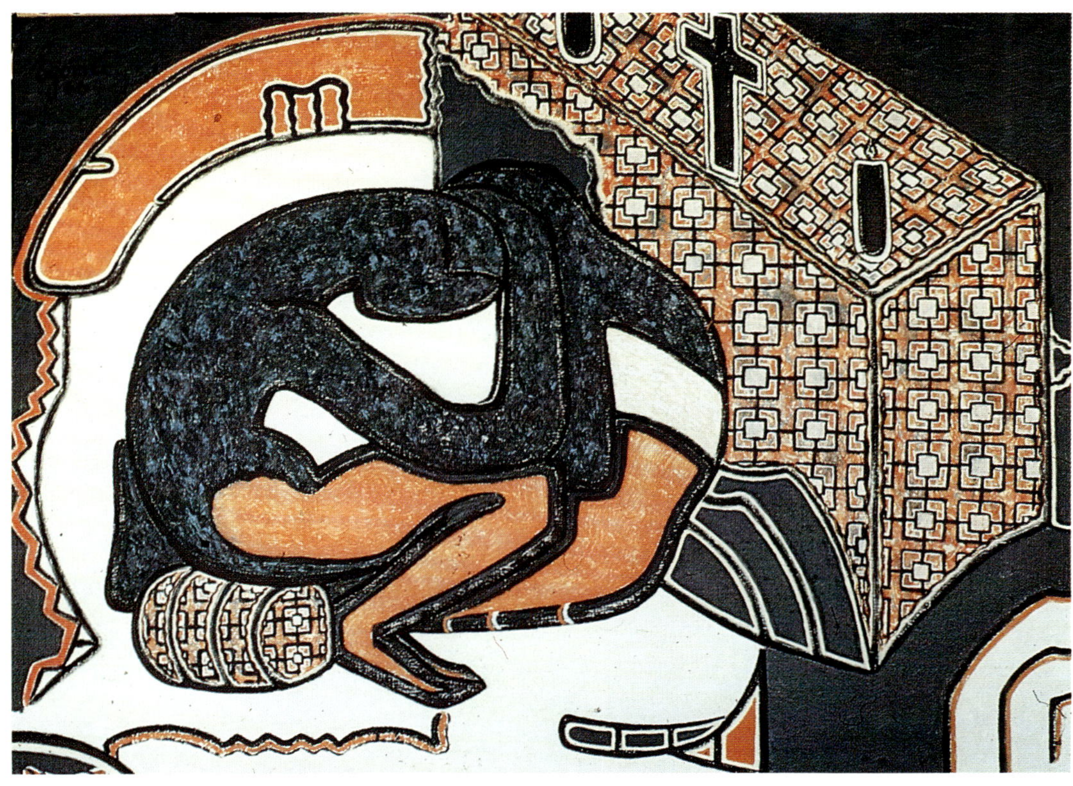

***Sanctuary in the Chapel*, 1966**
Oil on canvas
91 x 122 cm

'Universal Mosque' and which is the one visual clue to the identity of the building. The painting is obviously a night scene, providing atmosphere for fluorescent light to issue from inside the mosque through its windows and door. To the left of the mosque is the outline of a tree, and the curve of the dome is echoed in the background in the reclining stem of a shrub which resembles the edge of a platform and ends to the left in what might be a little pool.

On one level, the ambiguous nature of the structure resists sectarian specificity and points to the universality which the artist means to establish through the title of the painting. It not only demythicises the mosque as a religious symbol, but through that the faith as well. On this level therefore, Egonu seems to register a pluralist argument by rejecting traditional forms in favour of an indeterminate, arguably innovative one. Because difference in the particular context is architecturally encoded, Egonu replaces a regular code with one which challenges otherisation.

At the same time, Egonu subordinates nationalist sectarianism to the unifying vision of the nation-state. Within the state the 'sect' is a threat, a primordial residue which must be relegated and subdued, if not completely dislodged. Egonu's vision, as gleaned from this painting, is the Bakhtinian ideal whereby the *natio* overrides sect and "the period of national languages coexisting but deaf to one another, comes to an end". At the time putting sectarian units under check seemed a prerequisite for the survival of the emergent postcolonial state, especially in its power struggle with the vestiges of Empire. The fragility of new nations such as Nigeria, the uncertainties of their disengagement from the formidable structures of Empire, and the pressures of legitimation, all underlined the vulnerability of such nations — should they adopt a rather tolerant disposition towards sects within — to disruptive and divisive internal conflict which resurgent sectarianism perpetrates. In envisioning a neutral space of worship in *Universal Mosque,* a theatre of faith open to all convictions and sects, Egonu sought to locate all such sects within the democratic commonwealth of the state, and thus diffuse their disruptive potentials.

As the conflict in Nigeria escalated, leading to the massacre of thousands of the Igbo, a shift emerged in Egonu's concerns and in his work. His initial anxiety over nation and self polysemously 'masked' in the universalist arguments of *Universal Mosque*, gave way to concerns over broad questions of the human condition. As violence became an actuality rather than a mere threat in Nigeria, Egonu became more concerned not for the somewhat abstract issue of nation as for individual lives. And although his broad nationalism did not disappear entirely, the fact that more lives were being lost from his section of the country naturally lent a bias to his worries. For him, also, the borders of nation became unclear. One could see in his work the beginning of that process by which, according to Timothy Brennan, 'nation' and nationalism undergo a "semantic shift".[6] In the face of conflict allegiance to 'nation' sometimes undergoes a pragmatic transfiguration, shifting perhaps towards nationalist extremism, or recoiling into the self.

In *Sanctuary in the Chapel*, 1966, Egonu began to image the tragedy of national chaos and disintegration not within the intangible frames of an invented community, but in the harsh arena of individual, human anguish. At this stage the human figure made its reappearance in the paintings. In *Sanctuary in the Chapel* we find a lone figure in an enclosure, a raised hand over its chest, effectively obscuring its gender. The figure is presumably a refugee in search of sanctuary. The structure in which the figure is placed is positively marked as a Christian space by its image of a cross. Whereas *Universal Mosque* encoded the more philosophical discourse of faith and universality in architectural anonymity, *Sanctuary in the Chapel* moves away from such idealism. The lone refugee in *Sanctuary* represents the persecuted, the weak, and would reappear in a later painting, *No Place for the Weak*. The cross in *Sanctuary* seems to reflect the Christian religious affiliation of the majority of the persecuted Igbo. Egonu's use of a chapel as a space of refuge and sanctuary, signifying both desperation and vanquish, seems to indicate the failure of the ecumenical argument of the earlier painting, the failure of the universalist-neutralist discourse. It seems as if the artist was granting that an unsubdued sect, represented by Islam, had overpowered the non-believers, while Christianity offered refuge. This was reverse sectarianism. But then, issues are never so simple and straightforward. Any such argument is undermined both by the artist's ambivalence over questions of faith — which in a sense partly informs his universalist argument — and the inconsistencies of any specific religious theories of the national crises which inform these works and the discourse which they engender. Egonu always viewed both Christianity and Islam and the history which they embody as irreconcilable with true cultural nationalism for anyone from his part of the world.

What we see in *Sanctuary in the Chapel*, therefore, is not the valorisation of Christianity, or the replacement of patriotism with sectarianism, but the proposition of a mediative body, one which could offer 'spiritual protection' to all. More importantly, the painting sought to call attention to the human suffering that was beginning to escalate in parts of Nigeria. Egonu's nationalism never gave way to religious sectarianism. Even when Nigeria broke up in 1967 and the artist's section of the country founded the Republic of Biafra, he never truly offered the breakaway nation his full allegiance.

If, in works like *Sanctuary*, the artist's inclinations seem to play down nationalist idealism, his subsequent works from 1966 and 1967 further de-emphasise it. In *Mother and Child*, 1966, it is no longer 'spiritual' protection that matters, but the even more urgent reality of battle and the miseries of war. Although when *Mother and Child* was painted full war had not yet broken out in Nigeria, there were enough signs that it was almost inevitable. A second coup had taken place in the country which claimed the second head of government in one year, and was clearly a campaign of vendetta against the artist's

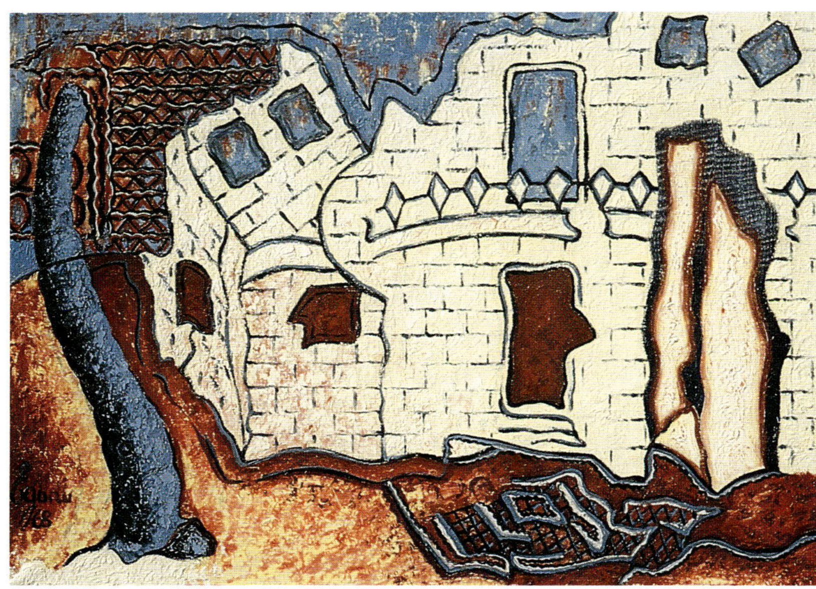

Bombed House, **1968**
Oil on canvas
56 x 76 cm

people. The guarantees of physical protection and safety which the people sought after massacres earlier in the year faded away with the new coup and the clearly sectarian government which it ushered in. From that moment spiritual protection was no longer sufficient. The millions of Igbo people, herded together in their home enclave in eastern Nigeria after being driven out of other parts of the country, began to fear possible annihilation, and many spoke of imminent genocide.

In what must be considered a masterpiece in the depiction of conflict as well as perhaps one of the artist's finest works, *Mother and Child* not only distils the irreconcilability of war and metaphysical idealism, the futility of the spiritualist argument in the face of brutal conflict, but also captures most deftly the complexities of conflict, violence and vulnerability.

The painting is dominated by the image of a mother and child in a roadside thicket. The two figures are in a state of discernible shock, the mother hiding her face behind that of her child. The atmosphere is one of agitation; the woman could be weeping. She clasps and covers her child protectively. In this position, she could be protecting her child from physical violence, a threat which hovers menacingly, since both figures do not appear adequately hidden from the cause of their anxiety and fright. In the upper left corner of the painting, in a bright clearing which could be a deserted road, a duel is taking place between two figures, one with red hair and the other with blue. The red figure towers above the blue who is down on one knee. The gesture is one of momentary loss of ground, but not of submission: the warrior is not fallen, only falling, with one knee bent as if about to rise. On the contrary, the towering figure in red is looking down on the falling duellist, but his knees are partly bent, and so is his body; as if, having received an unexpected blow, he is in the process of an anguished doubling-over. From his other side protrudes an object like a club, which is not in use at the moment of portrayal.

The presence of this potentially harmful object, even if inert, indicates the possibility of use, before or after. The figure in red could be pulling up his victim for the final blow, or dragging him away, ready to employ the club or gun. Perhaps it is this frightening possibility which explains the anguished apprehension of the mother

***The End of a Tree*, 1967**
Oil on canvas
81 x 112 cm

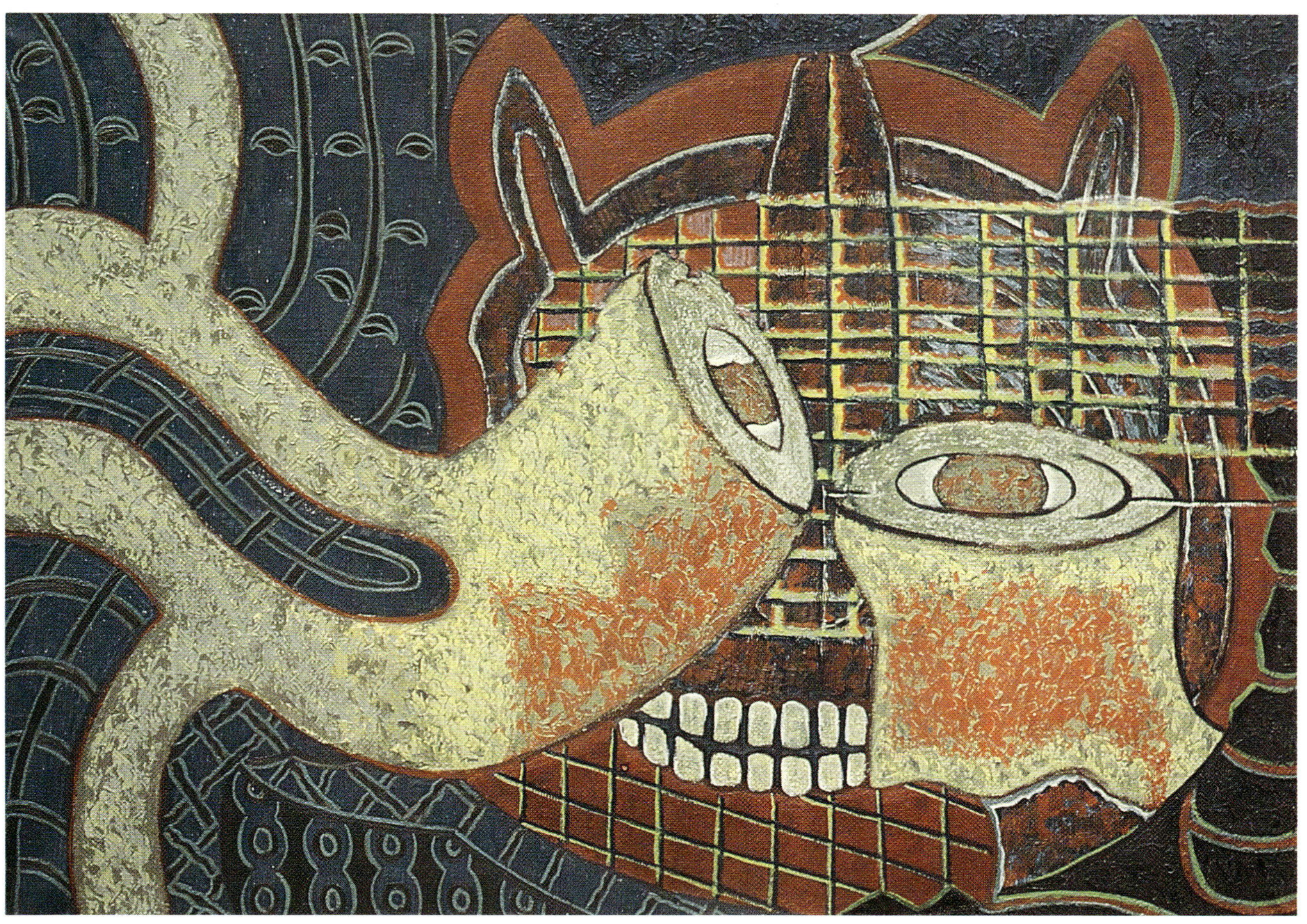

and child. By choosing this particular moment of ambiguity, rather than portraying the aggressive act itself, by leaving room for uncertainty and thus for greater anxiety, Egonu is able to de-sensationalise his representation. This he also does by employing images of faceless figures in everyday clothing rather than uniformed soldiers, for instance. Signification here is direct, discourse at its most philosophical, since it is the concept of feuding, rather than the act, which comes across. The artist seems to emphasise that war is about conflict and confrontation, not about soldiers, and the dialectics of conflict and confrontation, as well as their consequences, go beyond the fall of cities and death in the trenches to that of simple human terror, the warp and torture of the human soul.

In the painting the eyes of the child are shut tight in absolute terror, that terror with which every war child learns to live. Because the process of accepting or conquering this terror invariably robs a child of tenderness and subtlety, a generation grows up with a diminished appreciation of human worth, instituting a generational cycle of violence. Not only do children need protection from the physical violence of conflicts and war, they must also be protected from the traumas which embed a psychotic predilection for violence and threaten, much more than the immediate costs of war, the future of the community and nation. In essence, not only is Egonu concerned for the sacredness and security of human lives, he is also concerned for the future of his country, in whatever form it survives.

By ignoring clichés in the representation of conflict — arms, battle scenes and such images — Egonu is able in this painting and a few others, to steer contemplation towards the primary significance of the human element in war. To represent conflict and confrontation with guns and armaments, or with striding and falling soldiers, is to be reductionist. Our attention is directed rather to the costs of conflict not simply in terms of the material causes or repercussions, not even merely the loss of lives — what the US military now qualifies as 'collateral' losses — but in terms of the damage to the young who constitute the future and soul of a community. More significant than some of his later paintings on the miseries of war, and indeed more significant than Achebe's, similarly titled, prize-winning poem on the same conflict, 'Madonna and Child',[7] Egonu's *Mother and Child* returns the discourse of confrontation to its human foundations and addresses a dimension seldom examined, the relationship between conflict and the psychology and cyclicity of violence.

One significant rhetorical strategy in *Mother and Child* is Egonu's use of the theme of the Nativity, one that is historically associated in almost all traditions with fertility and birth, not death; safety, and not vulnerability; the promise of redemption rather than the imminence of annihilation. Egonu magnifies the power of his deposition by playing this very popular image against that of feuding and danger, and this way reverses its traditional symbolism. The result is an unfamiliarity which borders on the profane, and this way affects even more poignantly on our sensibilities.

The significance of this painting also lies in the fact that it opens up the discourse of conflict. Perhaps more than any other work on

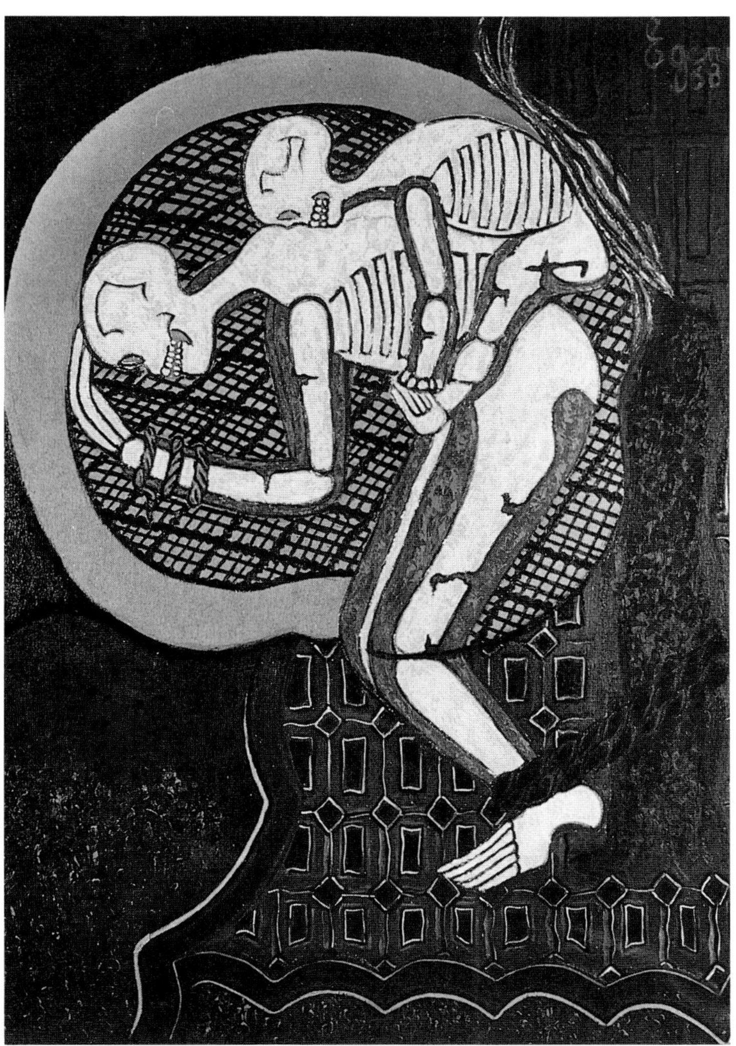

***Blind Eye to Tragedy*, 1967**
Oil on canvas
122 x 91 cm

conflict, *Mother and Child* draws attention to the masculinity of war. The gender bias of conflict, manifest in the male domination of armies and battles, has its roots in the specific gender configuration of state power which is the purveyor and protagonist of conflicts. This we discern in Egonu's imagery. Without positing absolute gender distinctions, the artist raises the discourse of gender relations. The dichotomisation of power and courage along gender lines, which we find, for example, in David's *Oath of the Horatii* is in line with a tradition which bell hooks has identified as "the central ideological component of all systems of domination in Western society".[8] We note, however, while the *Horatii* women are languid and limp, resignedly consigned to their 'rightful place', Egonu's woman is a centre of

***Death of an Elephant*, 1968**
Oil on canvas
71 x 91 cm

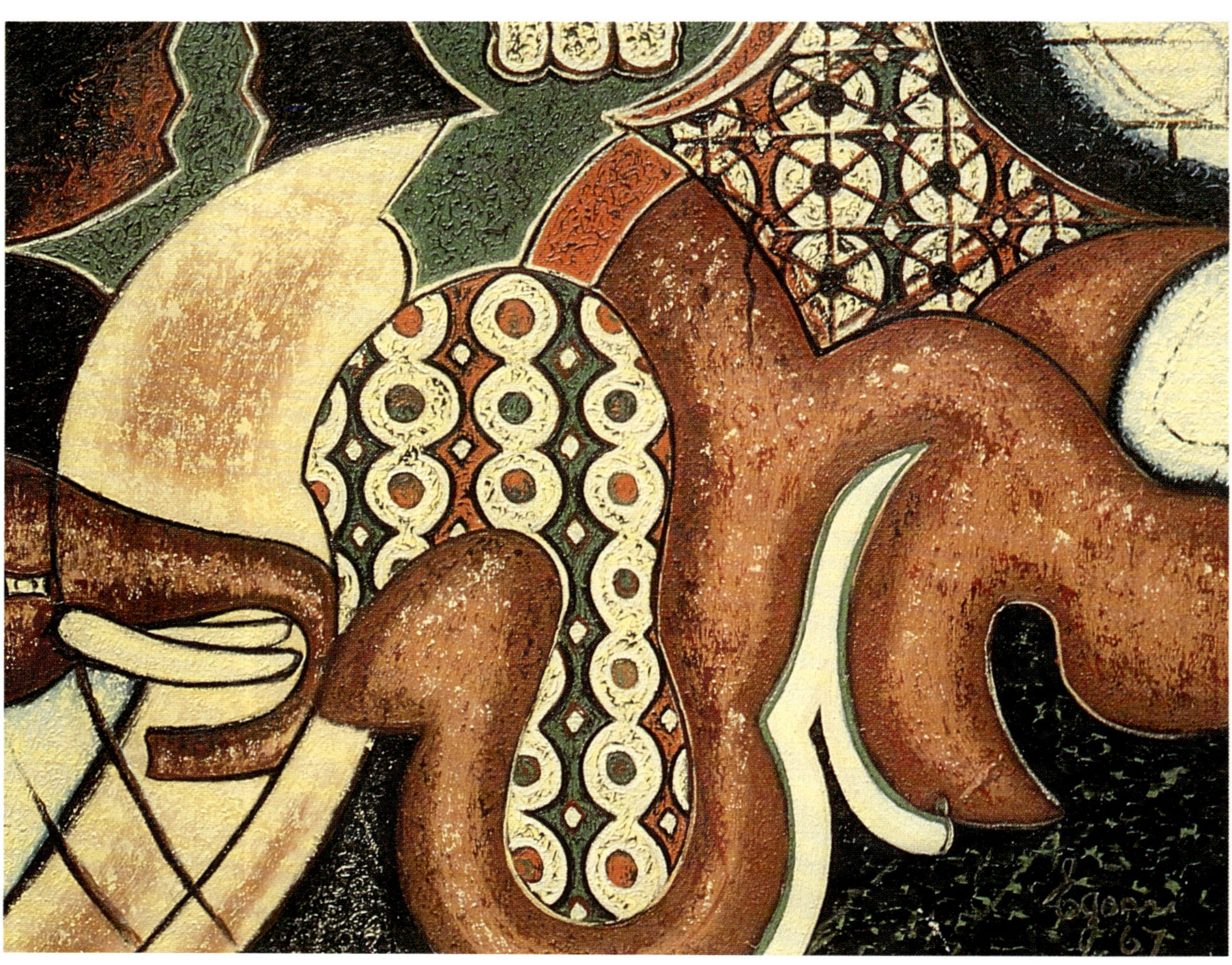

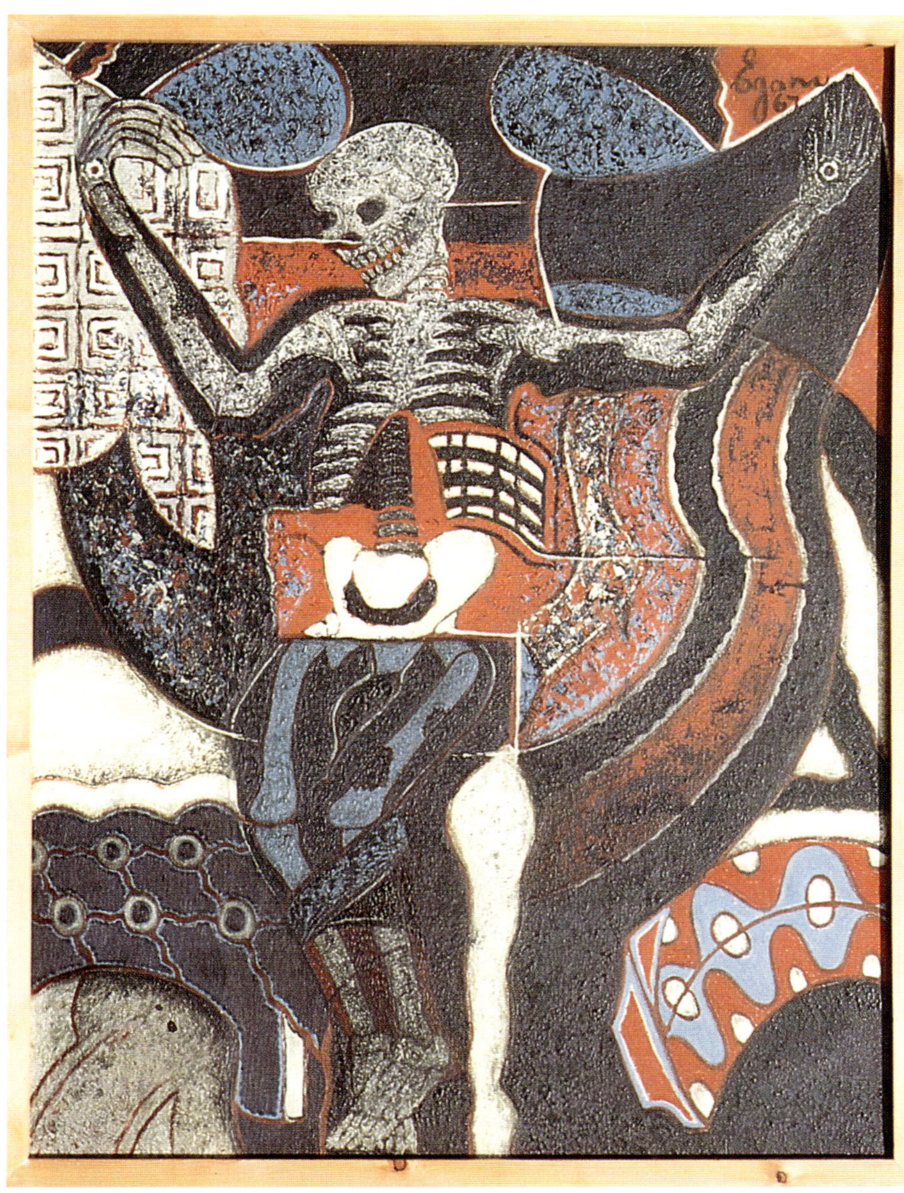

***Thirty Thousand*, 1967**
Oil on canvas
122 x 91 cm

dramatic anguish. She is stricken, and her terror is as impressionable as it is central to the logic of the picture. It is significant also that, though both compositions are built in two sections delineated both visually and psychologically, while the male space takes a larger section in the *Horatii*, Egonu's mother and child occupy the larger, central space; the dominant locus of the painting is the woman and child rather than the valorisation of the male.

War formally broke out in Nigeria in 1967, and Egonu's work of the war years, 1967-1970, all touch on the above themes, but never again in such precise and holistic terms. Other paintings from 1966 like *Bombed House* and *Battle* work within similar frames, but do not confront the phenomenon of conflagration in the same manner as *Mother and Child*. And the universalism, the 'humanism' of the stipulated discourse, Egonu consciously re-emphasised by freeing the figures of racial specificity.

The breakup of the Nigerian nation did not destroy Egonu's nationalism. Instead, it led him into what Aijaz Ahmad has described as the "nationalism of mourning", no longer a contemplation of what imperialism did to the colonies but of "what we ourselves had done, were still doing, in one way or another, to our own polity".[9] At this time a certain element of hysteria entered Egonu's imagery, especially as fighting in Nigeria became fiercer and figures of the level of human

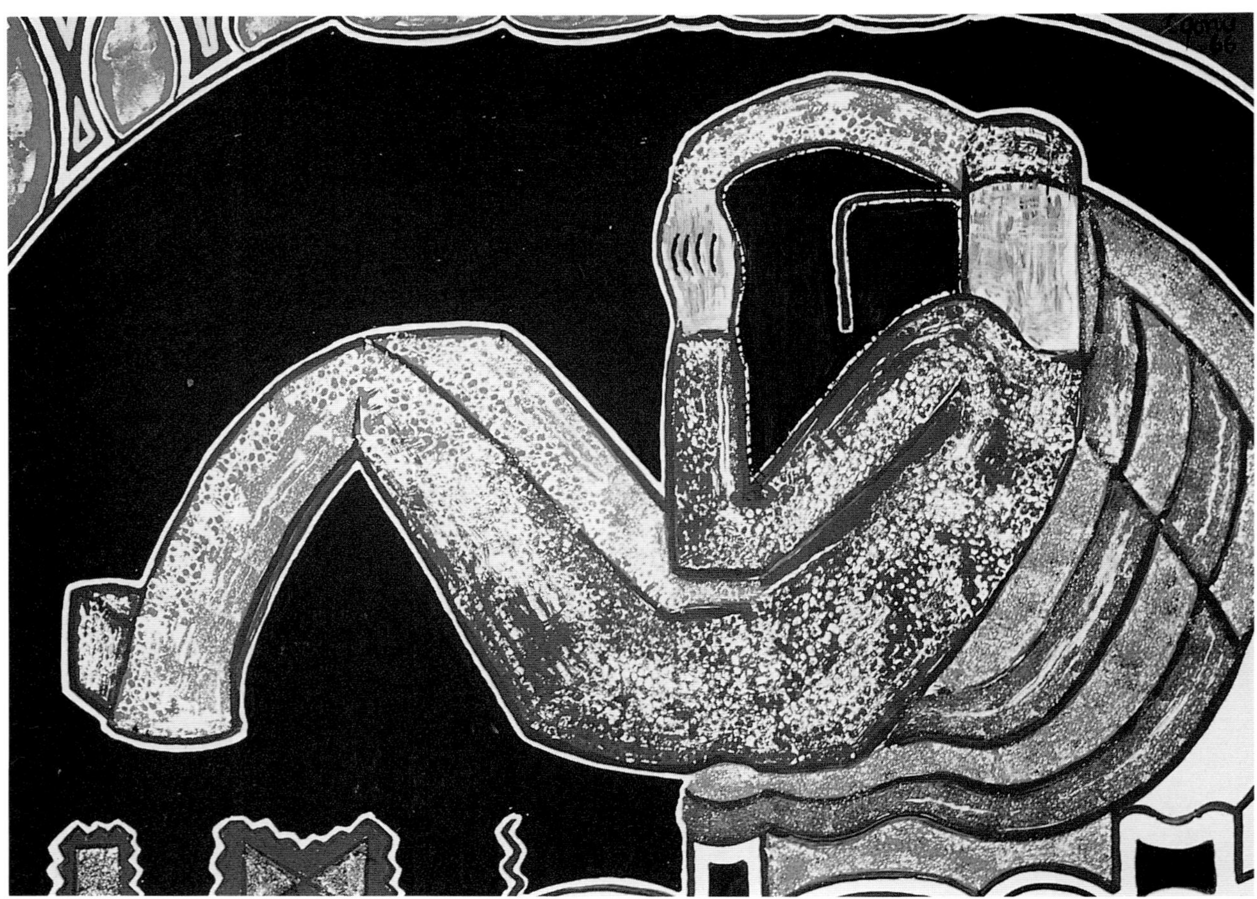

***A Soldier Resting After Battle*, 1966**
Gouache on paper
51 x 76 cm

loss became available. In his allegories the historical symbol of war and death, the skeleton, began to replace the human figure. Egonu's awareness of the danger of sensationalism and his efforts to avoid it show in his initial choice of metaphors for this phase of his work. As in the beginning of the apocalyptic phase in 1965, he began with non-human metaphors in such paintings as *The End of a Sheep* and *End of a Tree*, metaphors which stood for the annihilation and, with a tone of apocalyptic finality, the demise of his country. It is important to note that the tree in *End of a Tree* is felled not by machinery but by teeth, signifying the human element in conflict. The culprit here is a rodent, woven into the design behind the tree, its teeth located at the base of the trunk. The tree is not felled in an instant of sudden brutal severing, but through a gradual gnawing at the base, a cumulative and therefore predictable and avoidable process of destruction.

From 1968 Egonu shifted from the role of observer and contemplator to one of active campaigner, and from chronicling the war at home to agitating for international support. His exhibition at the Upper Grosvenor Galleries in London, in 1968, 'The World in Perspective', was given to this purpose. Not only did he appeal with his imagery, with the human skeleton as the leitmotif, he did so also through titles such as *Thirty Thousand*, *Blind Eye to Tragedy*, *No Place for the Weak*, and so on. *Blind Eye to Tragedy*, 1967, is a direct and embittered response to what the artist saw as international indifference to suffering in Biafra, especially the suspect role of the British government. Again, the artist employs the image of mother and child, though in this case they are direct victims not of the traumas of war but of its physical violence. To direct attention to the specific and brutal peculiarities of the war against Biafra, Egonu creates an extreme image of carnage and savagery: a lynched mother and child. He does not spare us the horror of this situation as he takes us through the history of the incident, showing us figures not merely tied to a tree but lynched and abandoned to rot. The skeleton of the woman leans forward, with that of the child still clinging to it, as the body rots and the ropes on her hands snap. We are shown part of the flesh sticking to the lynch tree, and in what looks like a nightmare at dawn, the two figures are thrown into highlight by a pale, blue sky — the woman's fingers are unnaturally placed on her forehead, a gesture which in life signifies lamentation and in death, defiance.

The painting encodes the embattled nation and its people: the

Flight, 1966
Oil on canvas
122 x 178 cm

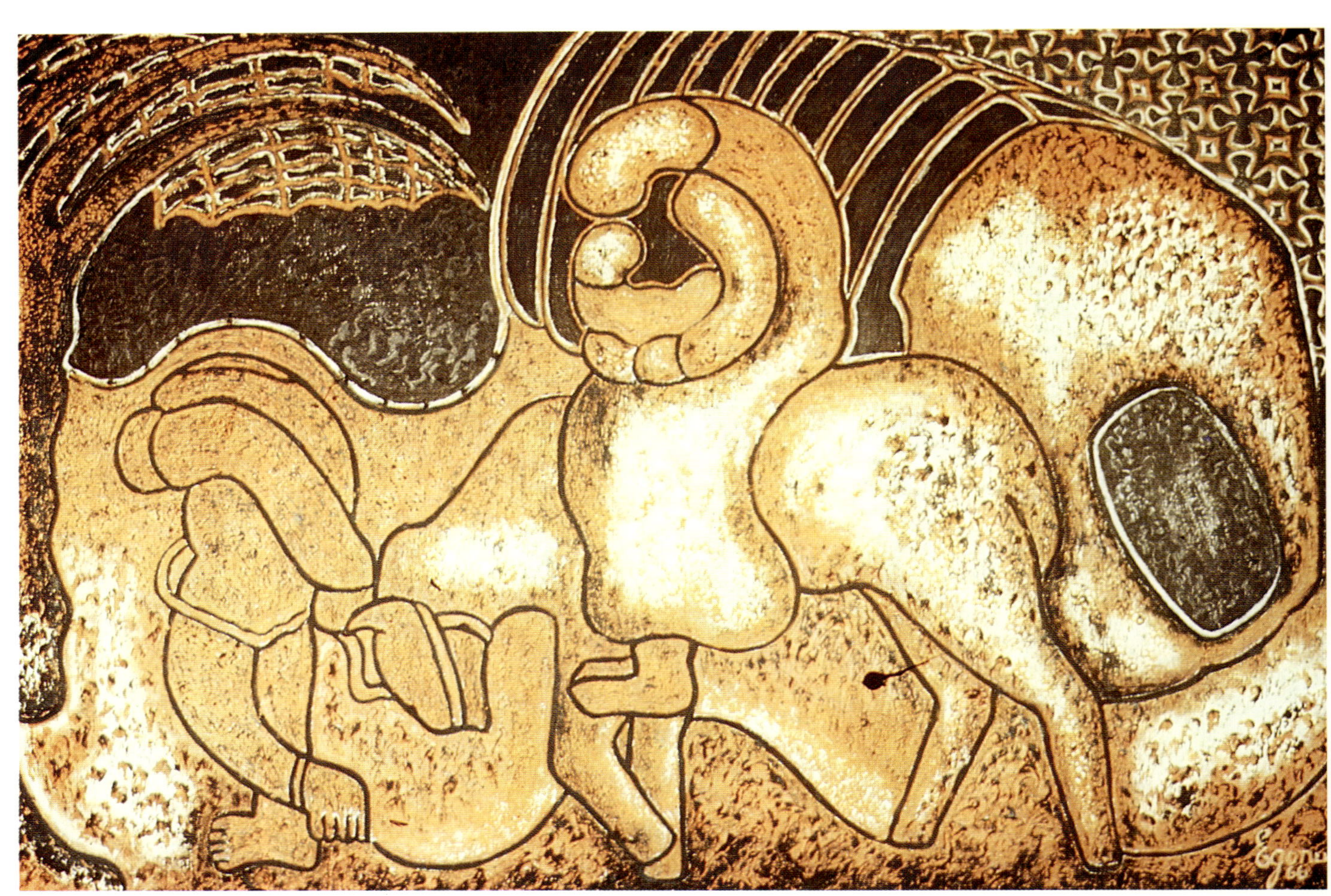

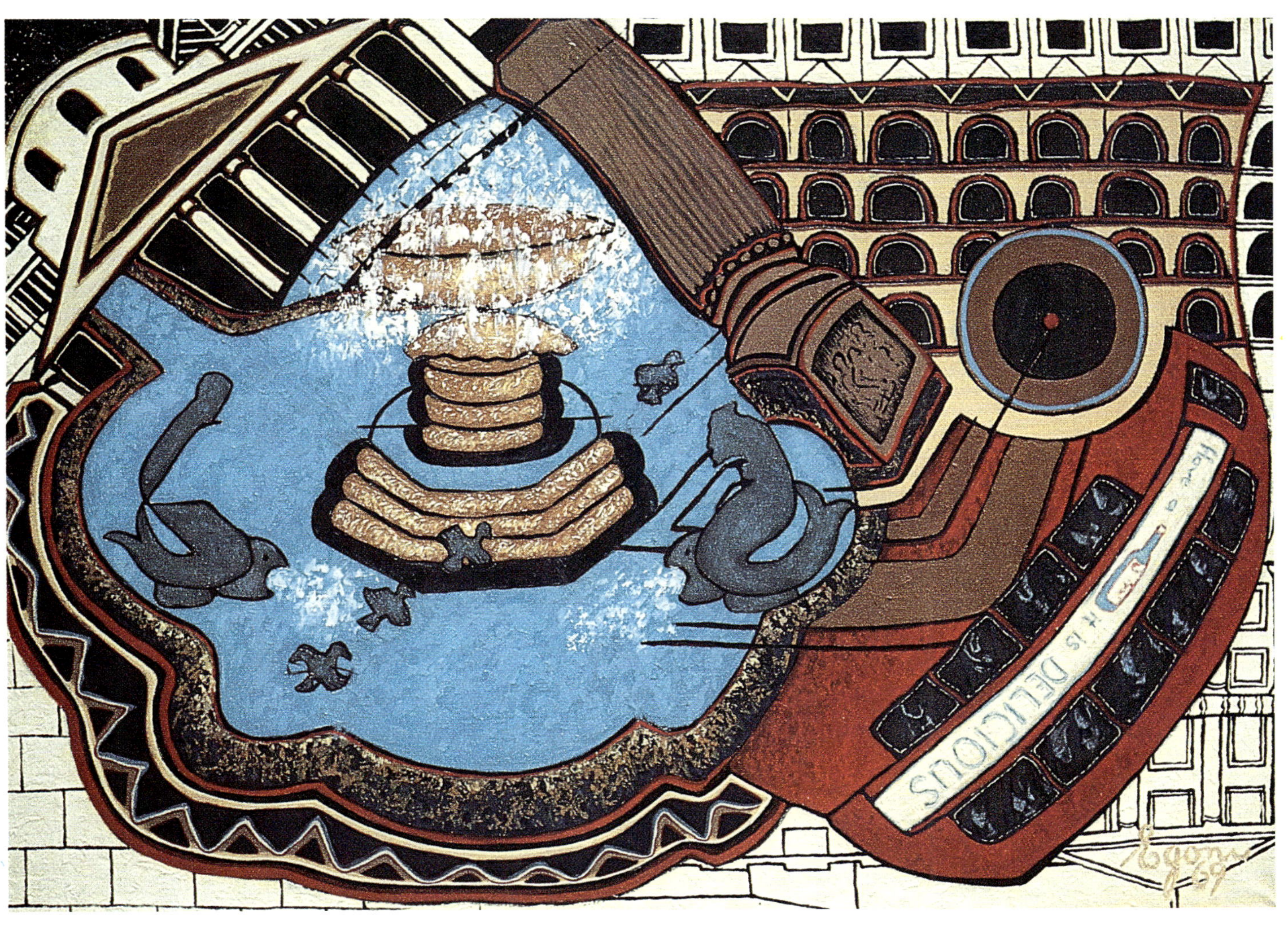

Trafalgar Square, 1968
Oil on canvas
82 x 115 cm
Spencer,
Stuart & Associates Ltd.,
London

woman and her child are also the nation and its children, and the tragedy of the war is not only individual but national as well. By 1967, despite some ambivalence, Egonu, like other intellectuals from the persecuted Igbo group, had come to accept the new boundaries of national identity which secession in Biafra dictated, and the nation mourned in *Blind Eye to Tragedy* and other paintings of the period is as much the disintegrating Nigerian nation as the threatened Biafra Republic. Also, the defiance expressed in *Blind Eye* replicates the artist's own struggle with these conflicting identities and boundaries. There is a contest for his loyalty, but it is not the particularities of this loyalty that matter so much as the objects of his multiple allegiance.

The year 1968 was Egonu's cross-roads in several respects. Having made his contribution to the war effort, and increasingly possessed of a sense of futility, he returned to philosophical contemplation. Again, this transition is marked by the return of animal imagery in his work. In *No Place for the Weak*, 1968, the valediction to this phase of his work, the artist positions two animals of indeterminate species locked in a fatal duel. The colour-symbolic schema of the 1966 *Mother and Child*, that is, the use of red, green and white for the duellists, is again employed to denote aggressor and aggressed. The aggressor is red, the aggressed green and white, and partly skeletal. The sense of combat without resolution of *Mother and Child* is abandoned for the absolutes of victory and vanquish as the red beast embeds its teeth in the neck of the other animal. Clear power relations are established here, with the strong triumphant over the weak, seemingly synonymising strength and victory. The idealism of the ecumenical paintings of 1966 yields to a new realism, a recognition of the dialectics of power as manifested in the concrete realities of confrontation, in the final submission of the body. *No Place for the Weak* refrains from making a value judgement, and simply states one man's perspective of reality through experience, one which is understandably cynical: conflicts are decided not on moral grounds or those of universal, inalienable rights, but by strength.

Two Fighting Cocks, from the same period, is a less cynical, more philosophical painting. In choosing the metaphor of fighting cocks to represent the Nigerian conflict, Egonu drew an analogy between cock-fighting and the phenomena of violent conflict and disintegration which has been the fate of postcolonial nations. A cock-fight is brutal, bloody, fatal: once in the cock-pit the two animals are bound inextricably to battle until one of them is dead. The pit is therefore a determinist, inescapable arena of suicidal confrontation. On this level, cock-fighting mirrors the history of countries locked in self-destructive combats, the dialectics of which are determined not necessarily by their own internal dynamics, but often by the machineries of western intervention and manipulation. This in itself parallels the political economy of cock-fighting; the sport is both sponsored and manipulated to arouse and exploit the combatants' weaknesses to the cock fighter's gain. Thus, in the simple image of two fighting cocks Egonu provides a most appropriate metaphor for emergent nations and their place in international politics. In the specific case of the Nigerian conflict, historians have since argued that it could have been aborted if not for the role of Britain which gained enormously through arms sales and oil deals with the Nigerian government, and the export of mercenaries.

In 1969 Egonu moved into a new phase in his work in the series, 'War and Peace' which was concluded in 1972. In 1970 he painted a second study of the flight of the Igbo from other parts of Nigeria at the beginning of the conflict in 1966. While the first study, *Flight*, 1966, made reference to the Biblical flight of the Virgin and Child to Egypt, the second is less allusive, drawing directly from the chaos and bleakness of the Igbo exodus.

The Nigerian civil war came to an end in 1970 with the defeat of the secessionist Republic of Biafra. The loss of the war signalled a momentary break in Egonu's preoccupation with it, while he moved on to other engagements. His pessimism during these years seems to have carried into the aftermath. But what is most important, however, is that it was the war years which permanently defined his role as an expatriate in the metropolis and set his work on a different path to that of formalist modernism, aligning it within a tradition of socially committed art. As his contemporary Uche Okeke put it in a speech of 1968, 'Art and Revolution', war demands of art that it "takes on a new but different line of action. The dreamer must turn activist...".[10]

In Nigeria the war transformed Egonu's entire generation. It turned the poet Christopher Okigbo from an eccentric symbolist and dedicated neoclassicist to a romantic *engagé* artist. Okigbo not only produced one of the corner-pieces of committed work in 20th century literature, the *Path of Thunder* cycle, he also enlisted in the war and became one of its earliest casualties, as if to validate Okeke's radical contention that in times of threat the artist "must speak out

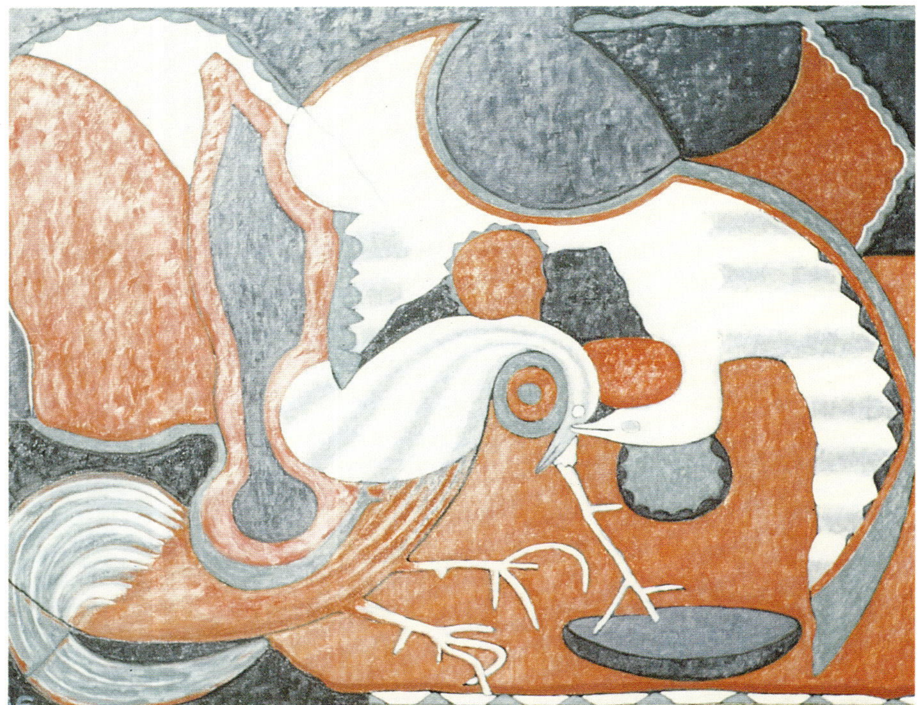

***Two Fighting Cocks*, 1967**
Oil on canvas
64 x 76 cm
Coll: M Flint, London

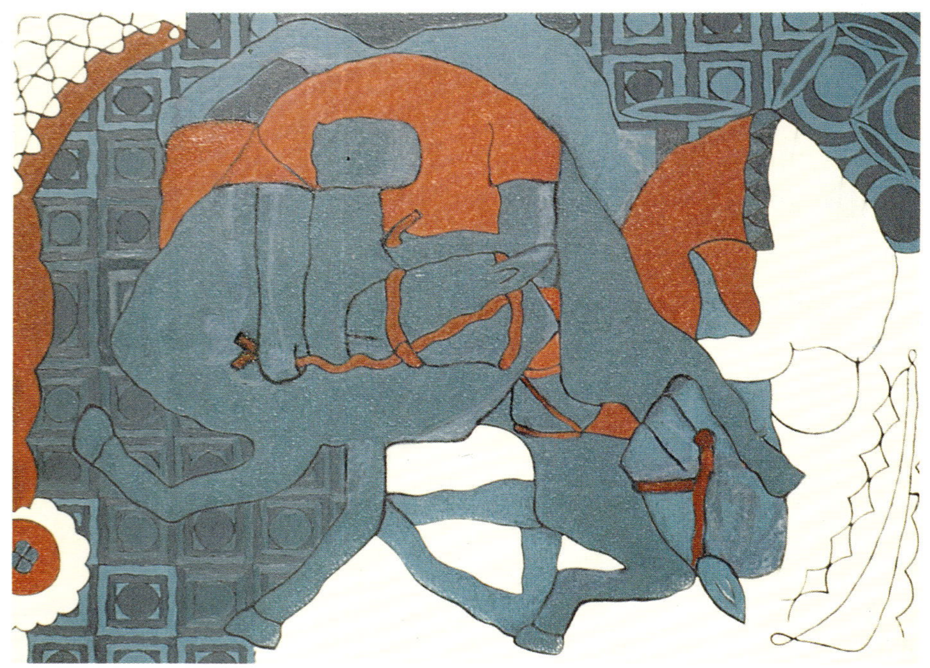

***Second Return After the Exodus*, 1974**
Oil on canvas
107 x 143 cm

with all the forces at his command, fight if he must and die in order to safeguard liberty and survival''.[11] For the novelist Chinua Achebe the war had a far-reaching effect, sowing a most sinister cynicism which kept him from producing novels for twenty-two years. What emerged at the end of this long regime of silence was the novel, *Anthills of the Savannah*, 1987, described as his angriest yet ''wisest book to date''.[12] Although Achebe had stood out clearly as an artist of commitment with a unique sense of community, creating in his first novel a story in which he breaks the rules of the 'novel' by placing the community rather than the individual as protagonist,[13] it is his post-war novel that finally embodies the maturation of his vision.

Egonu's war works are equally significant within his entire oeuvre because they provide exceptional insight into the personality and anxieties of the émigré whose allegiances to his country are inevitably refracted by distance. Egonu's perception of aesthetic essence took shape in response to historical exigences both in the host society and in his home country. When these historical imperatives demanded it, he took up and played his role as an emissary, using his art to bring to the attention of the world the specificities of an anguished moment in his country's history. In an interview a few years ago Egonu revealed that it is his wife's belief that the origins of his ill-health in the 1980s lie in the anxieties of the war years.[14] Memories of those years have continued to preoccupy him, surfacing again and again in such works as *First Return after the Exodus* and *Second Return after Exodus* of 1974. At different moments he has, through his work, resumed the role of emissary and visionary. It is this role that he returns to in the 'Addiction' series, 1970, 'Stateless People', 1980-1982, and 'Will Knowledge Safeguard Freedom?', 1985-1988.

Woman in Grief, 1968
Oil on canvas
48 x 22 cm

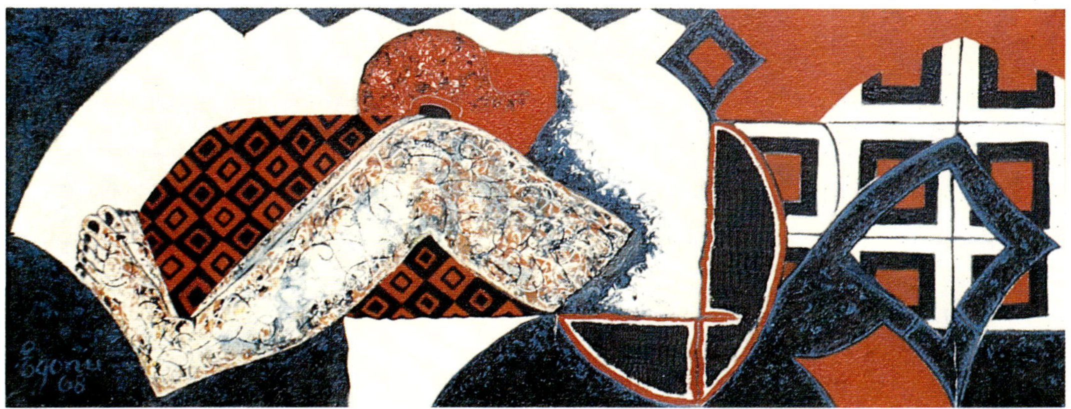

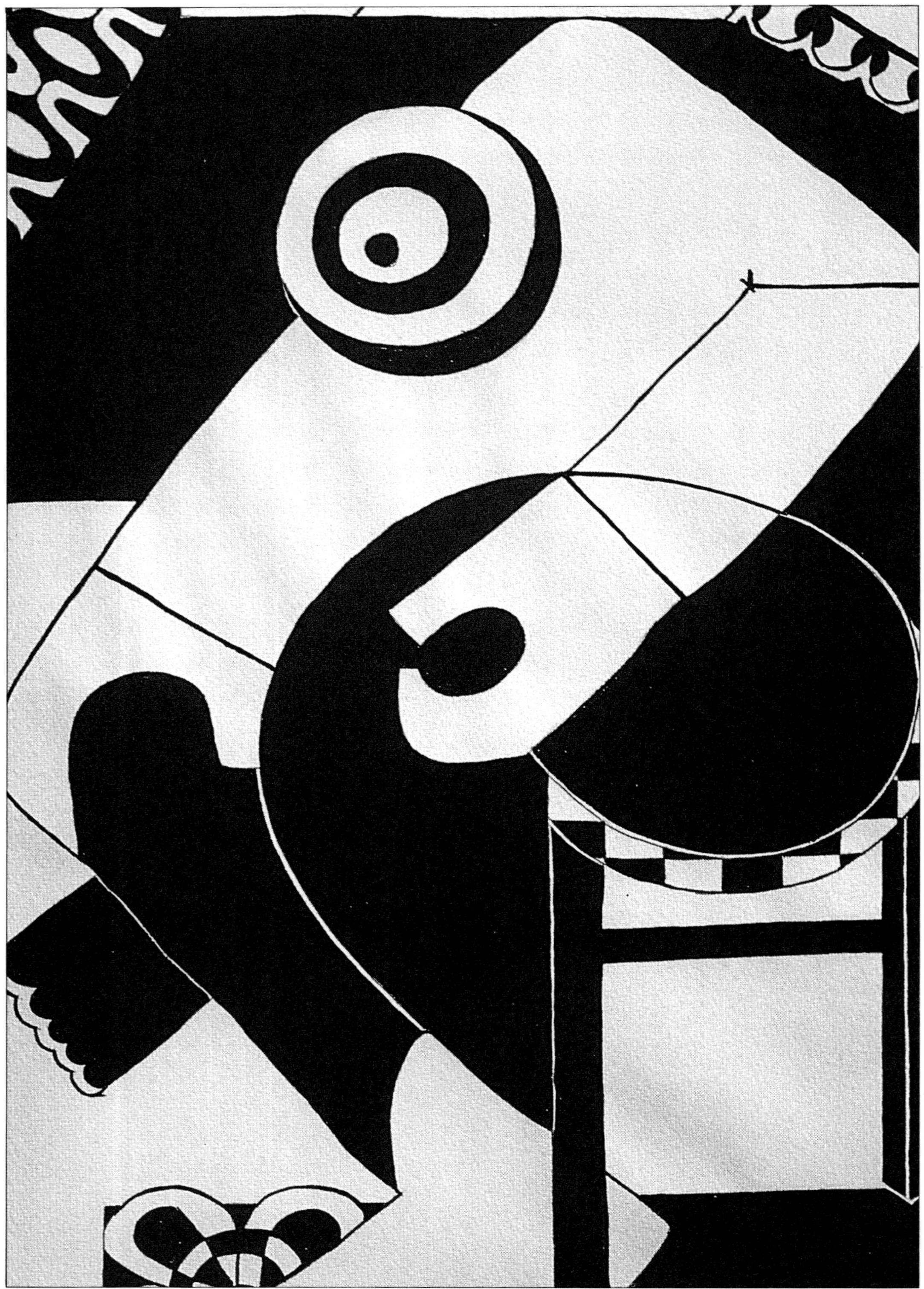

Beyond the War Years

The paintings of 1969 and 1970 which culminated in the 'War and Peace' series, formed Egonu's lever of ascent over tragedy. The evening classes he took in printmaking in 1970 not only fulfilled an old longing to improve his skills in graphic techniques, it was also a way of struggling out of the war years by going into a work environment which offered a different kind of company. The company of artists and printmakers at the Working Men's College in Camden, London, helped direct Egonu's mind and creative preoccupation away from the bitterness of the war. Discussing art and making art, learning new techniques and exploring possibilities, presented a new and different challenge.

Out of the exercise came Egonu's first major body of post-war work, the 1970 portfolio of five lithographs which he called 'Addiction 1-5'. The 'Addiction' series begin with *Addiction One*, a stark lithograph in an edition of 70 which recalls not only the immediately preceding work of the war years but also Egonu's paintings and drawings of the immediate post-bridge period in the mid-1960s. Its circular composition alludes to the paintings *Piccadilly Circus*, 1965, and *Exodus*, 1970. In terms of form, *Addiction One* is rather conventional, attempting to capture in chiaroscuro a semblance of the texture and patterning of Egonu's paintings. In *Addiction One* the artist summarises the message of the series by assembling metaphors for the different addictions which he addresses in the rest of the prints: gambling, alcohol, drugs and indulgence. The predominant elements in the lithograph are a bottle of wine and two leaves of indeterminate species.

***Stateless People (An Artist)*, 1980**
Gouache
75 x 56 cm

Slightly off-centre is an object resembling a glass or cup. Extending from the wine bottle and terminating in the bottom right of the lithograph is a spider web, symbol of entanglement, loss of direction, imprisonment, and imminent destruction or consumption. *Addiction One* prefaces the series and establishes the direction and concern of the body of work.

In *Addiction Two* there is clearer, more detailed figuration. One of the two figures in the print, positioned right at the compositional centre, leans over a surface covered with what seems to be crushed tobacco. The figure to the right holds a bottle and underneath it are suggested a car body and wheel, or perhaps a wheelchair, referring to a number of situations linked directly or indirectly to alcohol abuse. To the left of the print the composition is disjointed along a long

***War and Peace #4*, 1969**
Gouache on paper
51 x 66 cm

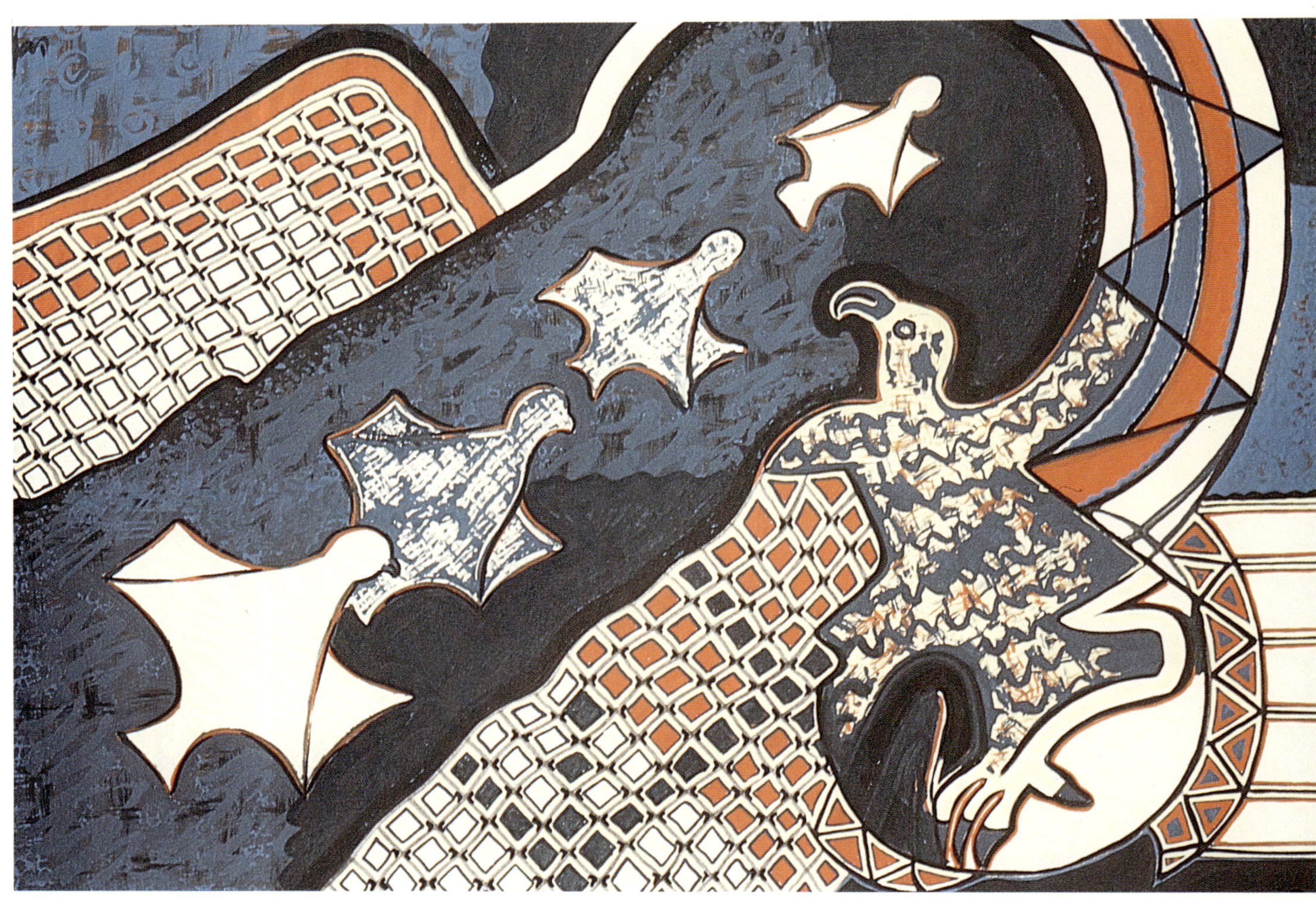

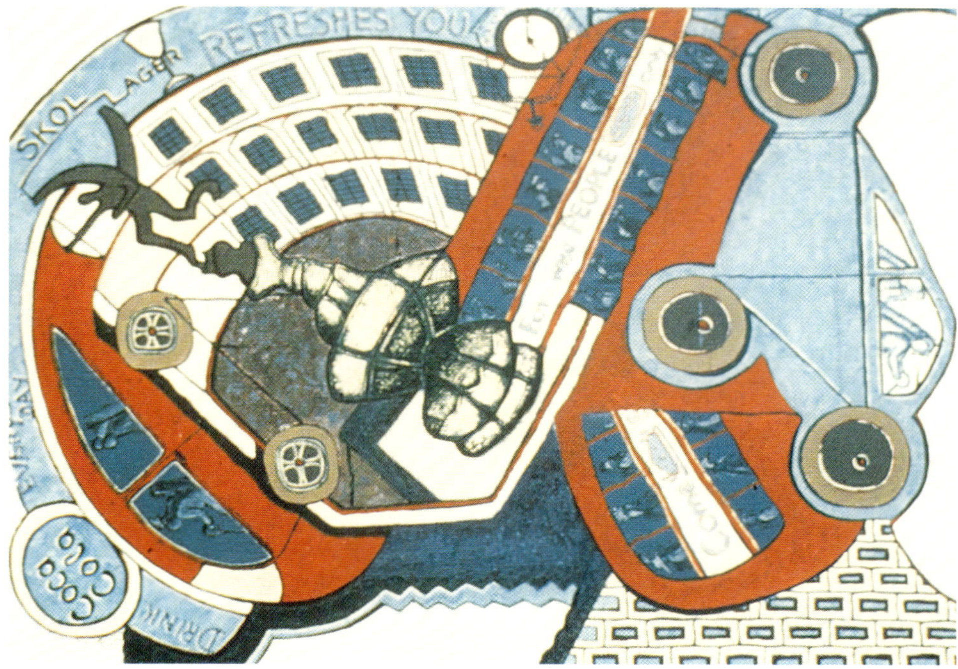

***Piccadilly Circus*, 1966**
Oil on Canvas
82 x 115 cm

diagonal, creating a very prominent fault-line. This fault-line could be read conceptually as a stairway or as a sign of disjunction, of disruption and dislocation. In *Addiction Two*, therefore, the artist represents addiction as a rupture or descent. *Addiction Three* reintroduces colour to Egonu's work from this period, and sets the stage for his eventual foray into silk screen printing with which he would produce some of the most visually stunning works in his entire oeuvre. The print lends itself more easily to reading, since it deals only with a specific addiction, gambling.

In the rest of the series composition is progressively simpler, figuration stronger and more clearly defined. The fourth print deals again with alcohol and drugs, and figures are shown either injecting or sharing drugs. One figure is shown in a posture of supplication and submission, kneeling before two giant bottles as if in worship. The fifth print, *Addiction Five*, shows an indulgent party at table. In it the colourfulness of the third and fourth prints is replaced by a greyness which is as sedate as it is simple.

In all the prints one recurring element is the facelessness of the human presence, an anonymisation which focuses attention on their theme, emphasising the metaphorical rather than the representational or descriptive. On another level, this anonymisation universalises the

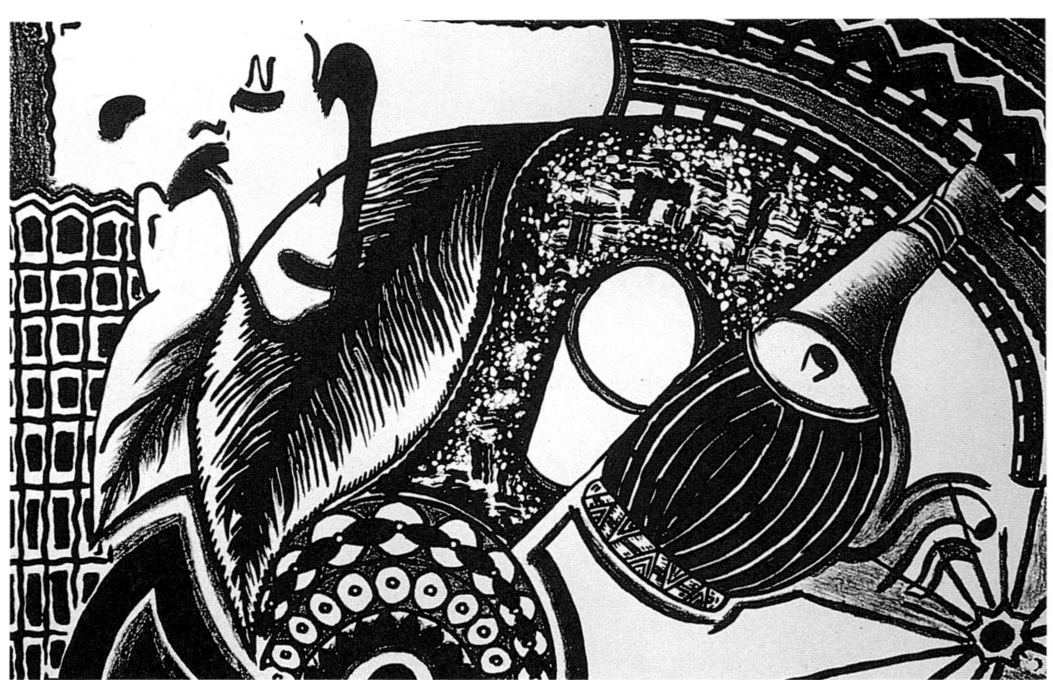

Addiction One, 1970
Lithograph
57 x 79 cm

problem which the prints address. Egonu replaces individual identity with a social one, thus conceptualising addiction as not specific to or characteristic of any particular community, but rather a human problem, crossing the borders of nation, class and ethnicity.

Between 1979 and 1983, however, Egonu's partial blindness returned him to angst and contemplation. It was during this period of anxiety and uncertainty, during which he worked under painfully trying circumstances, that he again turned his mind to the questions of nation and identity, the result of which was a series of philosophical works entitled 'Stateless People'.

By 1980 when he began 'Stateless People', Egonu had lived in England for thirty-five years, a long period during which he had moved through several phases of life. The cessation of hostilities and the post-war reconciliations in Nigeria brought a new period of renewed hope and visions of growth and progress. The oil boom in Nigeria gave the country a new status. Egonu revisits this period with a mixture of nostalgia and anguish, recalling how Nigerians, and by association Africans and black people in Europe, began to hold their heads high as a result of the country's prosperity. ''From their airport hotels they could buy up whole shops on the phone, and wherever you went, people went out of their way to attend to you if you were

Nigerian."[1] Grand visions and grand projects, what came to be known as 'white elephants', were all part of this brush with greatness. The 1977 FESTAC was one such project with which Nigeria tried to live up to its assumed image and prestige. At the end of his term in office in 1979, the country's military Head of State confidently projected that "Nigeria will become one of the ten leading nations in the world by the end of the century".[2]

With time, however, it was clear that such projections were more delusion than genuine vision. The period of Nigeria's boom was characterised by hyper-consumerism rather than productivity or concrete infrastructural development. No solid foundations were laid, no meaningful investments were put in place. On the contrary, corruption and decadence boomed. By 1983, when the country came close to collapse for the second time in its short life as a nation, the situation had grown so critical that Chinua Achebe, in an unusual outburst of irate pamphleteering, stated starkly: "Corruption in Nigeria has passed the alarming and entered the fatal stage; and Nigeria will die if we keep pretending that she is only slightly indisposed."[3] By the end of that year the country had careened into chaos and the Second Republic had collapsed.

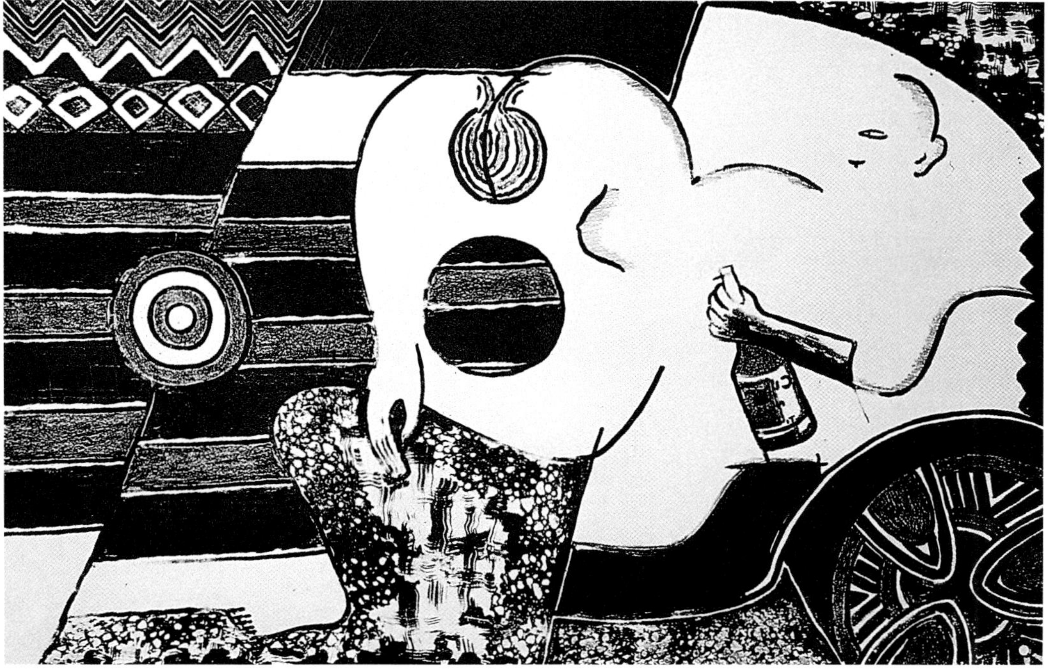

***Addiction Two*, 1970**
Lithograph
57 x 79 cm

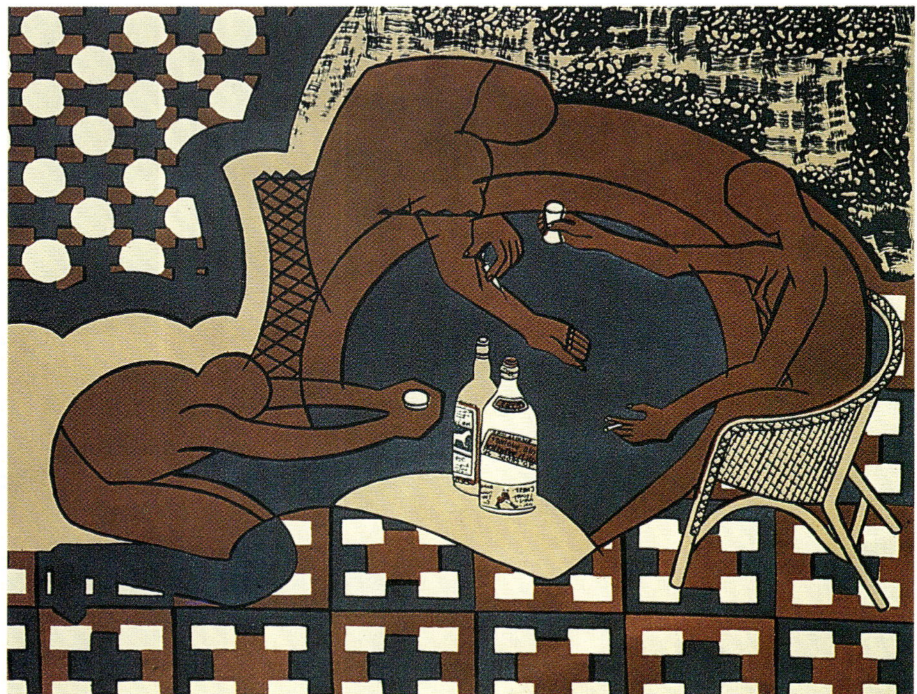

***Addiction Three*, 1970**
Lithograph
69 x 81 cm

The period of Egonu's partial blindness between 1979 and 1983 coincided with Nigeria's chaotic and farcical experiment with democracy, and thus was for the artist a period of anguish, both physical and spiritual. With a failing physical vision confronting him, and a failing national vision too, Egonu again brought his life and history under scrutiny with clarity and sobriety.

On the face of it 'Stateless People' is not a particularly unique body of work. The paintings formally follow a similar pattern to Egonu's colour screen-prints from the late 1970s and early 1980s, with large, flat areas, fewer and bolder patterns, decorative restraint. They are brilliant yet possessed of an austere schematisation, which is understandable given the artist's failing sight. For one critic they are reminiscent of Fernand Léger, ''that great French political propagandist''.[4]

The human figure is a recurrent motif in the series. Although no longer faceless as in the 'Addiction' lithographs, in most of the paintings the figures are nonetheless portrayed face-down. The posture of each figure is consistent with the activity in which it is engaged. The stooping, downward gesture, however, symbolises a state of dishonour, shame, disgrace, humiliation, regret or sorrow. It is significant that this posture is replicated in another work from the same period, the ink drawing, *Man with Stick*, 1980, in which a crouching, turbaned figure leans on a thick stick, his head buried between hunched shoulders. The face-down gesture in *Man with Stick* is a reflection on the agonies of blindness, a personalised exploration of pain, sorrow, and resignation, rather than a general pronouncement on disability. In 'Stateless People' also the gesture is symbolic of a statement on a specific phenomenon, part of the artist's visual mapping of his theme.

Each of the figures in 'Stateless People' is engaged in an activity or profession: a musician, an artist, a writer and, in the painting entitled *Stateless People: An Assembly* Egonu brings all the figures together in one composition. 'Stateless People' works on two levels: first, the archetypal, using as its metaphors a section of society traditionally

***Stateless People (an Assembly)*, 1982**
Oil on canvas
142 x 215 cm

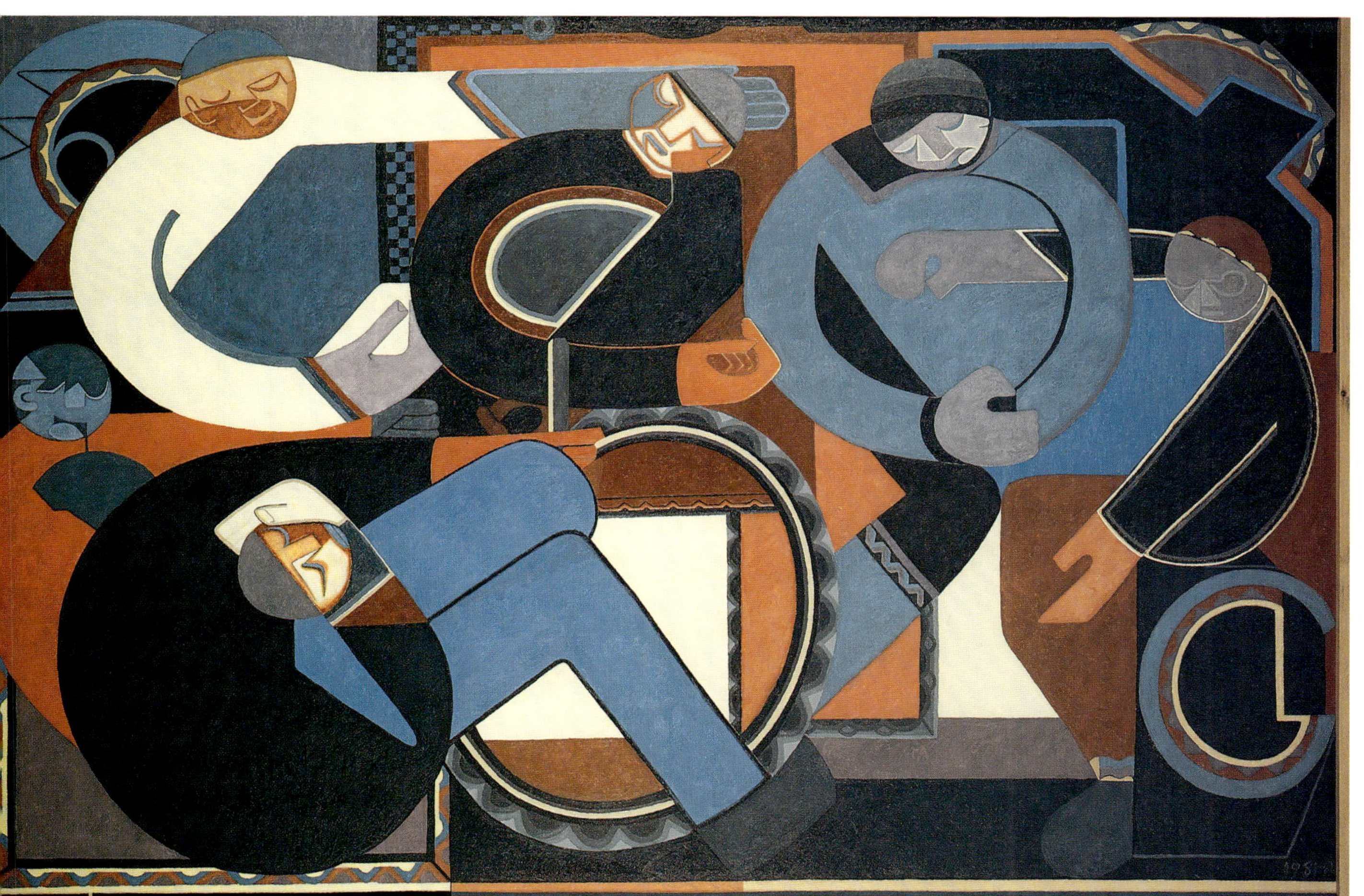

associated with alienation and exile. We are reminded of the American exile-writer in 1920s Paris, of the street busker, the traditional outcast whose lifestyle and calling alienates him from the rest of society, or of the postcolonial intellectual or artist in exile, driven from his country by political or intellectual intolerance.

However, Egonu's 'Stateless People' deals not with émigrés but with those who are rendered stateless by what is today generally recognised as the disappearance of the postcolonial state, the disintegration of structures and machineries of governance and accountability in new nations. In a statement at the opening of the Royal Festival Hall exhibition of the series in 1986 Egonu noted:

> It is always assumed that 'Stateless People' are people who, through the consequence of their political activities (in opposition to the establishment) or who suffer victimisation due to their religious conviction in their original countries, either escaped or were forced out by their authoritarian regime. In this case, people who belong to this category cannot go back to their countries, and consequently end up without nationality.
>
> My stateless people are far from being political or religious refugees. They are people who are symbolically stateless. How can a person who has a country and lives there, of if he lives outside, can go back any time, be regarded as a stateless person? If a country exists just in name without a permanent foundation, foresight, commonsense and ambition for the good of the country, in other words dwells in chaos and stagnation, it is non-existent...

***Artist's Studio*, 1969**
Oil on canvas
48 x 122 cm

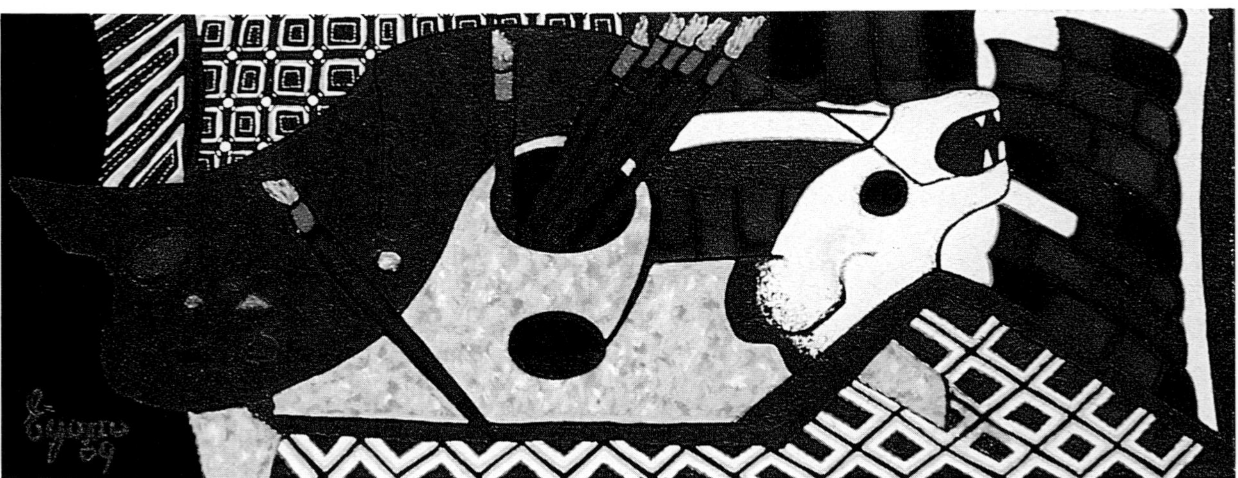

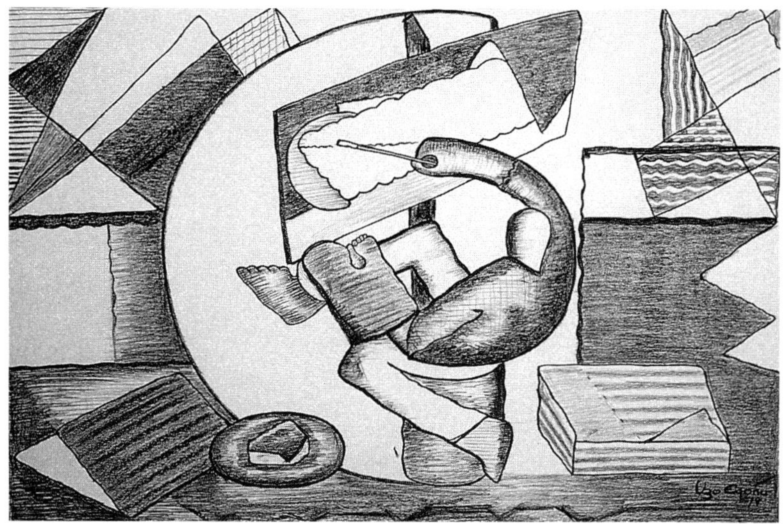

***Artist at Work*, 1978**
Pencil and charcoal
51 x 72 cm

> In this modern age, it is not good enough for a country to feel that because it is not a colony of another power this fact in itself is commendable. What is commendable is what a country is trying to achieve and what it has accomplished. If symbolically a country does not exist, and if logic of existence is applied, anyone who inhabits such a country is stateless.[5]

Jean-Jacques Rousseau argues in *The Social Contract* that the state dies when the legislative process is eroded.[6] When the social contract is breached, that is, when the citizen is denied the right of moderation over the activities of the sovereign, the right of democratic intervention, and government withdraws from its responsibilities to the citizenry, the state ceases to exist. It became clear to Egonu, as a keen student and observer of politics, that this degeneration and severance of social bond had occurred throughout the postcolonial world. This was indicated not necessarily in the replacement of democratic structures by those of force in these countries, especially since "one can define the modern state sociologically only in terms of the specific means peculiar to it, namely, the use of physical force".[7] It was indicated precisely by the gradual failure of those states to provide physical and material security for their citizens. It is remarkable that Egonu devoted a series to this problem when he did, for it would take another decade for political scientists and sociologists to agree that the state had indeed collapsed in most parts of Africa.

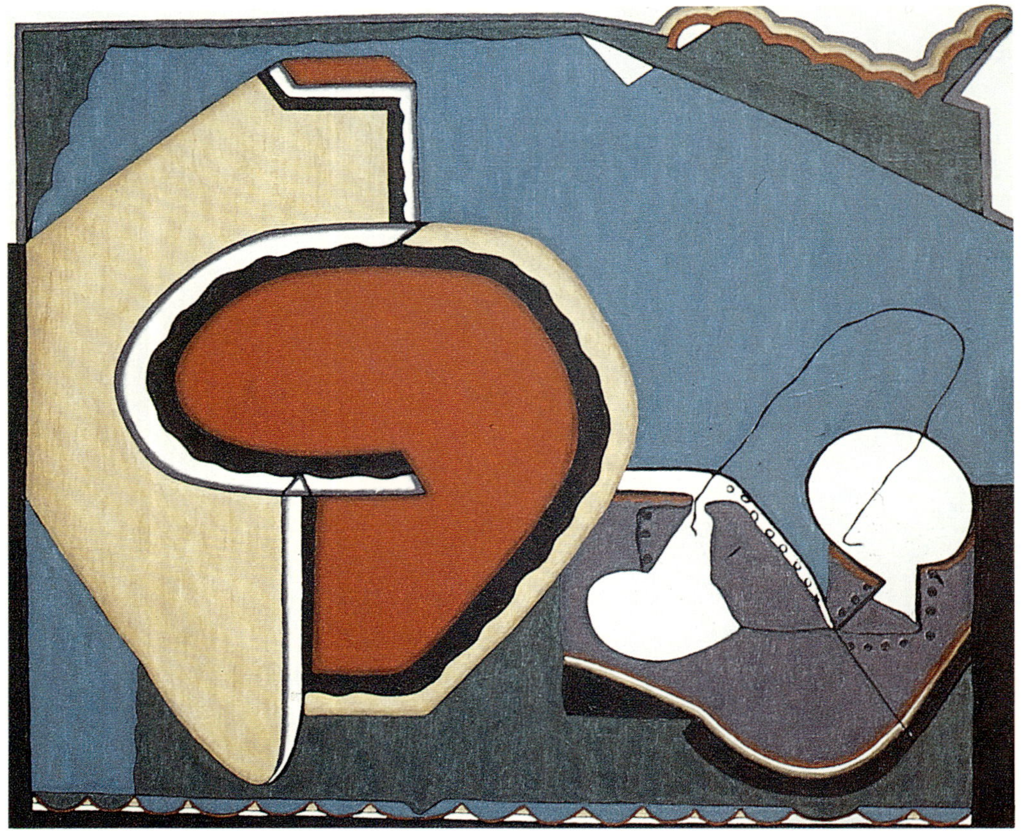

Vase with a
***Pair of Boots*, 1979**
Oil on canvas
78 x 91 cm

***Philosopher with Beret*, 1981**
'Poets & Philosophers' series
Oil on canvas
152 x 124 cm

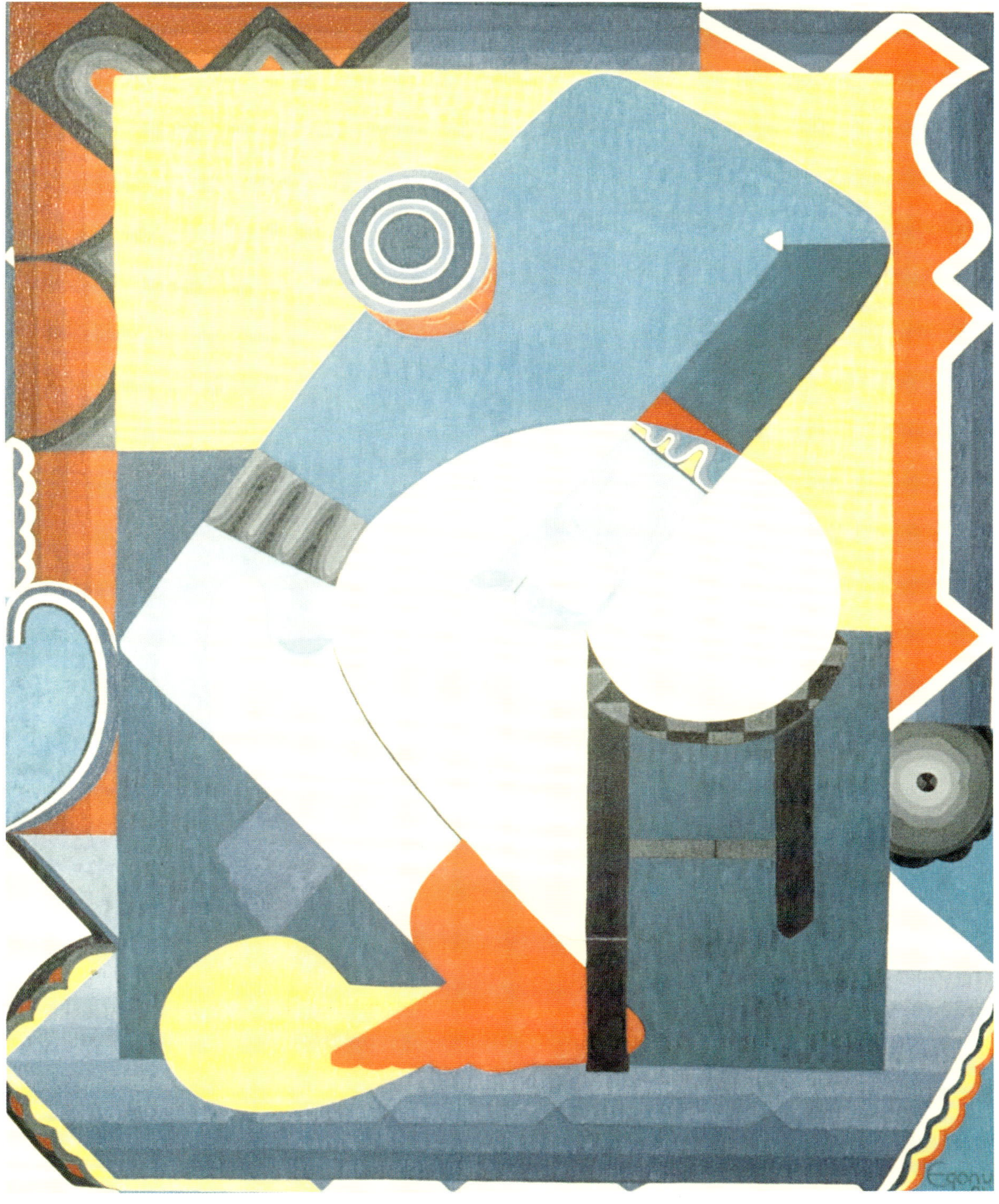

Nothing of the above is visually evident from the paintings, except the anguish, the scar which the protagonists' predicaments have left on them. This is represented by the brooding, broken posture of the figures, their gesture of despondence and defeat. Through this, however, the artist is able to communicate quite eloquently the dilemma of statelessness and how disenfranchisement and disempowerment break the individual spirit in a historical age when the individual is heavily dependent on the state. In extension we find also that Egonu's choice of iconography, his metaphorisation of disenfranchisement in the broken figure of the intellectual or artist plays on a different orthodoxy, that of the artist as the conscience and sensor of society. In a sense recent history — not only in Africa and the Third World but in Europe as well — lends credence to this concept, and artists and intellectuals rather than politicians remain the barometers of societies in crisis, defining what has been described as the prophetic aesthetic. Each society and situation, however, determines the concreteness of this aesthetic, and the sense of responsibility which lies at its centre. Egonu perceived the crumbling of the state in Africa as a tragedy with no visible willingness on the part of those involved to avert it, and his frustration occasioned his employment in 'Stateless People' of an aesthetic of melancholia rather than didactic or pedagogical strategies.

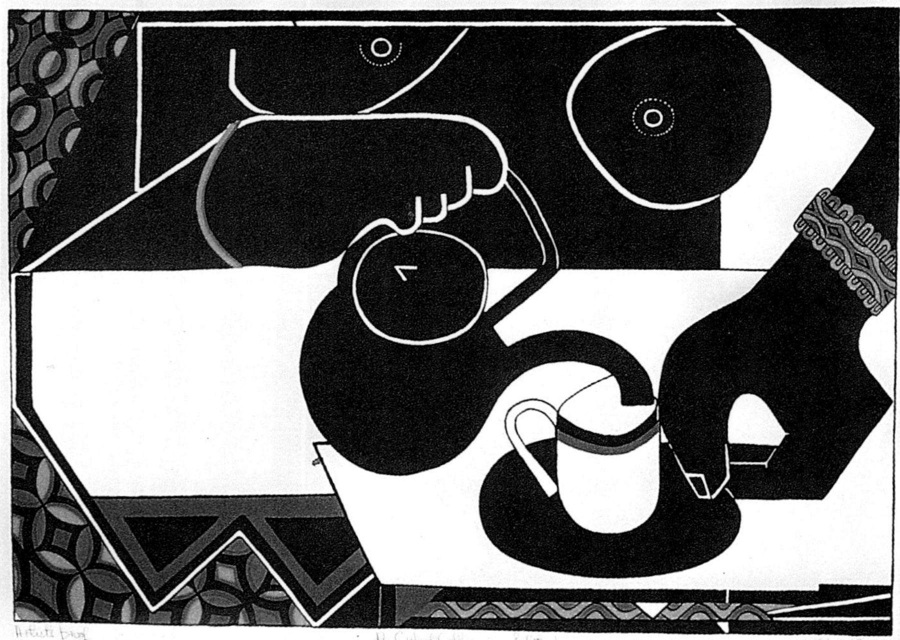

A Cup of Coffee in Solitude, 1981
Screenprint
64 x 88 cm

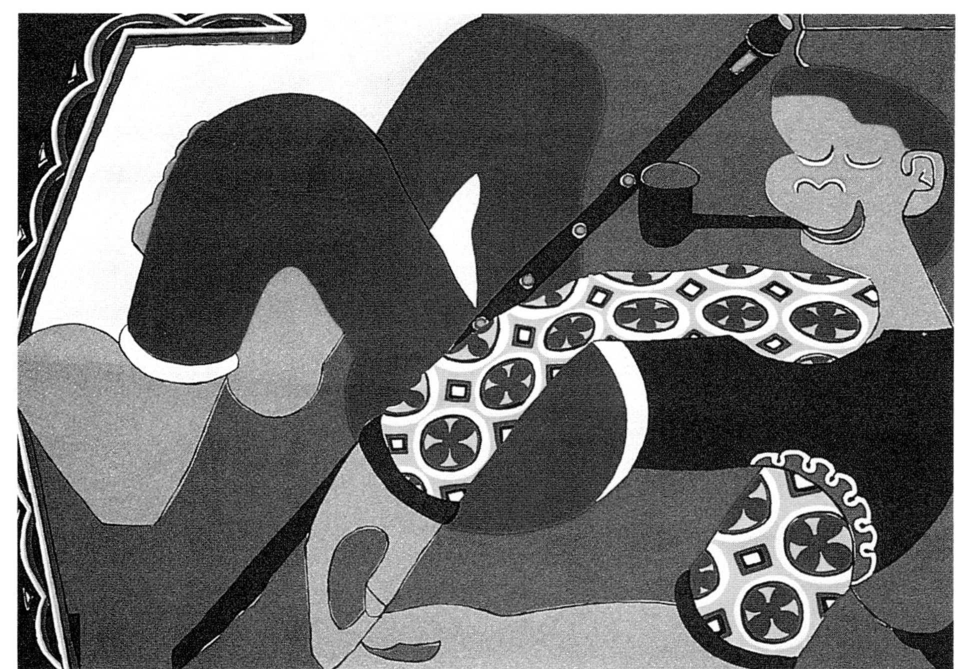

***Flute Player*, 1979**
Screenprint
66 x 84 cm

In 1979 also, Egonu began the sketches and preliminary drawings for a series of screen prints figuring the female figure in a domestic setting. Between 1979 and 1982, he produced *Lone Eater*, 1979, *Mending*, 1980, *A Cup of Coffee in Solitude*, 1981, and *Tasting*, 1980, *A Letter*, 1982, *Lone Player*, 1980, *Reading*, 1980, *Coffee Time*, 1979, and a number of ink drawings and related gouaches. These works, in their stunning simplicity, precision and power of evocation, belong with Egonu's most important work, as significant in his oeuvre as 'Stateless People', the 'Addiction' series, and indeed, to some extent, the war paintings. Like his earlier work, these are marked by a consistent iconography, the most prominent element of which is the lone, female presence, rhetorically figured in a pair of hands and a suggestion of breasts. In each work the artist depicts a specific chore or activity which corresponds with the title. The location in which these activities are played out is discernibly domestic, represented by patterns suggesting wallpaper and carpets. These are then replicated in the figure's apparel, providing a delicate formal cohesion which, together with the masterful manipulation of positive and negative spaces, belongs to the classical tradition of Igbo mural design. The shapes are bold, stark, aggressive and assertive, the figural patterns carefully hedged

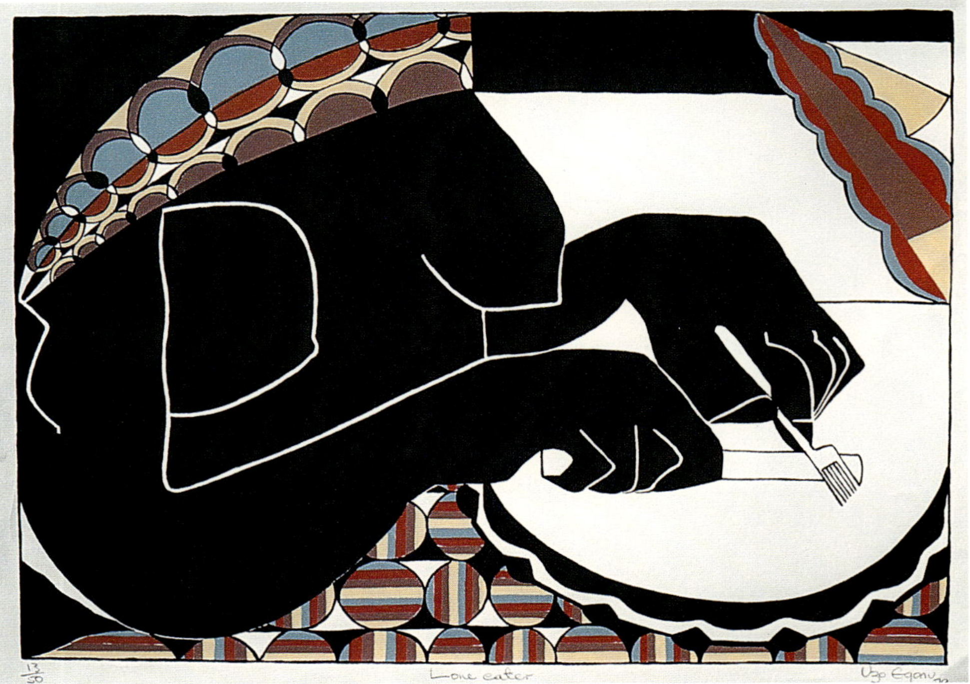

***Lone Eater*, 1979**
Screenprint
51 x 71 cm

into the corners except in the study *Coffee Time*, 1979, which eventually transformed into *A Cup of Coffee in Solitude*, and in the process lost its originally hesitant and profuse patterning. What emerges from these works with their precision, their almost brutal simplicity and overall coherence, is a carefully and consciously constructed system of signification with an overwhelming sense of logical intent. Throughout the series there is a consistent absence of the head, a feature which grows in significance because it does not occur in other works from the same period such as the screenprint, *Flute Player Resting*, 1979, or the ink drawing, *Man with a Stick*, 1980, both of which present a male figure. The immediate critical reaction to this, of course, is to suggest that, by singling out his female figures from this period for decapitation, the artist 'otherises' the female.

Barbara Erlich White has noted that Renoir's paintings of women from 1885 to 1887 contain "this quality of a woman being all body and no mind", since the women are "enormous in size", in one case with "partially exposed breast... [and] her face is devoid of expression or feeling".[8] What White fails to observe is that this absence of a mind, or of intellect, is signified much more strongly in the size of the heads with which Renoir invests these women, compared to

***A Poetess*, 1981**
Oil on canvas
152 x 124 cm

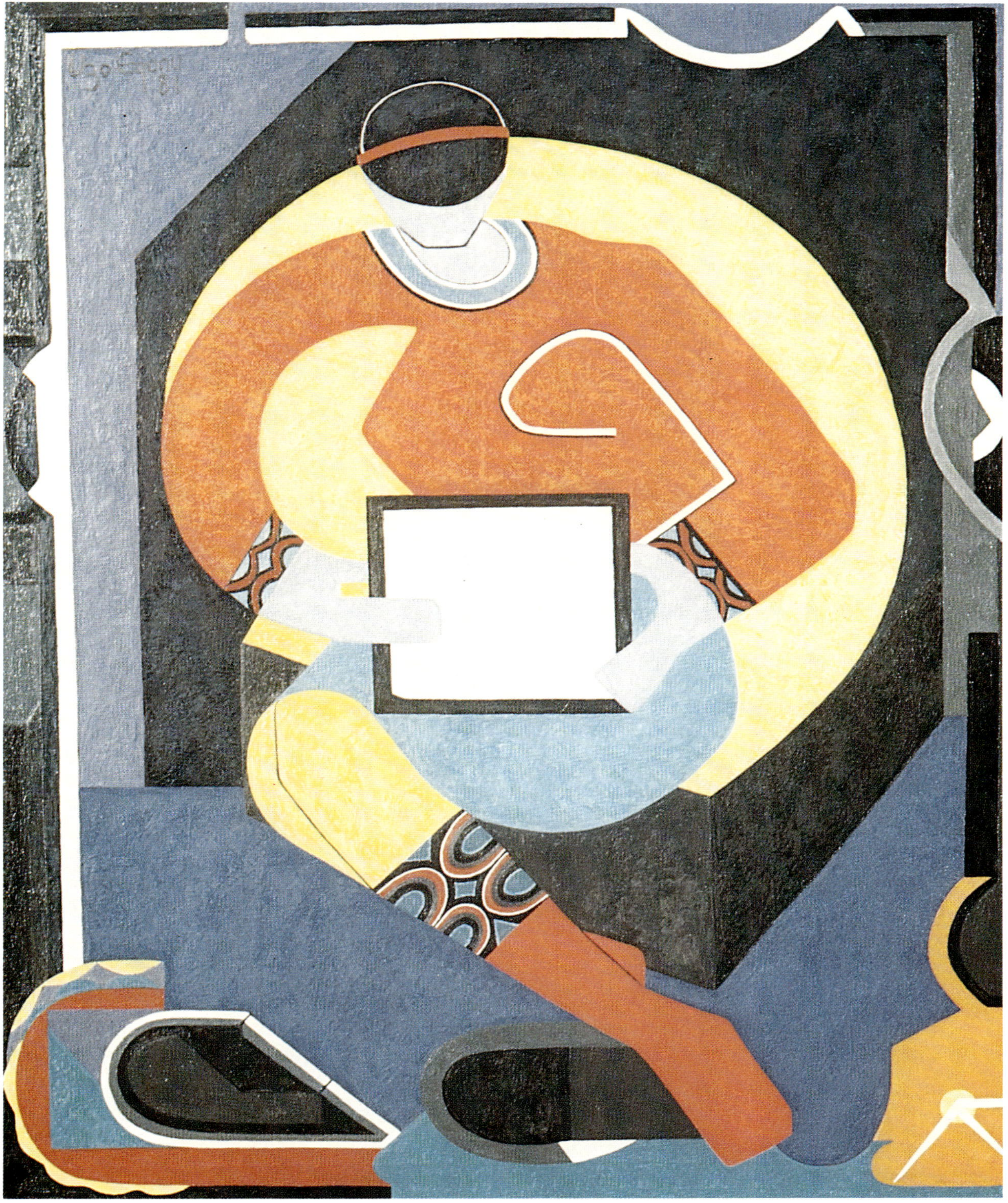

their buxomness. The head is proportionally diminished, impoverished, and the viewer's eyes seldom directed towards it. Renoir, a careful composer of pictures ennobled with a deep knowledge of the classical tradition,[9] also held very strong and backward views of women and their place in society, believing, as White points out, that ''men should be thinkers, artists and intellectuals, while women should be sources of pleasure for men — in sex, in mothering, in homemaking''.[10] His head-body proportions were therefore a conscious rhetorical device. It is tempting, then, to read the absence of the head in Egonu's images of women in these prints, as a parallel device to Renoir's.

But Egonu has no known gender views identical to Renoir's. Indeed, the first painting in a small portfolio called 'Poets and Philosophers' from the same period, is of a female poet, and, another oil from 1978 is entitled *Woman Reading*. A woman reading is also the subject of one of the prints in the series under consideration, *Reading*, and of the oil painting *Woman Resting* from 1980. Such a consistent identification of the female with intellectual preoccupation would be intolerable in Renoir's view.[11]

One could venture another explanation for the missing head in Egonu's prints; which reminds us of the economical concept of 'saturation' of Igbo graphic arts: a composition must contain only that which is necessary. There is a balancing situation of saturation which renders any additions redundant and disruptive to the wholeness and fragile coherence of the composition.

The locus of signification in all the prints is the hand-in-the-act, further highlighted by its location against an empty space. This structure is presaged in *Coffee Time*, 1979, which shows only the hands of the figure. The torso enters in the subsequent works only to define gender, and so the absence of a head is not a comment on feminine attributes, but a compositional device which focuses attention on the locus of signification.

What then is it about the activities in which the artist engages these women: mending, tasting, reading, drinking coffee? What are their circumstances and what aspects of the human condition are they meant to convey? What is the subtext of these narratives? Who are the subjects?

There are no singular answers to any of these questions. The overwhelming atmosphere in the series, as noted earlier, is one of solitude. However, because the figurative presence in each work is so dominant, there is also a feeling of authority and territorial control. We get the unavoidable sense that the figures in these works occupy their own spaces, at least physically if not socially or politically. There is no room for a second presence or for contestation, and there is little indication of transience or uncertainty in their possession of the space. Yet, there is an air of discomfiture, of entrapment and constraint, a feeling not of marginalisation but of restriction. In *A Cup of Coffee in Solitude*, in particular, the imposing presence of the figure extends to the picture's edges, leaving little elbow room. By bringing the frame to 'saturation' Egonu seems to represent a condition of constriction and immobility and, by extension, the staidness and boredom of domesticity.

The activities around which the works are constructed are all indicated in the gerund: mending, tasting, reading. Each is, in a sense, a state of expectation. Where the noun is indicated Egonu employs registers of isolation, as we see especially in *Lone Eater*, *Lone Player*, and *A Cup of Coffee in Solitude*. By employing these registers he insinuates an absence, and creates a sense of loss. The viewer is almost forced to wonder what this absence is, who or what is being missed,

Reading, 1980
Gouache on paper
58 x 79 cm

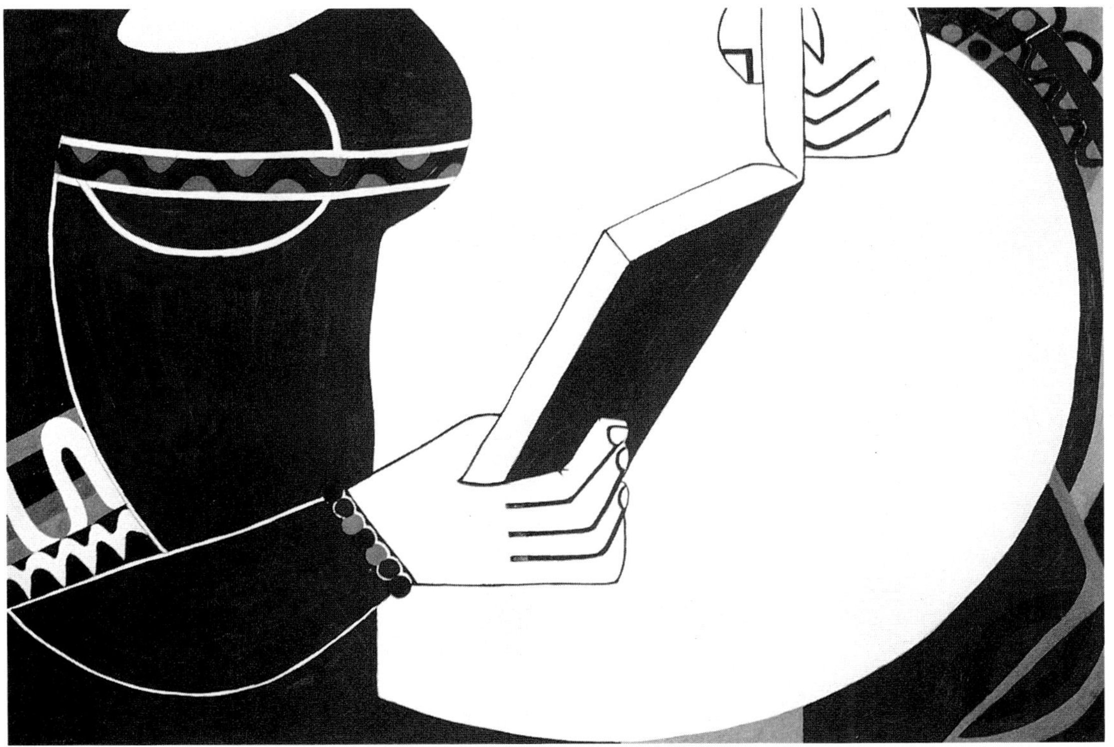

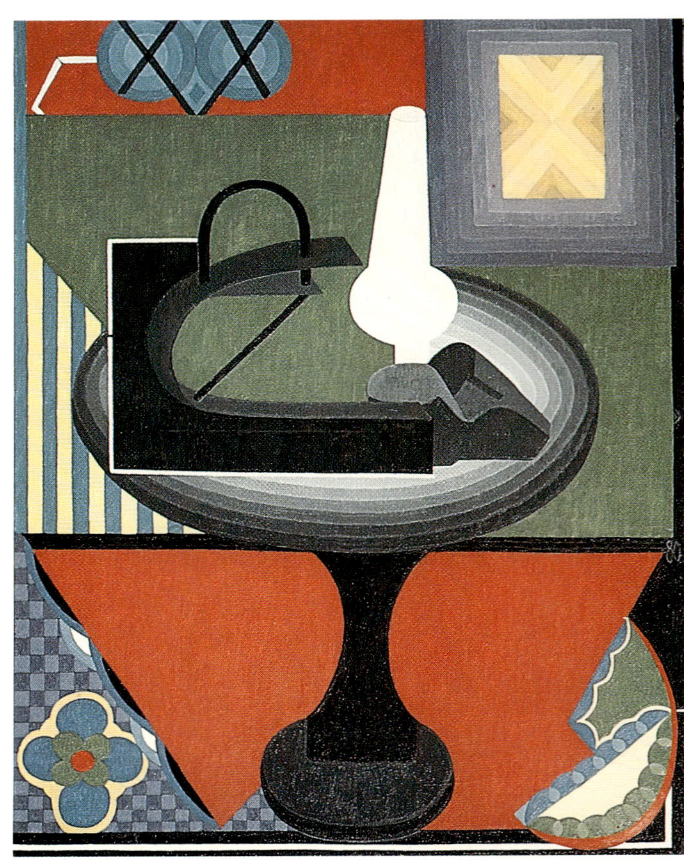

***Still-life, Pair of Boots and Lamp*, 1980**
Oil on canvas
145 x 106 cm

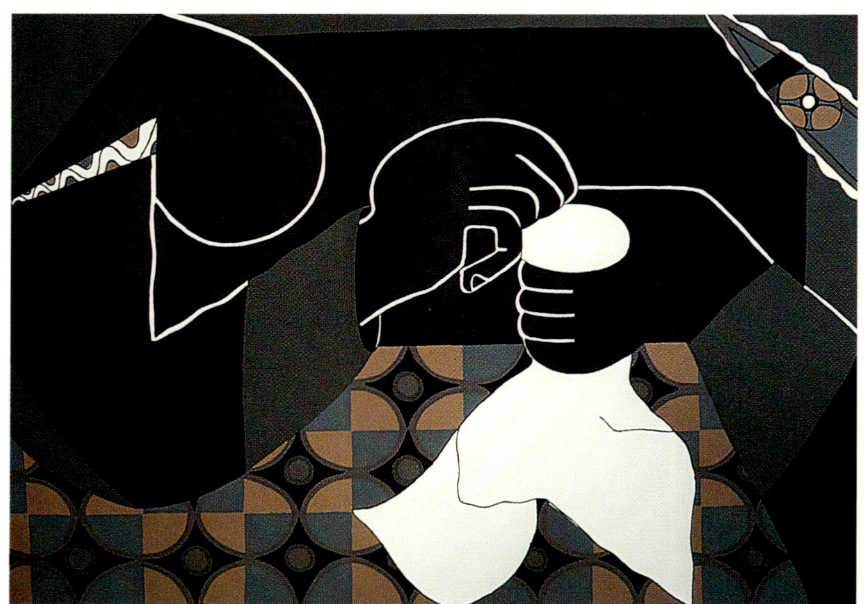

***Mending*, 1980**
Screenprint
65 x 85 cm

expected, or barred. The latter is particularly relevant since, in *A Cup of Coffee in Solitude* and *Lone Eater*, for instance, there is arguably also a sense of contentment with the solitary state, one of a fulfilling condition of peace and quiet, of eventually being in charge of own's own space. In which case it would not be loneliness we see, or a state of enforced solitude or alienation, but solitude in the Storrian sense of "a return to self" when "the capacity to be alone is a valuable resource".[12] Within the context of women's struggles to regain the right to their own space and control over their lives and bodies, the ability to be alone, to engage in chores for one's own satisfaction, even to drudge for oneself, is a positive gain. The feeling of constraint may then symbolise this struggle as women actively hold the borders of their space and defend it against structures of male control.

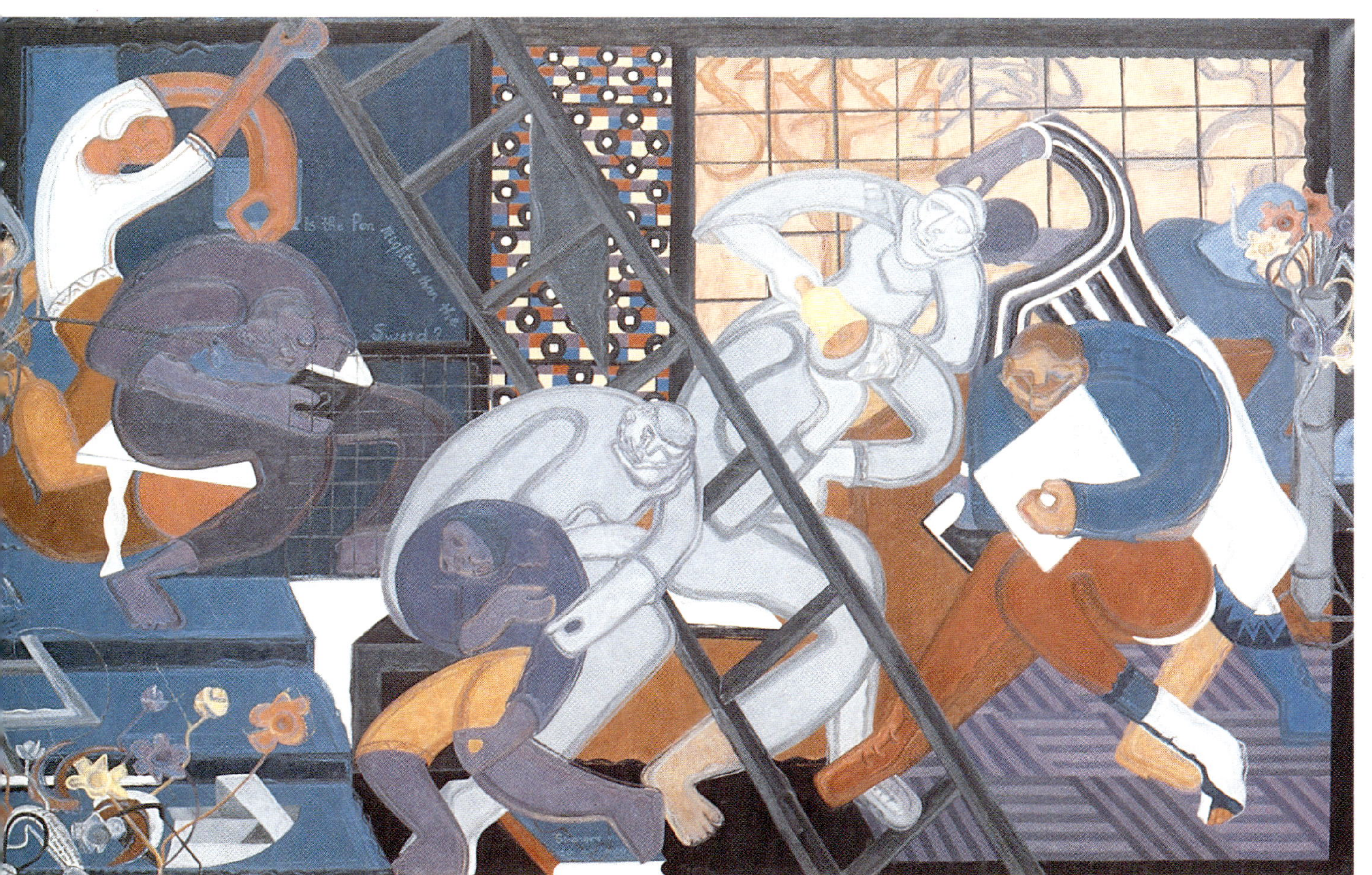

***Will Knowledge Safeguard Freedom #2*, 1985**
Oil on canvas
278 x 183 cm

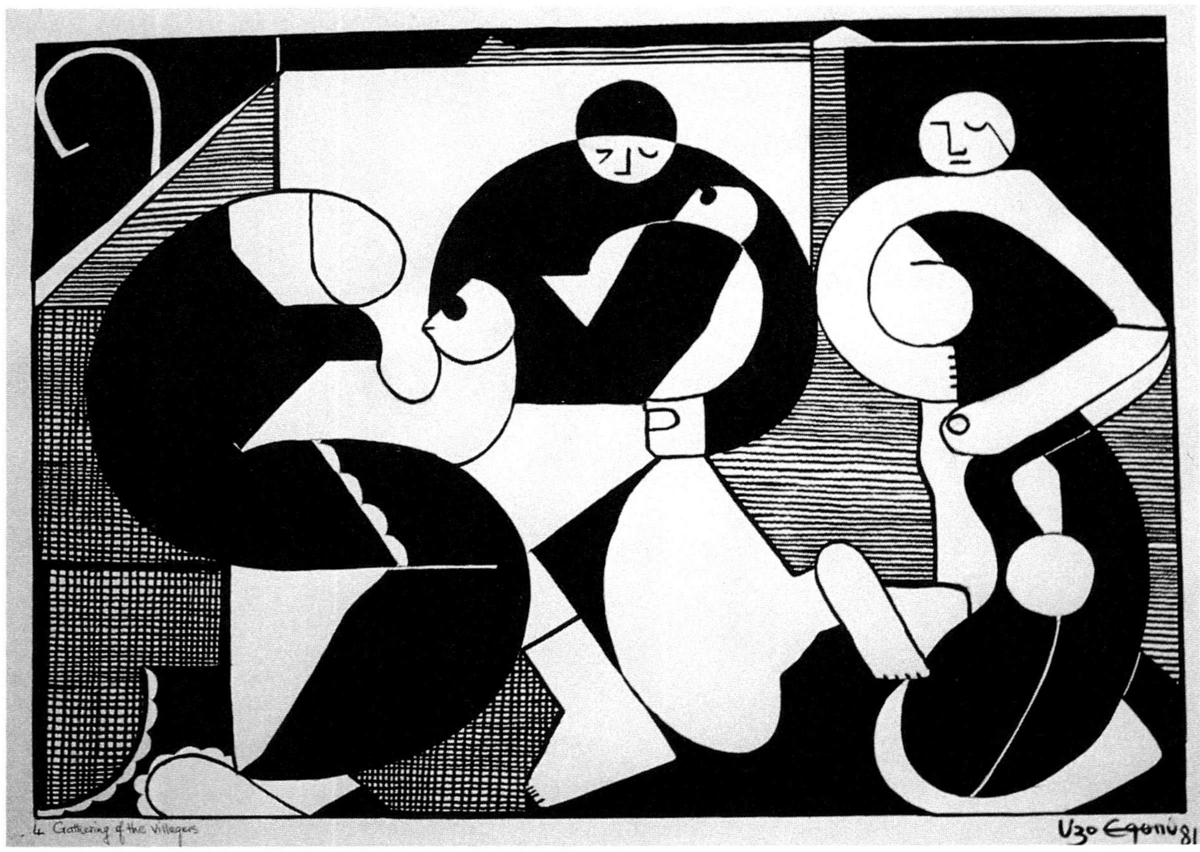

***Gathering of the Villagers*, 1981**
Gouache on paper
58 x 79 cm

This, of course, is only one reading of Egonu's images. Another is to pursue the path of alienation, longing, inadequacy, expectation, anxiety, dissatisfaction, loss, a construct which could be validly built on the same images. Whatever discourse they are meant to engender, these works stun us with their lyrical simplicity and poetic austerity, and through their stark visual power they engage us even more deeply in the indeterminate positions which they enunciate.

Egonu continued his preoccupation with social interrogation in his subsequent series of paintings from 1985 to 1988, 'Will Knowledge Safeguard Freedom?', in which, also, he abandoned the rhetoric of lament we saw in 'Stateless People'. The central theme of the series is the interconnectedness of power and knowledge, the ways in which scientific and technological advancement determine the fate and place of races, and the destiny of humankind. The failure of the experiment in modern state-building across Africa and the apparent lack of willingness to march with the times continued to cause Egonu personal anxiety and sorrow. In a conversation in October 1989 he reiterated his lingering concern and disappointment: "Although I am an artist," he wrote, "I am also interested in history. You look at Japan. If Japan had not tried hard, they would be a Russian colony today. But look at Ethiopia."[13]

Egonu always had a fascination for Japan, deriving less from any particular love of the country or its people as from an admiration of its technological and economic progress, its dogged recovery from the ravages of World War II through astute appropriation and mastery of technology and western civilisation while holding onto its traditions and ethics. Egonu's statement, quoted above, replicates that of an unpublished lecture note from 1986 where he wrote:

> My study of Japanese history helped me a lot in my art. I do not mean Japanese art, but Japanese studies of Western Science and technology and eventual industrialisation. Had Japan failed or ignored to acquaint herself with science and technology, she would have ended up as a Russian colony and could not have withstood the Russian Navy's onslaught last century, let alone defeat it.[14]

He takes deep interest in the technological miracles of South East Asia, in Hong Kong and Taiwan, and how these former pockets of backwardness rose in the second half of this century to the forefront of economic strength, while the entire African continent wobbled and crumbled, planting repression in place of progress, and corruption in place of development.

In all the paintings in 'Will Knowledge Safeguard Freedom?' the most prominent leitmotif is the ladder or staircase, symbol of ascent (or descent). The other recurrent motif is the human figure shown, in most of the paintings in the series, in different postures and gestures of engagement, ranging from reading to construction work. As in the 'Addiction' series, the first painting *Will Knowledge Safeguard Freedom?* summarises the whole theme. For each of the concepts there is a visual trope, which leaves the painting unusually crowded with symbols, reminiscent only of the *Exodus* of 1970 or *The Arts* of 1974-75. The figures are blindfolded while engaged in their occupations, perhaps symbolising the nascent stage of the quest for knowledge, the beginning of enquiry and labour, engagements which will eventually lead to discovery, knowledge and the light of advancement. The initial

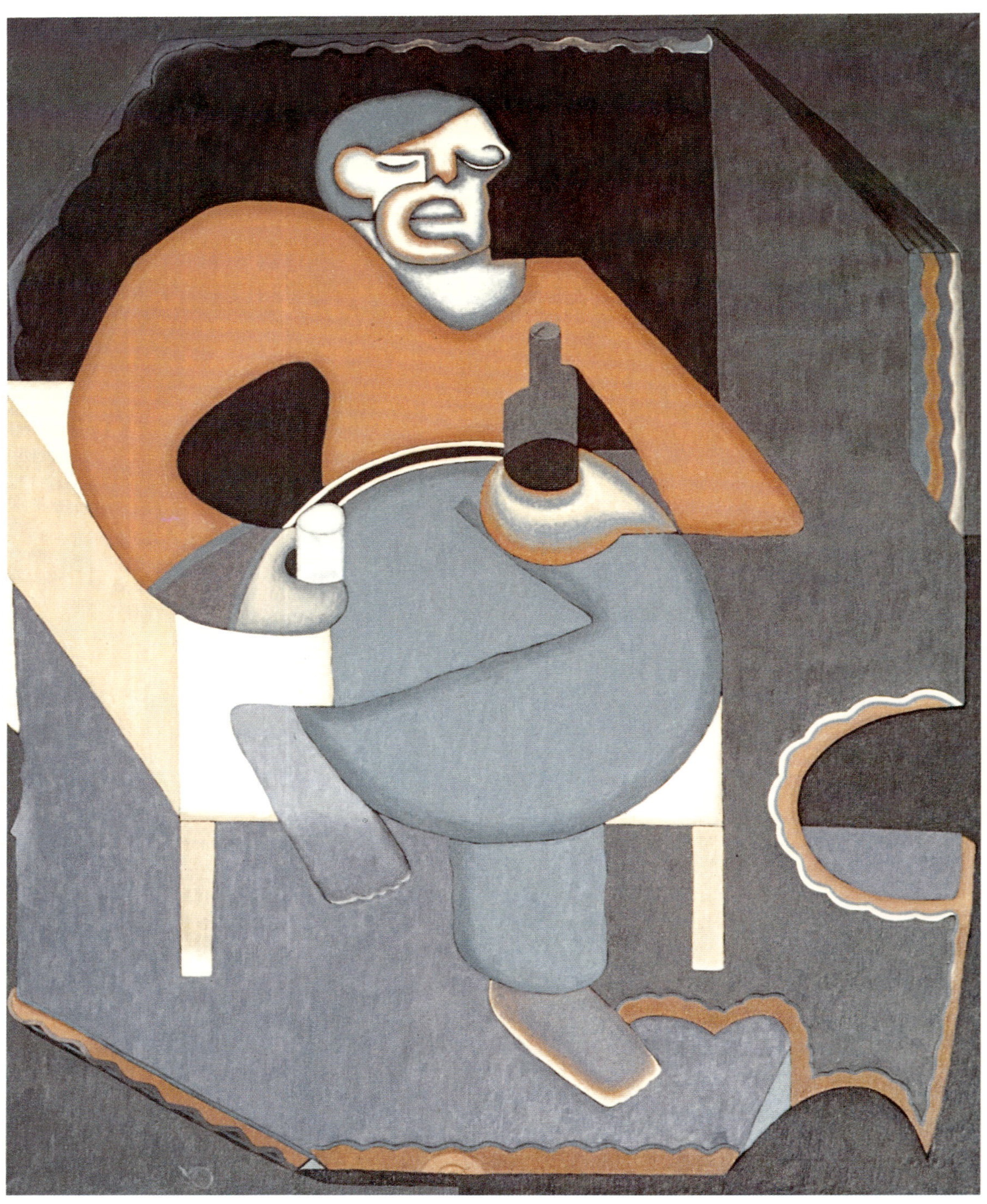

***Man with a Glass of Beer*, 1979**
Oil on canvas, 152 x 124 cm

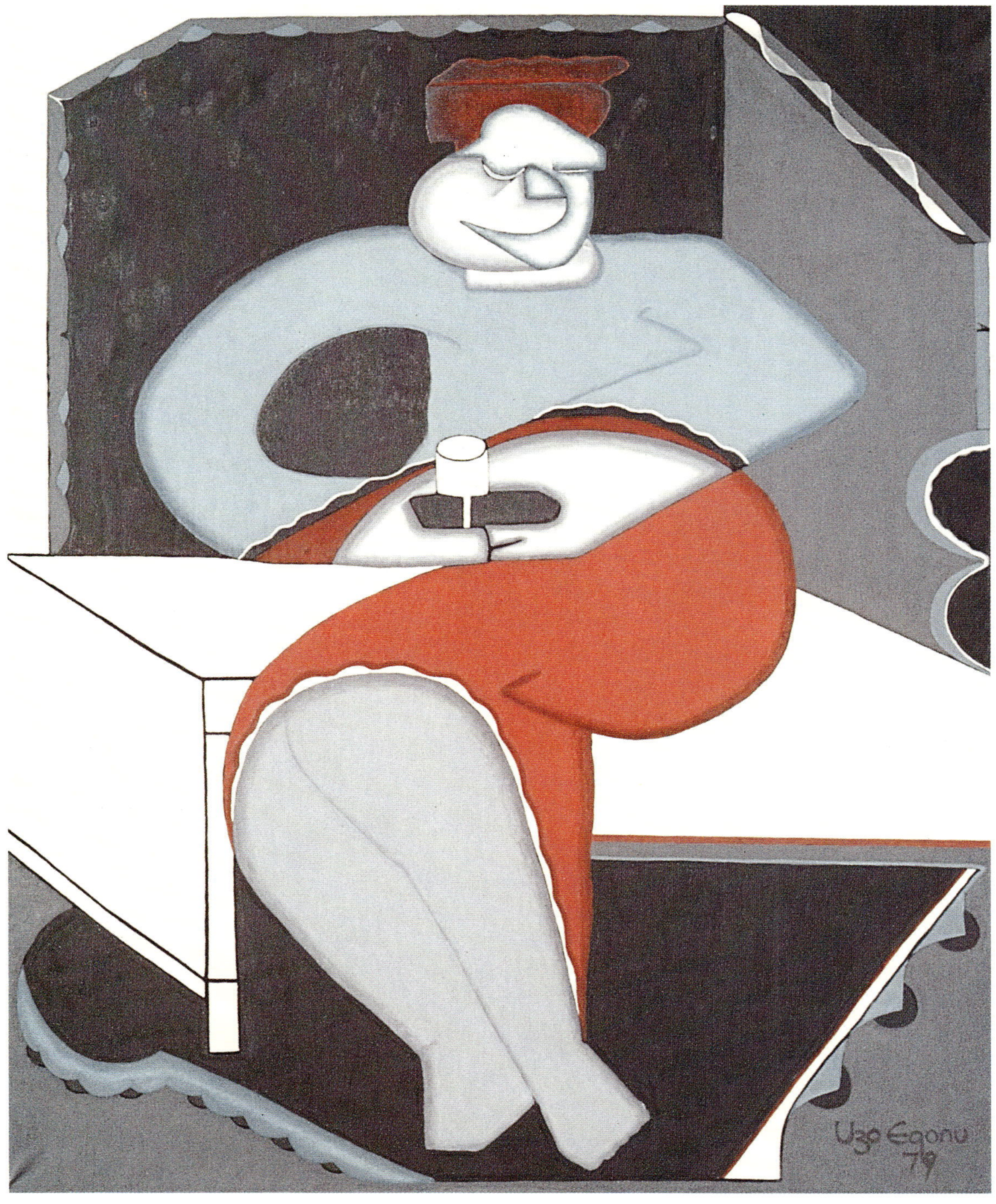

Woman with a Glass of Wine, **1979**
Oil on canvas, 152 x 124 cm

stages of enquiry are also a form of bondage — to ignorance, blindness, backwardness, the absence of enlightenment. In the painting a ladder rests within reach, but is not in use. Progress is at the disposal of humanity but only with knowledge does it discover this and ascend the rungs. The predicament of bondage which characterises this state is represented not only in the blindfolded figures but also by iron bars and steel girders.

With these elements Egonu creates a penal atmosphere, dispelled yet simultaneously reinforced by the image of a broken chain. While this underlines the absence of liberty, it also figures the necessity of struggle as an essential gesture, and it is to this that the artist alludes when he speaks of Japan's achievements. In his lecture note he insists that the progress achieved by Japan was "through hard work and determination", thereby theorising progress as a product of labour and the indispensability of exertion in the ascent to greatness, an ethic he apparently found lacking in the vision of his own people.

In *Will Knowledge Safeguard Freedom No 2* the artist challenges the determinist connection of greatness and racial superiority by inscribing the text: 'Who is created by a Great God?' Consistent failure, he seems to argue, cannot be excused through determinist rhetoric. Underdevelopment is neither genetic nor racial, but the product of ignorance and an unwillingness to strive. It is the inevitable consequence of the institutionalisation of complacency. In a short, unpublished essay explaining the symbolism of the ladder, Egonu writes:

> It is human nature for some people to feel superior because of their wealth or social position in life. Likewise, this applies to one country feeling superior to another, or one human race feeling superior to the rest. The logic behind the feeling of being superior because of wealth, social position, difference of race, is totally wrong.[15]

This would later be echoed by the opening sentences of Achebe's *The Trouble With Nigeria,* where he states categorically that "there is nothing basically wrong with the Nigerian character", a position which could be extended to the other peoples of Africa. And the failure to strive which Egonu locates in the individual, Achebe blames on the failure of leadership to affect positively the social behaviour of the citizenry and inspire the striving spirit, the "unwillingness or inability of... leaders to rise to the responsibility, to the challenge of personal example which are the hallmarks of true leadership''.[16]

In his paintings Egonu does not quite situate the problem with the failures of leadership or any sector of the race or population. He does not so much deal with failure as point to the requisites of success: science, technology, cultural freedom, the work ethic. Achebe, with usual insight, adds a cautionary note in his essay: ''Whenever two Nigerians meet, their conversation will sooner or later slide into a litany of our national deficiencies.''[17] This situation produced a period of intense social preoccupation in the visual arts in Nigeria, especially in the 1980s, and at the questionable level of 'litanies of deficiency'. Working from the distance of expatriation, Egonu rises above lamentatious rhetoric and finds room to philosophise.

It is perhaps the privilege of expatriation, also, which explains the optimism and vision in the series 'Will Knowledge Safeguard Freedom?', especially through the leitmotif of the ladder, and the symbol of the flower. Remarkably, the latter appeared several years later as a central image in the prize-winning novel by the artist's younger countryman and fellow émigré, Ben Okri. Although as a contemplation on the same theme, Okri's *The Famished Road* hovers between the genre of 'litanies' and that of critical affirmation, the motif of the flower persistently posits an optimistic present, as does the new-born baby at the end of Achebe's otherwise virulent novel *Anthills of the Savannah*. It is noteworthy that the expatriation shared by these three artists, helped them to transcend the stifling resignation and fatalism to which their fellow citizens at home fell subject.

In 'Will Knowledge Safeguard Freedom?' Egonu does not cast a damning eye but draws attention to universal lessons of history relevant for every people and race. There are a number of paintings in the series which the artist calls 'portraits'; each depicts a central figure and an inscription which indicates the race of the figure while also evoking others. Each figure clutches a ladder. Difference is erased while focus is placed on knowledge and the striving spirit, the prerequisites of progress and development. Effort and the quest for discovery, the artist argues through his imagery, are the keys to advancement and self-improvement for all humanity.

The series attains a level of correlation between intent and discernible visual symbolism comparable to that of 'Stateless People'. And yet the philosophy which it enunciates is one that is to some extent arguably simplistic, even deterministic. Many have challenged the valorisation of labour and the work ethic, and in deconstructing this

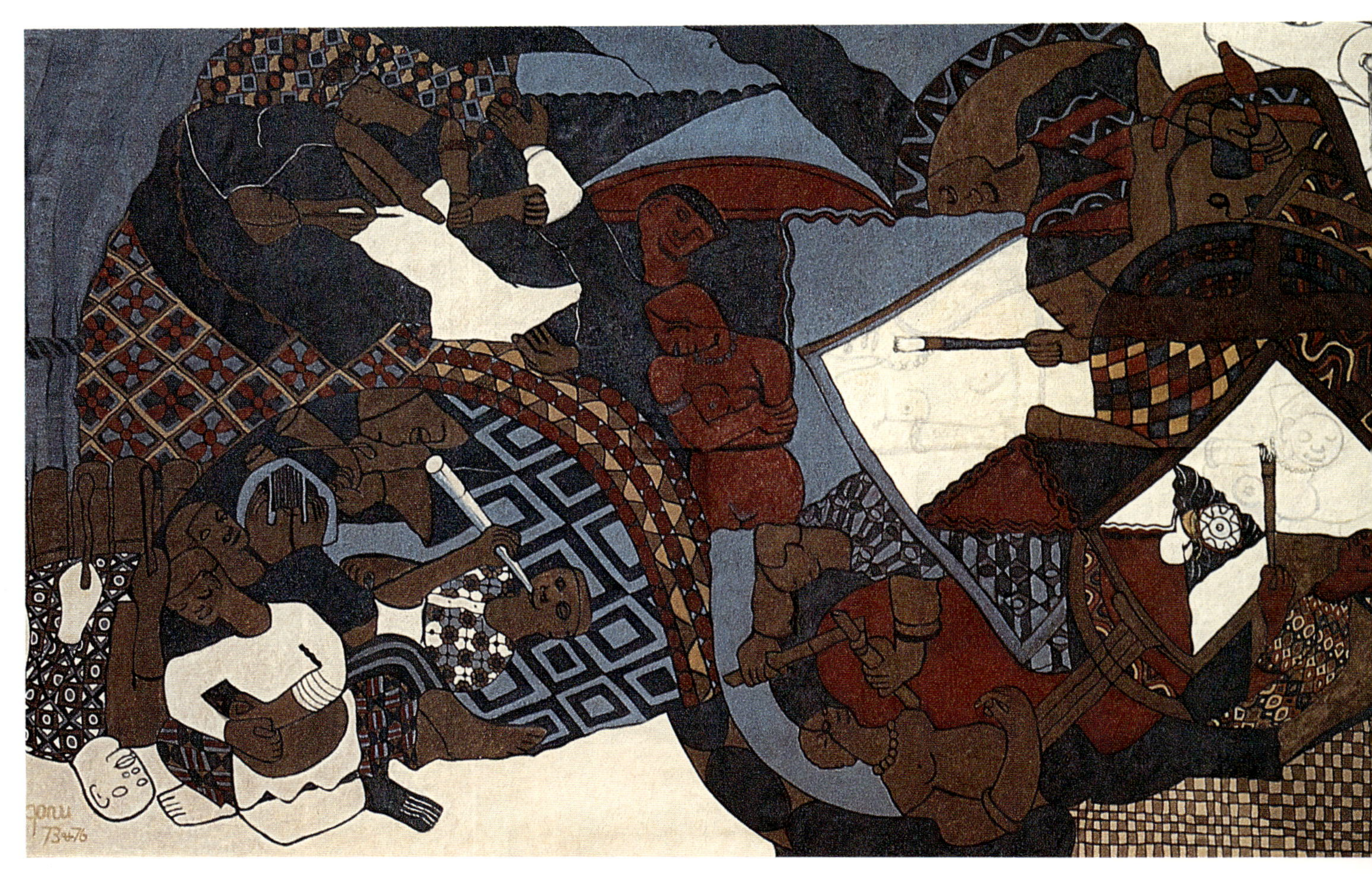

***The Arts*, 1973-74**
Oil on canvas
181 x 280 cm

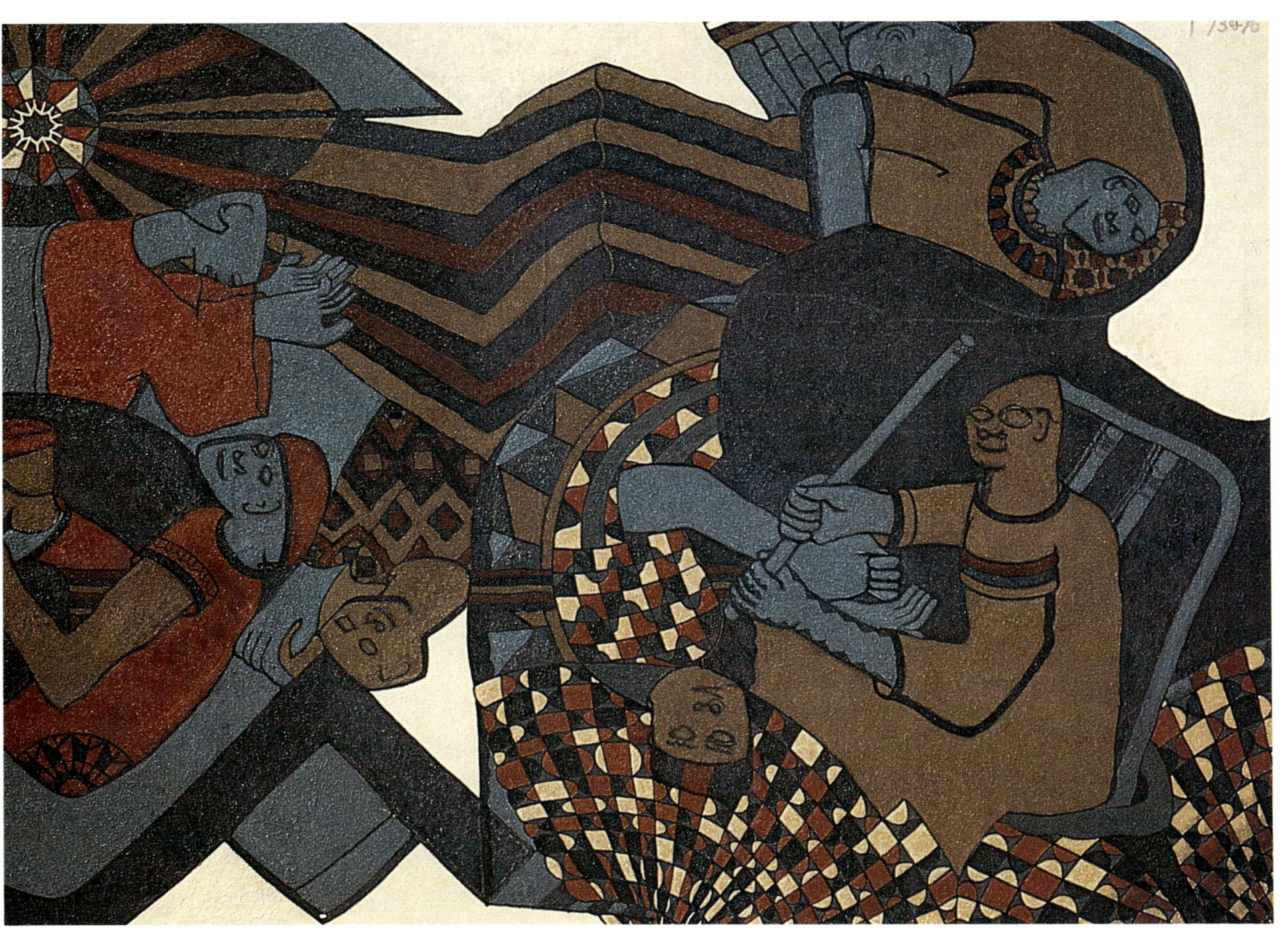

Enchanted by the Sunset, 1973-74
Oil on canvas
148 x 219 cm

argued that it is essentially oppressive against the lower social classes of society and is instituted by those classes which benefit most from their labour. Within the context and on the level that Egonu enunciates this philosophy, however, it can only be seen as most appropriate, even inevitable. To negate the argument for industriousness is a luxury which only societies which have attained a considerable level of development can meaningfully afford.

The significance of these paintings, however, is not simply in the validity of their contents as in the fact that, like 'Stateless People' and the war paintings, they demonstrate Egonu's predilection for committed art, art which, rather than turn into itself, contemplates the intricacies and inconsistencies of the human condition. It is this inclination which removes Egonu's work from Greenbergian modernism and places it at the centre of a modernism which combines the individualist articulation of form with a fervent nationalism and a traditional preoccupation with society. Egonu's work, like that of many Third World artists, contributes to the redefinition of the boundaries of modernism. Together, these artists steer modernism away from the decadent myopia of autonomism and pure formalism, and through their versatility and the breadth of their visions strip it of its Eurocentric pretensions. Also, Egonu's work from the late 1960s to the 1980s places him alongside the best known artists and writers of his generation and society. Like Achebe and Soyinka, he rested the greatness of his art on its overriding theme of humanity.

Anguish and Solitude

Between 1979 and 1983, when his sight was most severely impaired, Egonu produced a series of gouache and ink studies for painting and prints. Among these were four landscape studies in gouache called 'The Four Seasons', which were later translated to colour screen prints in 1983. They fall within what Simon Wilson qualifies as the classical tradition,[1] being essentially imaginative rather than topographical or illustrative. They represent Winter, Spring, Summer and Autumn, although it is not known in what chronological order the artist executed the gouaches or the subsequent prints. One of the first things that catches attention in looking at these landscapes, is that they are conceived as a continuum belonging to one body; in other words, as a single, composite tableau in four movements.

A unique feature of 'The Four Seasons' is that they neither follow the traditional horizontal orientation of landscape, nor the square favoured by, for instance, Gainsborough. Instead they are composed along the vertical or portrait axis. When the entire tableau is brought together, however, the horizontal format is restored. In this way, therefore, the paintings seem to play on both tradition and its subversion.

The paintings are not panoramic, as is typical of the genre, but focus on a limited, 'close-up' area, a perspective familiarised by nature photography and commercial graphics. In each painting there is the sparsest of elements, a sharp and severe use of contrast, as austere as Chinua Achebe's narratives, and a terse finish comparable to Miles Davis's *Sketches of Spain*. *Winter* depicts a tree and some shrubs, withered

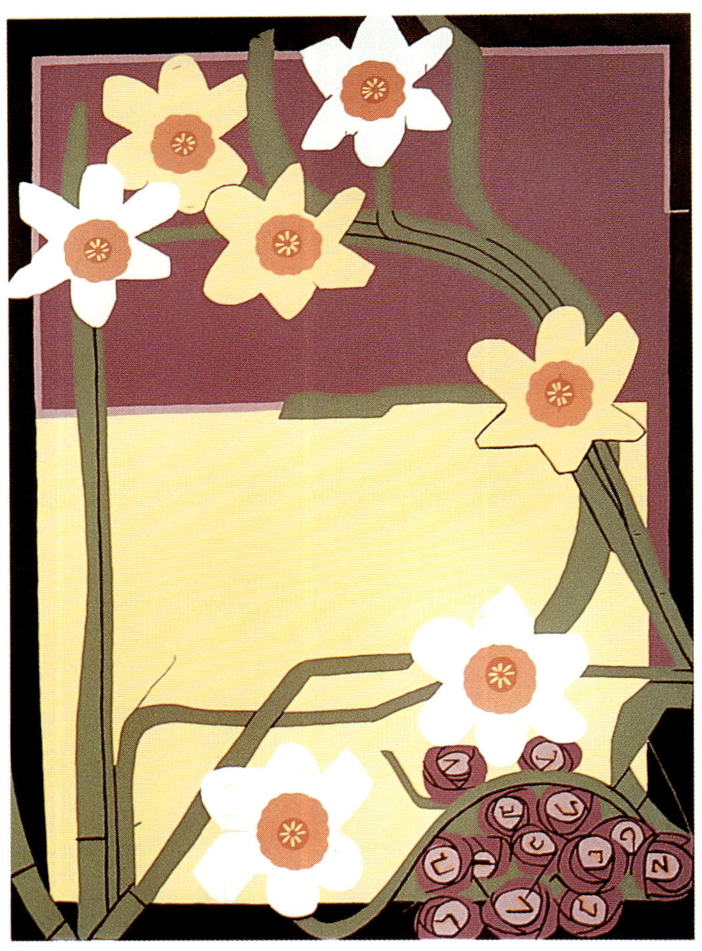

***Four Seasons: Spring*, 1983**
Screenprint
94 x 70 cm

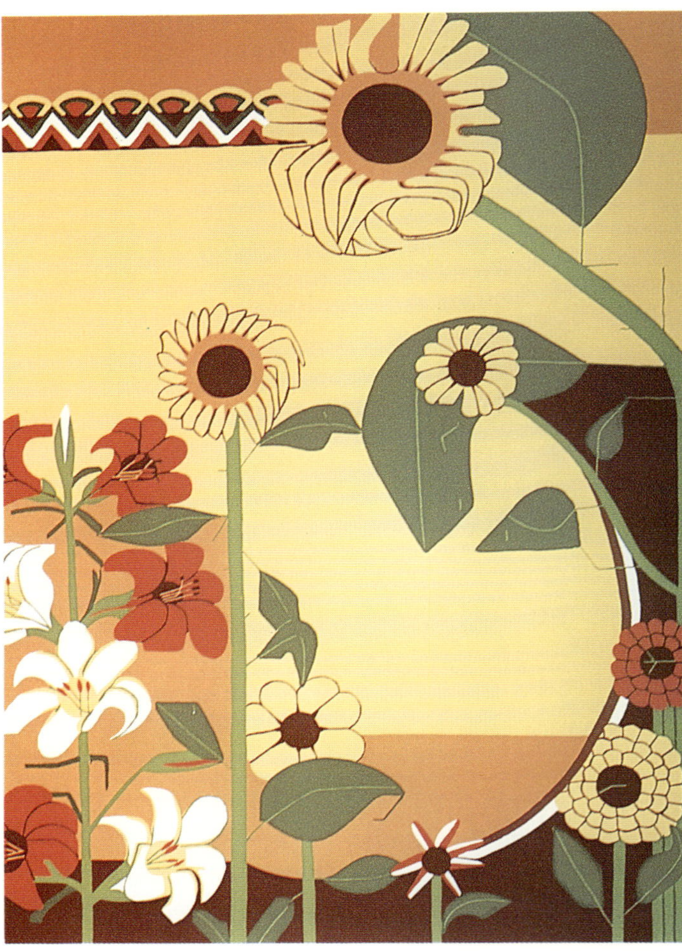

***Four Seasons: Summer*, 1983**
Screenprint
94 x 70 cm

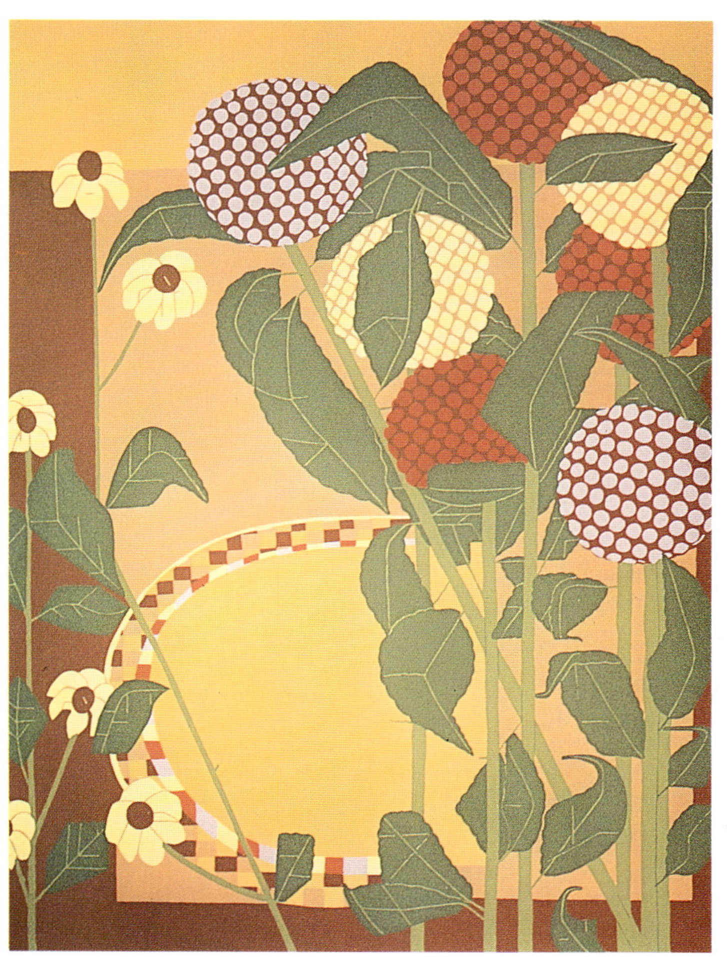

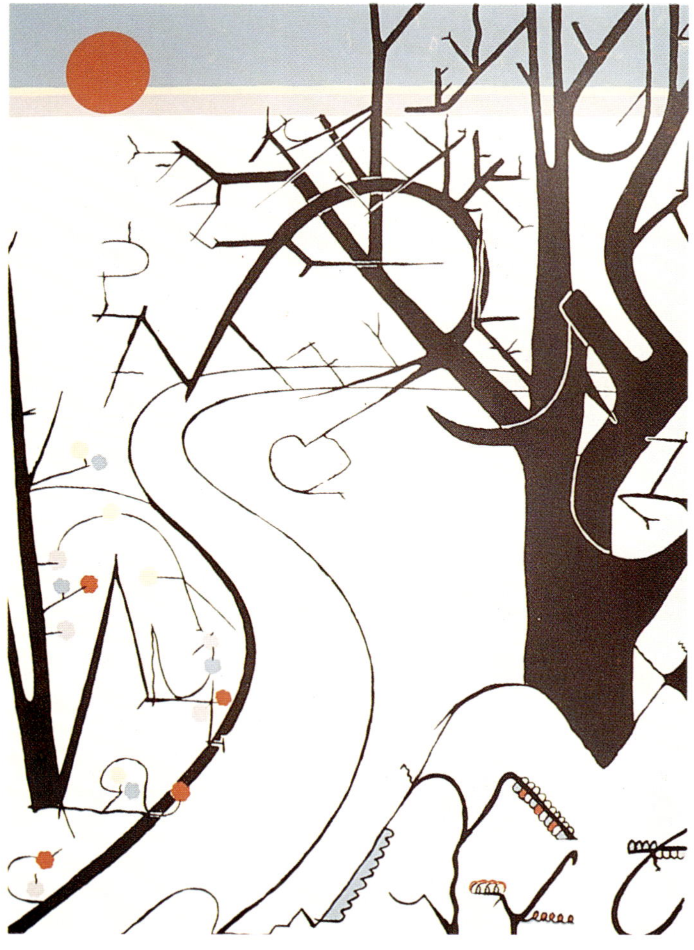

***Four Seasons: Autumn*, 1983**
Screenprint
93 x 70 cm

***Four Seasons: Winter*, 1983**
Screenprint
95 x 70 cm

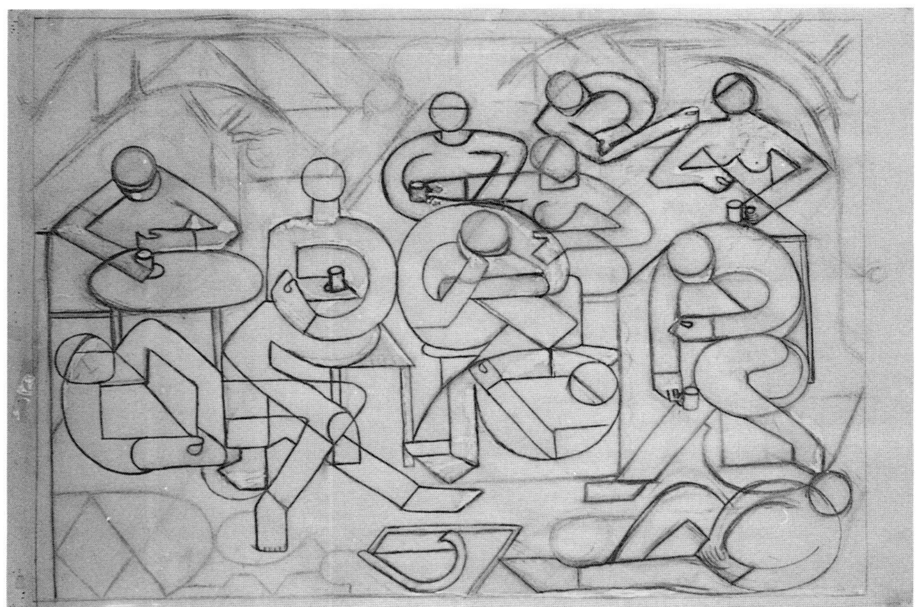

***Spring (study)*, 1983**

to bare branches, snow represented by a plain negative space, and in the middle distance, a suggestion of an automobile part-buried in the snow. In discussing the gouache study for *Winter* George Whittet relates it to Klee's use of line, severe and skeletal.[2] A closer parallel, perhaps, would be to Uli body painting from Egonu's own culture, especially in the deft and delicate orchestration of line, positive and negative space, which in *Winter* creates a saturated and pleasing composition. The other paintings in the series follow this austere aesthetic of a few details sufficiently charged with the mood of the subject. In 'The Four Seasons', therefore, we find a complex combination of elements of several traditions, from European landscape painting and modernist design to Igbo mural art.

What also distinguishes these paintings is that other, hardly definable quality of great landscape painting, that economy of statement which distinguishes the poetic from the prosaic. The notable absence of narrative frees the paintings from literary or historical conjectures, placing only nature at the centre. The sheer evocative power which issues from them, the artist's ability to distil the different moods and stations which constitute their subjects to appropriate visual metaphors, imbues these paintings with what Read calls ''excess of poetry, a quality which poetry would express, but lacks the means''.[3] A cleanliness and serenity elevate them above the genre and transform them into supreme celebrations of nature and its inherent poetics. This serenity lies not in the scenery or atmosphere, but in the form, and yet succeeds in communicating, with a symbolic power, the essence of its subject.

Egonu's most colourful works were done in the 1970s and 1980s. It was during this period that he worked with silkscreen, giving him the opportunity to explore colour in ways impossible with lithography or etching. The polychromatic possibilities of silkscreen in turn influenced his paintings from the period, some of which, like the gouaches under discussion here, were executed with a view to translating them into screenprints. 'The Four Seasons', however, are unusually colourful even for the period; with the exception of *Winter* which employs an appropriately severe palette, the paintings vibrate with exaggerated colour and warmth. There is a preponderance of yellow and orange which one does not normally identify with the English climate.

Although the artist produced the paintings from observation,[4] evidently from his top-floor studio, his failing sight was such that he could not clearly see the scene. In his brief on the work of this period, 'Painting in darkness', Egonu admits that he "could not see the colours clearly, but each time I had in my mind the colours which I had

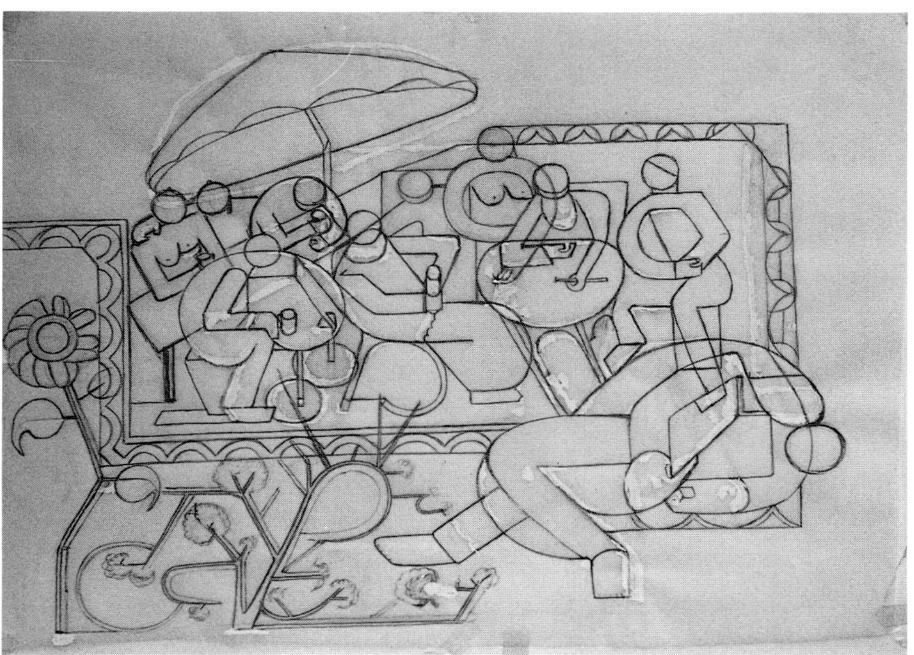

Summer (study), 1983

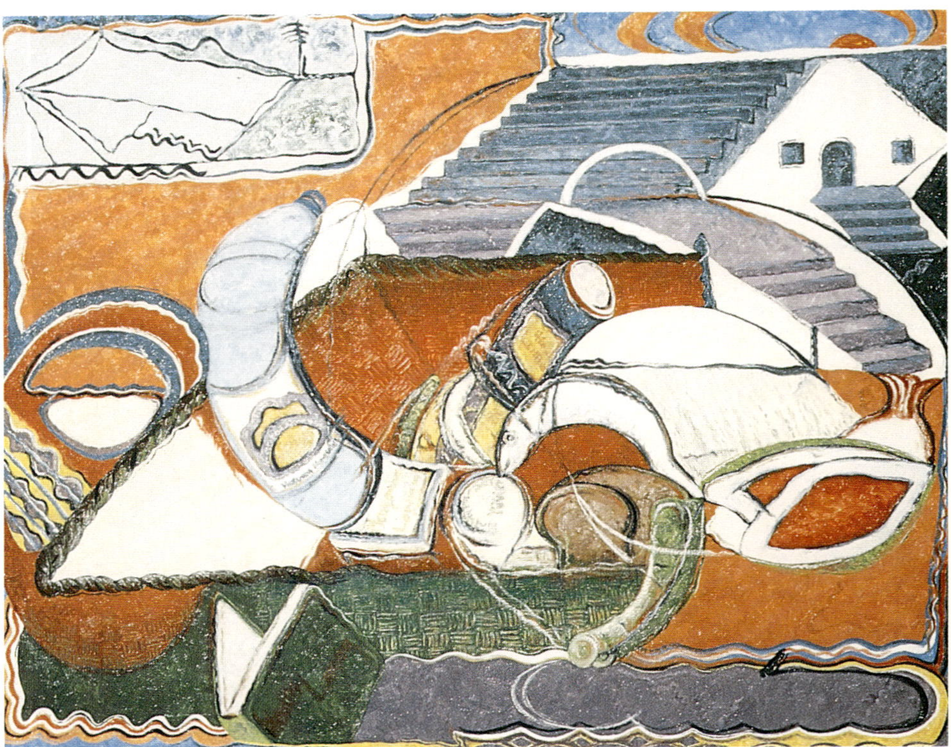

***A New Lease of Life #1*, 1988**
Oil on canvas
102 x 127 cm
Coll: Arts Council of England

already composed in my memory and through my imagination and means of looking and trying to judge the colours''.[5]

In this regard Egonu's 'Four Seasons' remind us of Monet's 'Water-lilies', painted after the latter's sight began to fail in 1908. Bernard Myers observed that the ''astonishing colour and splashing brushstrokes'' of the artist's post-1908 paintings ''are in no small part due to Monet's failing sight''.[6] The reduced sensitivity to light induces a tendency to compensate by using a brighter palette, and it is this which possibly explains the colour saturation of 'The Four Seasons'.

'The Four Seasons' contemplates nature on a particularly personal, poetic level. In 'Painting in Darkness' Egonu defines a relationship between himself and nature which seems to preclude much social interaction. 'The Four Seasons' is his private conversation with nature and commemorates his discovery of the latter. There is a note of solitudinal internalisation, a serene adventure which excludes the public. The paintings are a reverie and remind us of Constable's insistent desire to retire to the countryside, to ''take up my Viol de Gamba and walk off to some sweet Village where I can paint landskips and enjoy the tag End of Life in quietness and ease''.[7]

In the press release for the exhibition of 'The Four Seasons' at the Bhownagree Gallery in London in 1982, Egonu is quoted as saying: ''In my paintings and other works, I am trying to capture the chaos, yet beauty and discipline, of the changing face of nature.''[8] This interest in the dialectic between chaos and discipline in nature relates to the parallel dialectic between his failing vision and his will to transcend disability and persevere with creative work. He describes the period as one of ''pulling through'',[9] and notes that blindness signals material insecurity for an artist who lives by his work. This would have brought initial shock and a period of considerable anxiety. 'The Four Seasons', then, records a struggle to overcome internal anguish through a rediscovery of the beauty and warmth of nature.

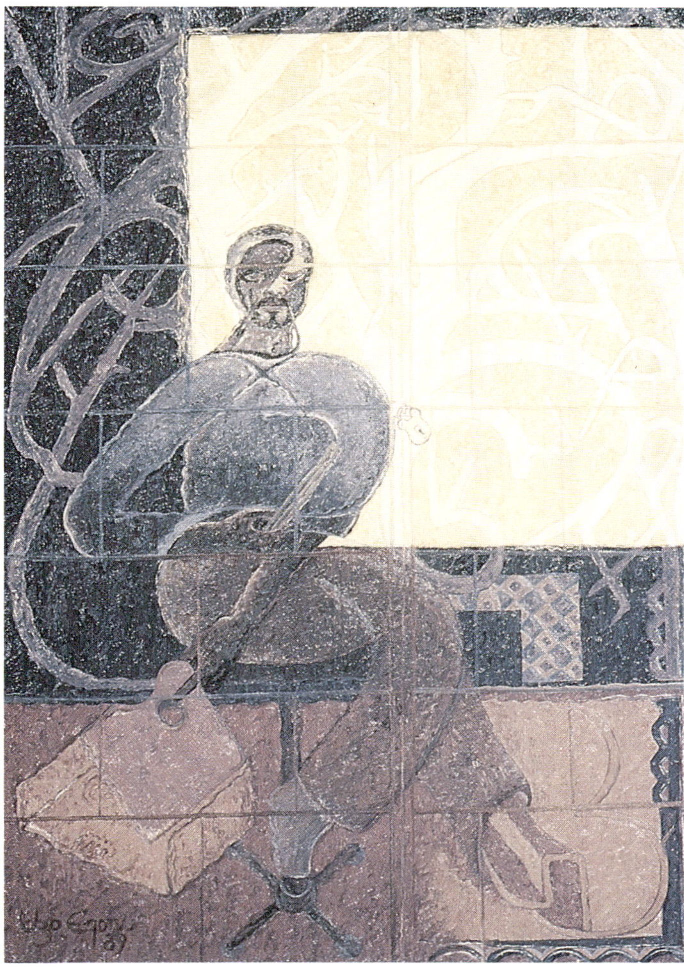

***Self-Portrait*, 1989**
Oil on canvas
178 x 124 cm

Rather than signify resignation, this work registers a courageous engagement with personal adversity, and a transition from anxiety to tranquillity.

In 1983 he had the final operation to restore his sight. Two years later, however, while in Germany for his show at the Galerie Neue Horizonte in Frankfurt Maine, he had his first heart attack. After considerable recuperation in Bedburg, he returned to London only to have a repeat attack in 1986. This time doctors predicted he would have less than a year to live.

Egonu always referred to these incidents as his 'traumatic experience'. They marked the beginning of a period of deep solitude for him, during which he finally withdrew from the world and resigned himself to the imminence of death. He began to sign and authenticate previously unsigned paintings and sketches, and to arrange his papers and estate in preparation. The certainty of death produced not terror nor undue anxiety but calm and collectedness, a desire to bring things to an orderly end.

Egonu survived doctors' predictions to begin what he has called "a new lease of life".[10] Also, his art went through a gradual but marked change. The new phase was marked by a pencil sketch which he made while in hospital in Bedburg in 1985. Titled *Uncompleted Journey*, the small sketch was made after a particularly feverish dream which left him palpitating when he awoke. In the dream he found himself travelling through an unfamiliar place, as if away from the living. Luckily he was drawn back from the trail when he was woken by Hiltrud. In his interpretation, he was symbolically rescued by this act, and brought back to life, and for him this meant that his mission as an artist was unfinished. His was still an uncompleted journey.

This was his opportunity to explore reality on a more personal level, to engage in a renewed philosophical contemplation of the self. After 'Stateless People' and 'Will Knowledge Safeguard Freedom?', it was time to withdraw from the arena of social commentary, though unexpected longevity would see him return to history and the public arena much later in the 1990s.

In 1987 he began a new cycle of work, a series of single-head studies which he also titled 'A New Lease of Life'. In each study the composition is taken up entirely by a huge and emphatic head. The thick, textured line which made its return in 'Will Knowledge Safeguard Freedom?' is also present, as opposed to the clean and precise line found in his work from the 1970s. The flat colour area of the screenprints and paintings of the Seventies and early Eighties, is replaced by the feel for texture of the work of the mid-Sixties; its stippling, tonking and the use of the palette knife. Almost all the elements associated with the refinement of the 1980s give way to the raw, impulsive emphasis of the artist's period of searching. However, the subject is now the head, the countenance, the individual, the singular face and its vagaries. One begins to sense the internalisation which Anthony Storr identifies with the valedictory period of an artist's life, when the objects of concern differ from those of the artist's previous work and, though they may relate to earlier preoccupations, do so in a different manner and on a different level.

The defiant solitude and self-assertion of this period is summed up in Egonu's *Self-Portrait* of 1989, the only work which directly identifies him as its subject. In the studio scene, Egonu divides the composition among his image', the painting, a huge canvas, the studio, and an outdoor view which he is painting. The composition masterfully lays out its elements to fill in every section of the work, which partly explains the position of the artist's palette, held down to his right while he wields a brush in his right hand in a particularly confident, even confrontational stance. The outdoor scene which the artist is painting is dark, with an outline of tangled vegetation reminiscent of winter. His studio and the canvas on which he paints are floodlit, and there is room for some decorative motifs. The entire painting is in violet chiaroscuro, and although the colour is applied to create a rough texture, with elements emphatically laid down.

Two things stand out about this painting. The first is that the artist and his work are locked in by padlocked metal gates. The second is that the artist faces the viewer full from his waist up, as if momentarily called to attention from his preoccupation, or as if posing for a quick press photograph. In this position he has his back the outdoor scene and the canvas, and faces the grid. When one looks closer, however, it becomes clear that he is integrated into the painting on the canvas, with a branch of the foliage painted directly across his face and torso. There is, therefore, an almost surrealist multiple registration, with the outdoor scene replicated on the canvas and on the artist, just as the canvas is worked into the artist's own image and helps constitute him.

Details of the artist's countenance are however not very clear. There is a recognisable semblance, but photographs from 1989 show that the figure in the painting is not a mirror image. The look in the eye is neither a stare nor are the eyes downcast. Instead there is a neutrality which defines the eyes not as tools of sight but as mere anatomical features. One is reminded here of David Bomberg's theory of *the eye* which he regarded as a stupid organ by itself.[11] The eyes here do not look, they do not regard, they do not register, their absence emphasised by the artist's position in relation to his canvas and the scene. The objects in the painting interweave out of the artist's sight, though not without his manipulation, symbolised by his poised brush. What one finds here, which is quite remarkable, is that Egonu seems to posit the possibility of creative occupation without sight, in this way registering his defiance of the threat of blindness which ruled this period of 'Darkness'. He seems to propose that creativity is largely an act of the imagination,[12] and the artist only a vehicle of the creative impulse. The image of the outdoor is on his canvas through both his conscious, manual application of paint, and by its imposition on his perception: the scene grows into him and through him onto canvas. A pattern of unity is established between reality, the artist's mind, and the work of art. To realise this unity of subject, imagination and medium or support, is the ultimate aspiration of every artist.

In this portrait Egonu begins a philosophical enquiry into the nature of the creative imagination. One can identify a shift, as Storr notes of the late period of artists' lives, from preoccupation with "life's

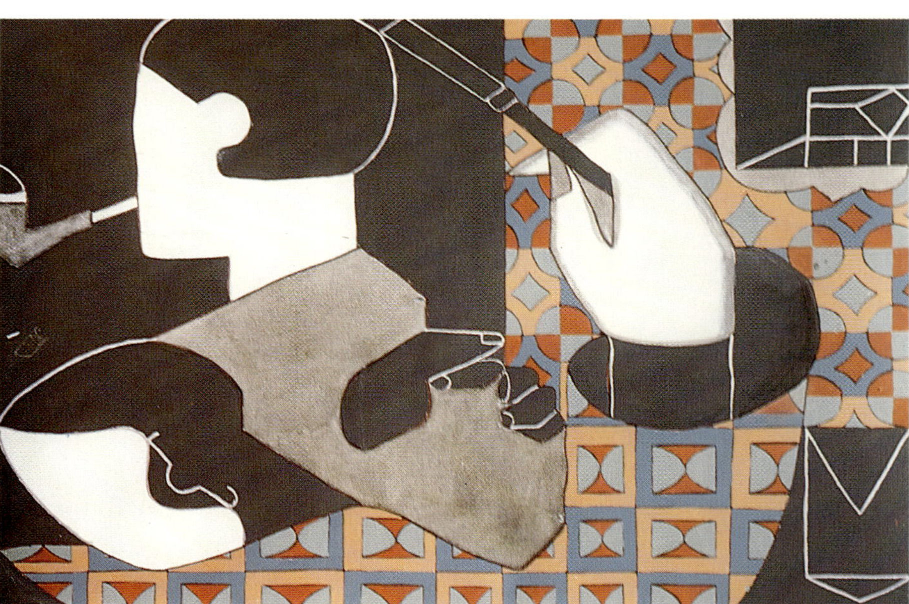

***Painter at Work*, 1979**
Gouache on paper
56 x 76 cm

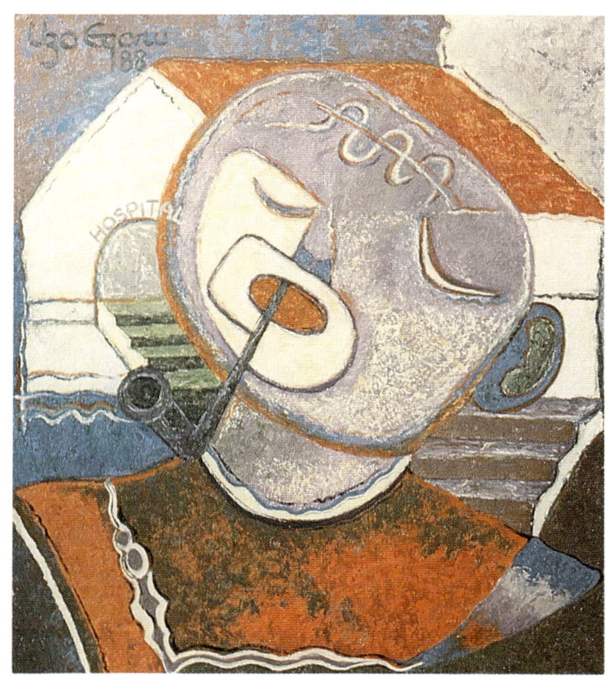

***The Man Who Does Not Listen to Advice*, 1988**
Oil on canvas
81 x 71 cm

dramas [to preoccupation with] life's patterns''. In Egonu's self-portrait the artist is as prominent as his tools, and as central as his subject: it is this unity which defines his being.

In his *Painter at Work*, 1979, Egonu shows an artist in the process of creating a self-portrait. The artist questions the disjunctions inherent in objective reality to unite his image on canvas with his working self; in other words, rather than show a representation of the artist on his canvas, Egonu shows the artist as existing simultaneous on and outside of his own support. The distance between object and representation is collapsed and the two are united. Egonu seems to imply that in contemplating a painting no frame of reference is valid beyond the image as painted. Every painting is autobiographical, having grown out of the artist's experience and the creative act. Autobiography, however, is fiction, a reconstruction of reality.

Painter at Work belongs to a self-portrait tradition which, from the High Renaissance to modernism is essentially an individualist tradition. Egonu's position is not, however, one of fascination with individualism, but to make a claim on western traditions, a claim which he returns to now and again as a reminder to us of his cross-cultural location. In the self-portrait of 1989, he avoids the individualist construct of the artist-as-centre or artist-as-hero, and redefines the artist as no more the creator than the created, and is therefore never fully realised except in conjunction with the subject and its representation.

Storr speaks of ''Third Period works'', those works produced in the late stage of an artist's life, as always striving to represent ''a new kind of unity between elements which at first sight are extremely disparate''.[13] Through the intermingling of seemingly disparate elements in the 1989 *Self-Portrait*, Egonu presents reality as unity in disparity, a totality of fragments in which no element is supreme, neither artist nor subject. This is the artist's valedictory, a testament summarising the experience of a life in creativity.

The ironwork depicted in the painting represents the physical conditions under which Egonu was compelled to live the rest of his life after his second heart attack. In the paper on the period he continues:

> There is a time in one's life that a change in life style either has to be voluntary, or circumstances might compel a change. A person may detest exercise or walking, prefers [sic] butter to low cholesterol margarine, likes drippings... but circumstances, due to the consequences of that particular life style which affects the health, may wipe out all the detestations... Either you keep to the old ways and bear the consequences, or you follow a new way...[14]

This was a new lease, a new phase of personal responsibility which nevertheless imposed certain restrictions on the artist. His triumph over death, so to say, placed his life back in his hands, requiring of him a level of discipline which, in its regimental nature, justified the hyperbolic imagery of incarceration which we find in this painting. Another painting from this period, *The Man Who does not listen to Advice*, plays on the dangers in ignoring the health precautions to which Egonu alludes in his paper.

The *Self-Portrait* of 1989 represents, therefore, both the anguish and the solitude of a regimented and fragile life. In the hold of this solitude, however, and the clarity of thought which all such conditions inevitably yield, Egonu found the peace to contemplate the deeper meanings of the creative life, and to distil into imagery the complex relationship between the artist, the subject and the work of art.

Past and Present in the Diaspora

Four years ago the thought of Christopher Columbus' voyage, which culminated in his 'discovery' of the Americas, prompted contemplation on the legacy of this discovery. Although usually a history only favours some people, nevertheless the episode may stimulate the minds of both those with opposing views and those whose interest is fulfilled by the event. The defeat of the combined Spanish and French Armada by the British Fleet may not be a welcome memory to the Spaniards and the French, yet the event may activate the minds of their scholars and artists.

Spain and Genoa may claim the glory of Christopher Columbus' voyage and the 'discovery' of the Americas — the former having facilitated his voyage, and the latter being his birth place — but people with the opposite view might say that the consequences of the legacy brought desolation and catastrophe to Africa south of the Sahara, the Incas and the Aztecs.

Although, as an artist, one is not cast in the role of a moralist, one feels, nevertheless, that this should not be a barrier to free thinking and inspiration derived from history; this should not prevent one from making a statement through one's work.

It was not the controversy, nor the sentimentalism attached to the consequence of the legacy of 'discovery' that provoked one's feelings to produce works which are inspired by that thought. What aroused one's feelings was the bewilderment of human behaviour and its contradictions. That thought was the inspiration and led to the visualisation of the event and its legacy. In reflecting upon the consequences of this legacy, a factor worth noting is that a strong will power strengthens human staying-power, and this determination is kindled by spiritual faith. To transform this thought into a picture: how can one represent spiritual strength and what metaphor befits its expression?

Uzo Egonu

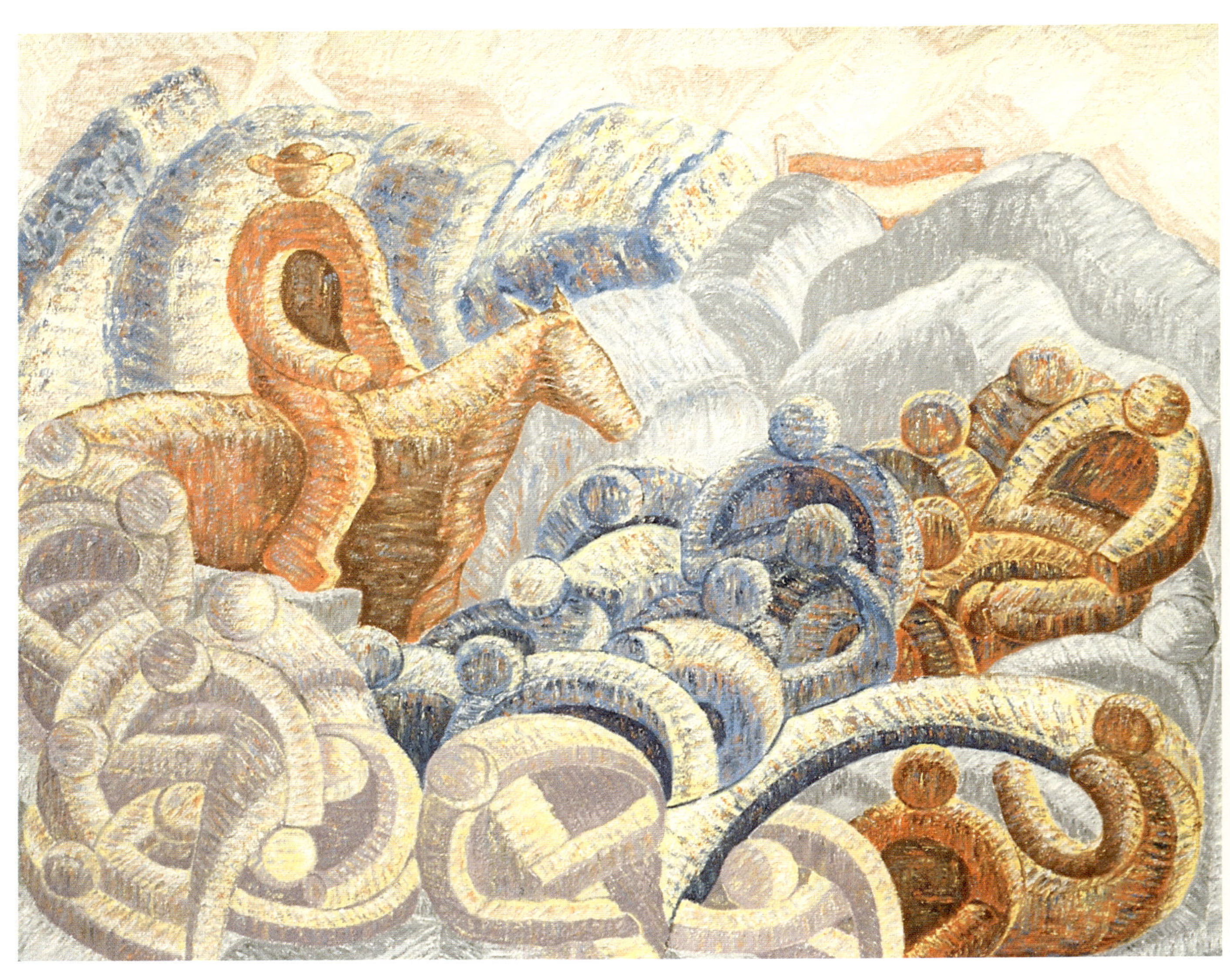

***Past and Present in the Diaspora #13*, 1991**
Oil on paper
63 x 79 cm

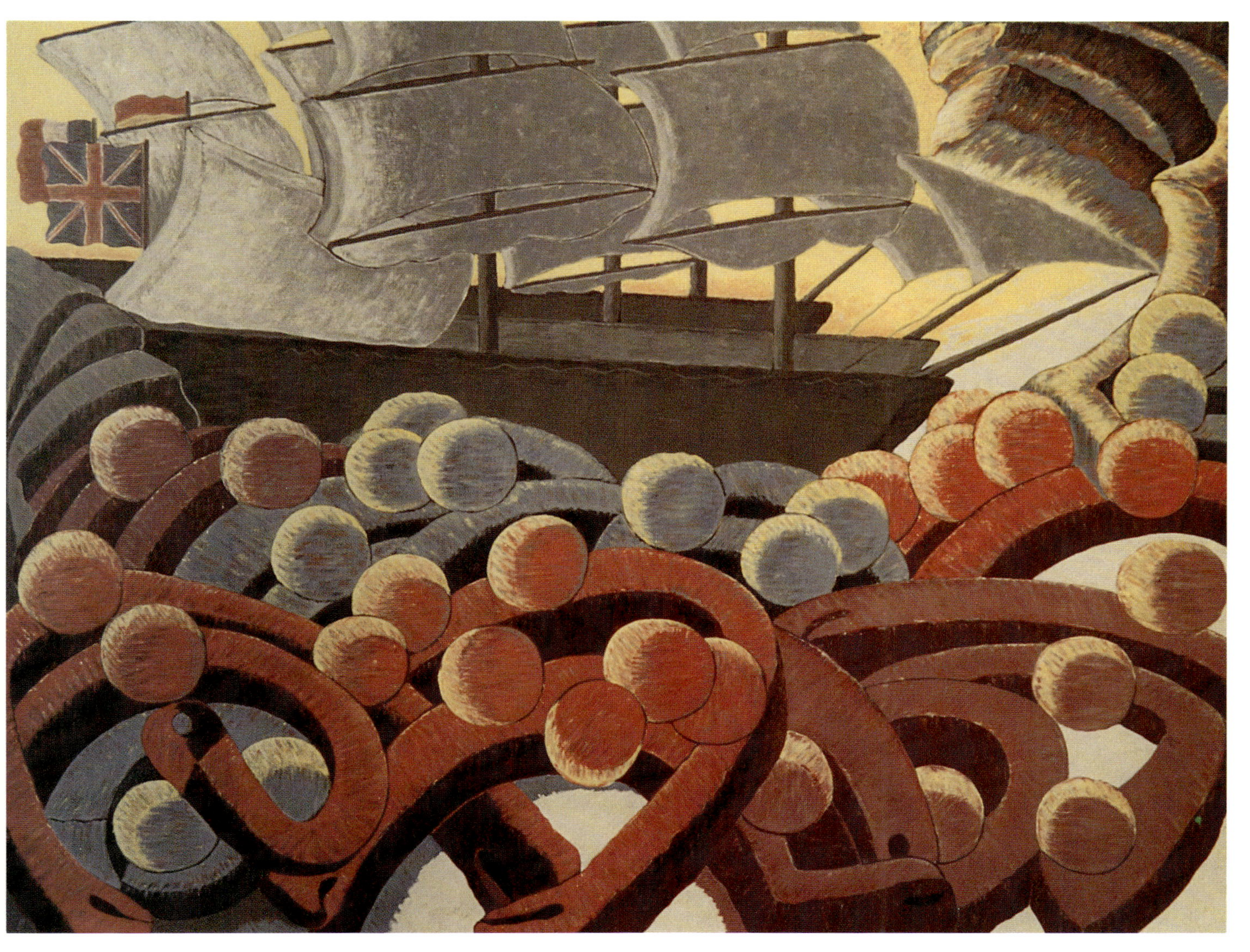

***Past and Present in the Diaspora #14*, 1991**
Acrylic on canvas
154 x 194 cm

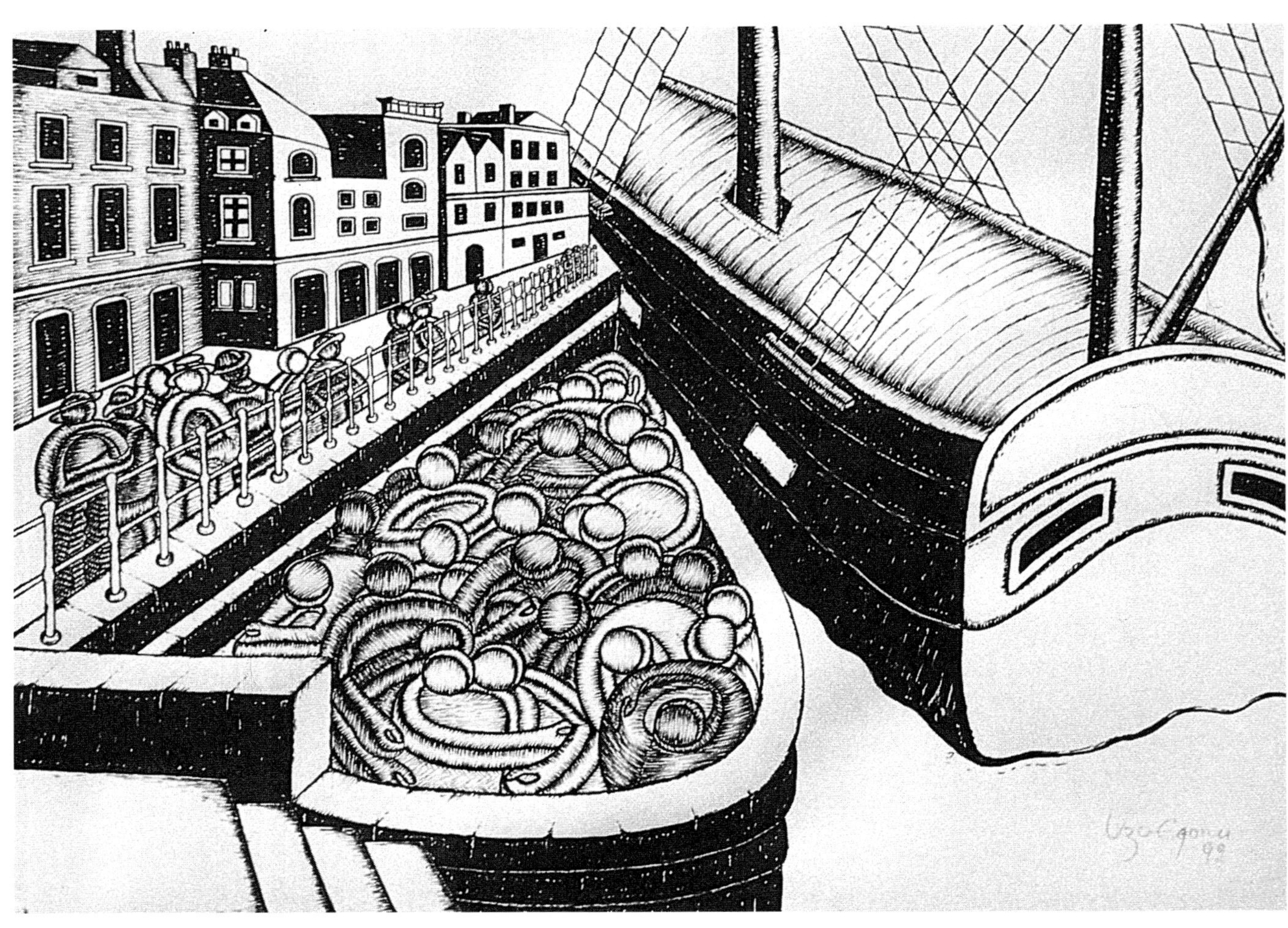

***Past and Present in the Diaspora #18*, 1992**
Indian ink on paper
63 x 79 cm

Postscript

Uzo Egonu's location in modernism would be that hitherto largely unacknowledged space in the centre where artists of non-European descent established their presence and practice by forging a conspicuous intersection between occidental and other cultures. Here modernism finally acknowledged its true nature as not that of the pedigree of western invention and genius, but of a syncretic amalgam of forms, idiosyncrasies and histories, that legitimates individuation and difference. Artists like Egonu reversed the dominant project of modernism by redefining it as not only a mere formal revolution in western art, or just another epoch in the evolution of western culture, but as the beginning of a new heterodoxical discourse within which modernity reveals itself as a shared terrain. Through their interventions on the formulation of modernism, and indeed their initiation of a plurality of modernisms, they changed the pattern of cross-cultural interaction away from the active/passive dichotomy between Europe and the rest of the world presented by the historically reductive colonial narrative, and finally made it difficult to ignore non-occidental impacts on the evolution of cultures. They effected a translocation of anthropophagy from the peripheries of empire into the belly of the whale, whereby colonial consumption of the centre posed itself against imperial appropriation and redefined the terms of centre-periphery discourse. Not only did artists like Egonu conclusively discredit the paradigm of non-occidental inferiority by exerting unquestionable standards of competence on practice in Europe, they also undermined existing power-knowledge relations and presented an unshakeable challenge to the authority of colonial command. In their work we find an almost calculated deconstruction of the language of modernism to reveal and register its true components and origins.

Uzo Egonu resides outside the locus of colonial mimicry because, rather than be formed in the image of empire under the conditions of a semantic slippage which preclude a perfect duplication of the European identity, rather than imitate Europe in order to comprehend or consume it, he has actively negotiated and dictated the terms of his relationship with it. He has formed his art and identity in his own image. He has shaped his form and defined his aesthetic by acquiring the tools and canons of the academy, and then consciously subverting them. There is a deliberate relocation of elements, a reformation and re-presentation of strands from a diversity of sources which are ultimately subsumed under a powerful individual vision. Egonu's work reveals a continuous and determined exploration of all the possibilities of form in order to, in his words, "subordinate it to my will [and] use it to express myself".[1] The result is a use of form which is

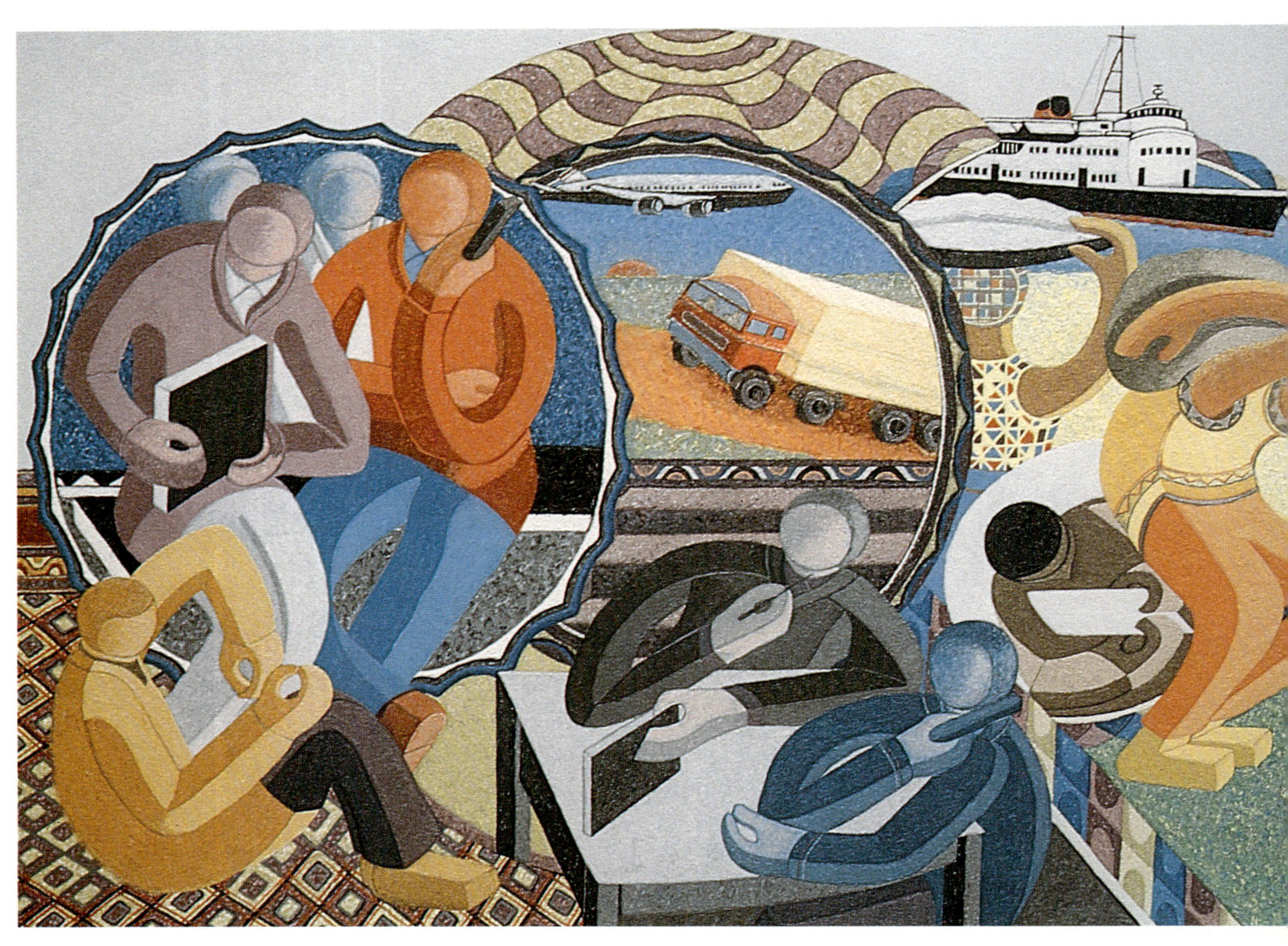

Universality, **1993**
Oil on canvas
145 x 211 cm
Commissioned by the International Maritime Satellite Organisation (INMARSAT), London.

entirely Egonu's and bears his unmistakeable imprint, a kind of visual signature which defies anonymisation and encodes the individual persona. While this may be difficult to describe or circumscribe in anything but a visual register, it nevertheless can be characterised by a number of formal devices, the most important perhaps of which are a unique virtual perspective, cyclic and multidimensional, the preponderance of borders, though occasionally inconspicuous, a particular feel for texturality and design. The aggregate of these devices Egonu has described as footprints.[2]

The architectonics of Egonu's work inscribe a unique, modernist interpretation of forms which derive quite considerably from Africa, and through these forms are projected important elements of those origins which further underline the artist's niche within his epoch. In interrogating form in his work, in looking closely at line or texture or colour, we discover the surface of elements and principles of design, or tropes of modernist confrontation with traditionality. We are almost forced to make a connection, albeit speculative in places, between these and non-formal, extra-aesthetic structures and geographies in a way that conventional landmarks of modernist art often fail to evoke. An experimentalist seizure and manipulation of old forms and the discovery and manufacture of novel forms and languages are consciously turned into potent signifiers of not just temporality, transience or rebellion, but more importantly of individual and collective histories. Form becomes writing, in a very practical sense of that which recollects, encodes and transmits, yet retains its nature as a visual and therefore perceptibly autonomous entity. In the documentation of 20th century British culture, Egonu's work falls within that unique part of modernist art where aesthetic ambivalence was restored to its place as an agent of cultural interrogation.

Egonu introduces to post-war British art a peculiar and privileged understanding of the sources which have considerably defined it indirectly but which are largely uncredited. Egonu is one of those artists who signalled a historical borderline beyond which the colonial experience no longer resided in anonymity together with the rest of the spoils of Empire.

With Egonu the African presence in British art changed from that of the mute and anonymous curio which David Dabydeen categorises as Hogarth's Blacks:[3] images objectivised, decontextualised, and ultimately consigned to the faded background of 18th century English portraiture. Egonu signalled the appearance of the African as an active player in the formation and interpretation of British reality, and in the conceptualisation and imaging of Europe. He introduced a new perspective, a new body of meaning and perception, and has contributed to the fragmentation of Europe's monological narration. In his work Africa becomes an affective presence in British art. The axis of imaging and representation is reversed, and not only is the gaze turned but its constitution also changed. Egonu's articulation of his own reality constitutes a different stream within the dominant narrative, as we see in his presentation of civil strife in his home country, which avoids the valorisation of tragedy and violence, as well as the stigmatisation of cultures which characterise popular western representations of others.

Egonu's work in the 1970s and 1980s initiated a migrant discourse in British art. In 'Stateless People' he introduces to art a theme hitherto explored only by the postcolonial writer in English literature, that of the fate and fortune of the peripheral immigrant in the metropolis. The alienation of exile and relocation is very effectively represented in his characters, lonely and nostalgic, alone or herded together in little café groups, or bonded to the tools of their trade, nursing an indeterminable loss.

For British art in the last quarter of the century, Egonu's 'Stateless People' signifies a doxa, the parallel of which takes us back to the immediate post-war period, to Moore's bomb-shelter drawings or Sutherland's agonised characters. Only, this doxa centres a different history and community, and so in a language quite different from the largely affirmative tone of much metropolitan or postcolonial discourse. Yet Egonu's themes cut across borders and the overall strength and enduring quality of his work reside in their humanism: nature and transience, strife and distress, nation and knowledge, the creative predicament. Individuals have been of less consequence in his work save where the personal serves as a symbol for the social, and yet he has brought to the imaging of his universal themes a concrete anchoring, identifying the individual as the ultimate site of the social. The tragedies of war, the agonies of addiction, the disorientation of relocation: these are invariably tragedies which are played out in the unbroachable interstices of individual existence, and their weight can only be gleaned within this localised space. Otherwise our ability to understand or empathise is lost in the voyeurism of the monumental gaze. Egonu particularises experience, and through his synecdochic strategies captures the broad ramifications of his themes.

Egonu's prints represent a confident command of language which has enabled the artist to step beyond formal experimentation and engage in a clear project of signification. They not only arrest, they communicate with directness, and unlike much modernist printmaking, their strength does not reside in cunning visual devices but in a stringent, almost elegiac manipulation of form. In them Egonu restores poetry to the print. It is this which George Whittet recognises when, in his assessment of 'The Four Seasons', he places Egonu alongside Paul Klee as one of the century's few masters of the graphic medium.[4]

Egonu progressed steadily from the tentativeness of his early work to the mastery we acknowledge in his work from the 1960s onwards, by a tenacious dedication to the studio and to his practice. In an age when late-modernist licence has created a severe polarity between skill and hype, Egonu could be said to belong to the old school which saw the artist's first duty as being to his or her craft, not to the market, the media, or ideology. Over the past forty years he has continued to work almost daily even through ill-health and hardship. In fulfilment of his childhood ambitions, art has remained his one consuming passion. His is a professionalism which is increasingly rare. He is constantly in the process of completing a work in progress, or conceiving new concepts and ideas, which he readily sets down in preliminary sketches. From the concept he progresses to fully realised drawings or colour sketches which form the prototypes for the final work. Many of these prototypes, especially from the 1980s onwards, stand as complete works in themselves, and this procedure the artist perfected while working in serigraphy.

Not only has Egonu worked in all conventional two-dimensional media, he has produced sculpture in bronze and terracotta, illustrated numerous books, and designed for the textile industry. Much of this work has yet to be studied, and though it constitutes a small part of his oeuvre, it nevertheless bears witness to a prodigious talent translated through skill and hard work. Egonu explores each medium to its fullest potential. He continues to engage new thematic and technical challenges.

In 1965 Egonu spoke of his career thus: "I have enjoyed what I have done, and [am] enjoying what I'm doing, and hope to enjoy whatever I may do in the future."[5] No summary could be more succinct for his life and practice as an artist over the past half century.

NOTES

Introduction

1 George Whittet, *Mudroon*, 1976.
2 Obiora Udechukwu, *Okike 10th Anniversary: An Exhibition of Drawings, Prints and Watercolours*, catalogue of exhibition, University of Nigeria, Nsukka, 1982.

Egonu: The Life

Biographical details derive from the artist's personal papers or conversations between the author and artist unless otherwise stated.

1 Samuel Adjayi Crowther, letter to J C Taylor, quoted in G T Basden, *Among the Ibos of Nigeria*, Seeley, Service and Co Ltd, London, 1921, p 289.
2 Chinua Achebe, 'Onitsha: Gift of the Niger', in *Morning Yet on Creation Day*, Heinemann, London, 1975, p 90.
3 F Deauville Walker, *The Romance of The Black River: The Story of the CMS Nigeria Mission*, CMS, London, 1930, p 212.
4 Achebe, 'Onitsha: Gift of the Niger', op cit, p 191.
5 Ibid, p 92.
6 Chike Akosa, *Heroes and Heroines of Onitsha*, Chike Akosa and Associates, Onitsha, 1987.
7 Achebe, 'Onitsha', op cit, p 92.
8 William N Geary, *Nigeria Under British Rule*, Methuen and Co Ltd, London, 1927, p 173.
9 Egonu, conversations with the author, South Kenton, September 1990, pp 15-16.
10 Conversation with the author, September 1990.
11 When the steamer *Empire Windrush* arrived in Britain from Jamaica in July 1958 with 492 Jamaicans recruited to help in the post-war reconstruction, the new Nationality Act of 1948 gave them and their families the right of permanent residence. The atmosphere of this gesture would be reversed in the next two decades, beginning with the 1962 Commonwealth Immigration Act.
12 Rasheed Araeen, *The Other Story: Afro-Asian Artists in Post-War Britain*, South Bank Centre, London, 1989, p 25.
13 Simon Wilson, *British Art: From Holbein to the Present Day*, The Tate Gallery & The Bodley Head, London, 1979, p 153.
14 Although the artist has always given 1952 as his year of graduation from Camberwell, this is mistaken. A testimonial signed by the Principal of the College, J W Wright, Head of the Printing Department at Camberwell, on 22 March 1962 (the original was lost with other documents earlier mentioned) indicates that he was at Camberwell between 10 January 1949 and10 October 1951, the normal course duration of 3 years.
15 Conversation with the author, March 1990. See also Egonu, 'My Metaphoric Journey in The West', paper delivered at the symposium on 'Neue Kunst aus Nigeria im Internationalen Kontext', Dusseldorf, November 7-8, 1991, p 1.
16 'Reflections of Uzo Egonu: Contemporary Nigerian Artist, Interviewed by Hiltrud Streicher', unpublished manuscript, 1966, revised 1975, p 30.
17 I owe this insight to the critic and art historian Dennis Duerden who discussed the period with me in his home in East London in 1990.
18 Conversations with Duerden, 1990. See also Guy Brett, 'Internationalism among artists in the 60s and 70s', in Araeen, *The Other Story*, op cit, pp 111-114.
19 Araeen, *The Other Story*, op cit, p 131.
20 Barbara Wright, 'Eight Artists', *The Arts Review*, 20 February-6 March, 1965.
21 'For Art's Sake', *Eastern Daily Press*, 19 April, 1965.
22 Ronald Moody, 'Uzo Egonu', *Magnet News*, 10-23 April, 1965.
23 'Chronique du Festival Mondial des Arts Negres', *Senegal D'Aujourd'hui*, April 1966. See also, *Federal Nigeria,* special issue dedicated to Dakar Festival of Negro Arts, Vol 9, Nos 3 & 4, 1966.
24 Reviewed by Max Wykes-Joyce for the *Arts Review*, 20 August, 1966. Egonu's *Two Fighting Cocks* was listed among the pictures the critic considered ''worth comment''.
25 Letter from H B Frankel, Organising secretary, Leicester University Arts Festival (Britain and Commonwealth), dated 28 June 1966. Artist's private papers.
26 *The World in Perspective*, Upper Grosvenor Galleries, July 1968.
27 Ibid.
28 Dennis Duerden, Uzo Egonu, *Arts Review with Auction and Gallery Guide*, Vol XX, No 14, 20 July 1968.
29 *Daily Mirror*, Wednesday 17 July, 1968.
30 See *Stroud News and Journal*, Thursday 19 November, 1970.
31 *Standard Bank Review*, December 1970.
32 *Arts Review*, Vol XXV, No 11, 2 June, 1973.
33 Emmanuel Jegede, 'The Vision of Uzo Egonu,' *West Africa*, No 2922, 11 June, 1973.
34 Adeyemo Adekeye, 'Uzo Egonu of Nigeria', *African Arts*, Autumn 1973, p 34.
35 Taiwo Ajayi, secretary to the United Kingdom African Festival Committee. Undated letter to Egonu. Artist's private papers.
36 Letter from Rudolf Mayer, Internationelle Buchkunst-Austellung, Leipzig, 16 August 1976. Artist's private papers.

37 Egonu, 'Painting in Darkness 1979-1983', untitled, undated manuscript, attributed to 1984 in *Uzo Egonu: Lithographs, Etchings & Screenprints* 1979-1983, catalogue of exhibition, Black Art Gallery, London, 1986.
38 Minutes of Jury, UNESCO Poster and Calender Competition, 16 March 1981, p 4. Artist's private papers.
39 Egonu, 'Painting in Darkness', p 2.
40 Ibid, p 2.
41 Obiora Udechukwu, 'Okike 10th Anniversary: An Exhibition of Drawings, Prints and Watercolours', catalogue of exhibition at the Continuing Education Centre, University of Nigeria, Nsukka, 1982.
42 Text of speech by Alhaji Abdulaziz C Ude, Nsukka, 16 January 1985, p 5. Unpublished. Artist's private papers.
43 Egonu, 'The circumstances leading to the creation of the work', undated manuscript. Artist's private papers. Also see Hiltrud Streicher and Uzo Egonu, 'Reflections of Uzo Egonu', *Third Text*, Autumn/Winter 1989, pp 173-182, into which the editors collapsed the above manuscript and others.
44 Letter from Rasheed Araeen, 14 November, 1986. Artist's private papers.
45 In Omotayo Afolabi, 'Our Nigerian: Uzo Egonu, Painting the Soul', *Nigerian Homenews*, 22-28 February, 1990.

The Egonu Aesthetic

1 The date of this painting is not very clear. The artist identifies it as having been done in 1964, but in his 1966 interview with Hiltrud Streicher it is dated 1965. The painting also appears in the review published in the *Magnet* by Ronald Moody in 1965, which suggests that it was either done in 1964 or early in 1965.
2 'Reflections of Uzo Egonu: Contemporary Nigerian Artist, Interviewed by Hiltrud Streicher', unpublished manuscript, 1966, revised 1975, p 10.
3 Uzo Egonu, *22 Prints*, exhibition catalogue, Nsukka, Department of Fine and Applied Arts, University of Nigeria, Nsukka, 1985, p 3.
4 Ibid, p 3.
5 A S Huffington, *Picasso: Creator and Destroyer*, Pan Books Ltd, London, 1989, p 61.
6 Ousmane Sembene declared it moribund at the Dakar Conference on French African Literature in March 1963. Other participants like Cheikh Hamidou Kane were of the same opinion. See *African Literature and the Universities*, Gerald Moore (ed), Ibadan University Press for The Congress for Cultural Freedom, Ibadan, 1965.
7 'Reflections', op cit, p 30.
8 Interview with the artist, South Kenton, November 1989.
9 'Reflections', op cit, p 41.
10 See also David Kunzle, 'The Corset as Erotic Alchemy: From Rococo Galanterie to Montaut's Physiologies', in Hess and Nochlin (eds), *Woman as Sex Object: Studies in Erotic Art, 1730-1970*, Allen Lane, London, 1973, pp 100-101.
11 Interview with the artist, November 1989.
12 For detailed discussion of the symbolism of this palette see Obiora Udechukwu, 'Lyrical Symbolism: Notes on Traditional Wall Paintings from Agulu', BA Thesis, University of Nigeria, Nsukka, 1972.
13 'Reflections', op cit, pp 8-9.
14 Ibid, p 11.
15 Ibid, p 11.
16 G I Jones has tried to explain Igbo village planning in terms of Igbo agriculture and has related social structures to the ecology with respect to the Central and North-Eastern Igbo. See Jones, 'Agriculture and Ibo village planning', *Farm and Forest*, No 6, 1945, pp 9-15, and Jones, 'Ecology and social structure among the North Eastern Ibo', *Africa*, No 31, 1961, pp 117-134. See also A E Afigbo, 'Prolegomena to the Study of the Culture History of the Igbo-Speaking Peoples of Nigeria', F C Ogbalu and E N Emenanjo (eds), *Igbo Language and Culture*, Oxford University Press, Ibadan, 1975, pp 41-43.
17 Chinua Achebe, Foreword to *Igbo Arts: Community and Cosmos* by Herbert M Cole and Chike C Aniakor, Museum of Cultural History, University of California, Los Angeles, 1984. Republished as 'The Igbo World and its Art', in Chinua Achebe, *Hopes and Impediments*, Heinemann International, 1988, pp 42-45.
18 Chinua Achebe and Ulli Beier, *The World is a Dancing Masquerade*, text of conversation between Chinua Achebe and Ulli Beier, Iwalewa, Bayreuth, 1991, p 4.
19 Achebe, 'The Igbo World and its Art', op cit.
20 The Booker Prize winning Nigerian novel, *The Famished Road* by Ben Okri, Jonathan Cape, London, 1991, is built on the theme of the endless Road and its limitless possibilities. It draws heavily from both the Igbo and Yoruba world
21 Achebe, 'Dead Men's Path', *The University Herald*, Ibadan, January 1953. Republished in Achebe, *Girls at War and Other Stories*, Heinemann, London, 1972.
22 Biodun Jeyifo profers that a reading of Achebe's *Things Fall Apart*shows that the narrative runs on two lines, one which deals with History capitalised and personified in '''the lords of the Land''' and another, the '''mini' narratives'' dealing with '''small people' in the community''. ''Among many of the ironic twists'' of the novel, he concludes, ''is the fact that while the main narrative line about Okonkwo (figure-symbol of the noble) leads to tragedy... the fragmentary stories

and motifs of the *efulefu* (the worthless) move this social class to restitution at the end of the novel.'' The fact is that it is this disjuncture, the sharpened dichotomisation and active repression of the 'mini' narratives, the progressive disregard for the worthless (the negative space) which Okonkwo rigidly pursued against the better judgement of the community, which leads to the tragic ending of the novel. See Biodun Jeyifo, 'For Chinua Achebe: The Resilience and Predicament of Obierika', K H Peterson and A Rutherford (eds), *Chinua Achebe: A Celebration*, Heinemann International and Dangaroo Press, London/Sydney, 1991, p 64. See also R N Henderson, *The King in Every Man*, Yale University Press, 1972.

23 T Uzodinma Nwala, *Igbo Philosophy*, Lagos, Lantern Books, 1985, p 57.

24 Cole and Aniakor, op cit, p 83.

25 Ibid, p 84.

26 A scene from the Smithsonian documentary, *Nigerian Art-Kindred Spirits*, Smithsonian World, Washington, DC, co-produced with WETA, 1990, illustrates this regard for standing space. In it the painter and theorist Uche Okeke is shown with his elderly mother who is producing an uli drawing for the programme. When she stops, Okeke observes that there are lots of open/fallow areas which could be filled with motifs, to which she replies that the drawing was already saturated. The fallow spaces are not to be trespassed for the fun of it.

27 Achebe and Beier, op cit, p 4.

28 Akin Euba, 'Nigerian Music: An Appreciation', *Nigeria Magazine*, special issue, October 1960, p 198.

29 W W C Echezona, 'Igbo Music', *Nigeria Magazine*, No 84, 1965, p 50.

30 Achebe and Beier, op cit, p 5.

31 Onuora O Enekwe, 'Igbo Masks: The Oneness of Ritual and Theatre', *Nigeria Magazine*, Lagos, 1987, p 79.

32 Achebe and Beier, op cit, p 5.

33 Egonu, 'About Myself and My Work', 1970, published in *Egonu, 22 Prints*, catalogue of exhibition, 1985.

Community and Commitment

1 Critical literature on this is vast and in the Seventies the discourse expanded into such other questionable constructs as 'Commitment and the Third World Writer', 'Commonwealth Literature' and so on. Peter Nazareth, Alastair Niven, Gerald Moore, are some of the authorities in these fields. In the visual arts this has manifested in such constructs as Susan Vogel's 'New Functionality'.

2 Leopold Sedar Senghor, *Prose and Poetry*, selected and trans. by John Reed and Clive Wake, Oxford University Press, London, 1965, p 82.

3 Chinua Achebe, *Morning Yet on Creation Day*, Heinemann, London, 1975, p 19.

4 Regents' Lecture, University of California at Los Angeles, 1984. Later published in *Hopes and Impediments: Selected Essays 1965-87*, Heinemann, London, 1988, pp 32-41.

5 Wole Soyinka, *Art, Dialogue and Outrage: Essays on Literature and Culture*, New Horn Press, Ibadan, 1988, p 16.

6 Soyinka, *Myth, Literature and the African World*, Cambridge University Press, 1976, p 61.

7 Soyinka, *Art, Dialogue, Outrage*, op cit, p 113.

8 Interviews with the artist, South Kenton, November 1990.

9 Achebe, *Morning Yet*, p 19.

10 Emmanuel Ngara, 'Achebe as Artist: The Place and Significance of Anthills of the Savannah', in Peterson and Rutherford (eds), *Chinua Achebe: A Celebration*, Heinemann and Dangaroo Press, London/Sydney, 1991, p 113.

11 For example, none of his works written in English, which is almost all of his writing, are available in translation in his own language, and an appreciable percentage of the Igbo population cannot read English.

12 Peterson and Rutherford, *Chinua Achebe*, op cit.

13 Achebe, *Hopes and Impediments*, op cit, p 43.

14 Ngugi wa Thiong'o, *Homecoming: Essays on African and Caribbean Literature, Culture and Politics*, Heinemann, London, 1972, pp 127-144.

15 George Lamming, *Of Age and Innocence*, Joseph, London, 1958, p 73.

16 Interview with the artist, October 1989.

17 Interview with the artist, October 1989.

The War Years

1 Raymond Williams, *The Year 2000*, Pantheon Books, New York, 1983.

2 See Frantz Fanon on 'The Pitfalls of National Consciousness' in *The Wretched of the Earth*, trans. Constance Farrington, Penguin Books, Middlesex, 1967.

3 Basil Davidson, 'Peace at Stake in Battle of Nigerian Poll', *Daily Mirror*, 30 December 1964.

4 Christopher Okigbo, *Path of Thunder: Poems Prophesying War in Collected Poems*, William Heinemann, London, 1986.

5 Uzo Egonu, *The World in Perspective*, catalogue of exhibition, 1968.

6 Timothy Brennan, *Salman Rushdie and The Third World*, Macmillan, London, 1989, p 18.

7 Chinua Achebe, *Beware Soul Brother*, Nwamife Publishers, Enugu, 1971.
8 bell hooks, *From Margin to Center*, South End Press, Boston, 1984, p 29.
9 Aijaz Ahmad, 'Jameson's Rhetoric of Otherness and the "National Allegory"', *Social Text*, Vol 17, Fall 1987, pp 3-25.
10 Uche Okeke, *Art in Development: A Nigerian Perspective*, Asele Institute and African American Cultural Centre, Nimo/Minneapolis, 1982, p 16.
11 Ibid, p 16.
12 Ben Okri in *The Observer*, 20 September, 1987.
13 Nelson Wattie, 'The Community as Protagonist in the Novels of Chinua Achebe and Witi Ihimaera', in Daniel Massa (ed), *Individual and Community in Commonwealth Literature*, Malta, University Press, 1979, pp 69-74.
14 Conversation with the author, South Kenton, 1990.

Beyond The War Years

1 Interview with the artist, South Kenton, December 1989.
2 General Olusegun Obasanjo, quoted in Chinua Achebe, *The Trouble with Nigeria*, Fourth Dimension Publishers, Enugu, 1983, p 9.
3 Ibid, p 38.
4 Colin Moss, EADT, 28 August 1987, p 8.
5 Uzo Egonu, 'Paintings (Stateless People)', unpublished statement, London, 1986. Artist's private papers.
6 Jean-Jacques Rousseau, *The Social Contract*, Penguin, 1968, first published 1762.
7 H H Gerth and C Wright Mills (eds), *Max Weber*, Routledge and Kegan Paul, London, 1970, p 77.
8 Barbara Erlich White, 'Renoir's Sensuous Women', in Hess and Nochlin, op cit, p 175.
9 Renoir wrote the preface to a translation of Cennino Cennini's 14th century treatise in 1911 in which he venerated time-honoured ideals in art from Pompeii to Corot. See Michel Drucker, *Renoir*, Paris, 1944.
10 White, op cit, p 169.
11 Renoir, in a letter of 8 April 1888 to Catulle Mendes, states that "women are monsters who are authors, lawyers... bores who are nothing more than five-legged beasts". See François Daulte, *Auguste Renoir Catalogue Raisonné, Vol 1, Figures 1860-90*, and White, ibid, p 171. There is of course Renoir's 'Girl Reading' (c 1876) at the Louvre, but a close study of the painting quickly shows how its focus is on the lady's face and hairstyle and the casual style of the work underlines the artist's attitude to the activity. On the contrary, Egonu effaces the figure in his treatments of the theme and attention is focused inescapably on the activity and idea.
12 Anthony Storr, *Solitude*, Ballantine Press, New York, 1988.
13 Interview with the artist, October 1989.
14 Egonu, unpublished paper, 1986.
15 Egonu, unpublished and undated paper, artist's files.
16 Achebe, *The Trouble with Nigeria*, op cit, p 1.
17 Ibid, p 2.

Anguish and Solitude

1 In Simon Wilson, *British Art: From Holbein to the Present Day*, The Tate and Bodley Head, London, 1989. Wilson qualifies the classical tradition in landscape painting as 'imaginative' and occasionally historical, while the narrative or 'natural', that which represents a particular and existent scene, he defines as 'topographical'.
2 See Chapter Three.
3 Herbert Read, *The Meaning of Art*, Pelican Books, London, 1949, p 115.
4 In the introduction to the catalogue for his 1986 Print Retrospective at the Black Art Gallery, Egonu is quoted thus: "The autumn and winter of 1982 revealed to me what nature can place before an artist who, like me, has nearly lost his sight."
5 Uzo Egonu, 'Painting in Darkness 1979-1983', undated manuscript, p 2. Artist's private papers.
6 Bernard Myers on Monet's 'Water-lilies: The Japanese Bridge', oil on canvas, 1918-24, in Myers, *Methods of the Masters: Monet*, Brian Todd Publishing House Ltd, London, 1990, p 112.
7 Thomas Gainsborough, letter to William Jackson, quoted in Simon Wilson, op cit, p 40.
8 'Africa's Top Artist Shows in London', London Press Service, August 1982.
9 Egonu, 'Painting in Darkness', op cit, p 2.
10 In Egonu, 'The Circumstances leading to the creation of the work', undated paper. Artist's private papers.
11 Recalled in Peter Fuller, *Beyond the Crisis in Art*, Writers and Readers Publishing Cooperative, London, p 145.
12 Compare the artist's evocation of memory and the imagination in 'Painting in Darkness', op cit.
13 Anthony Storr, *Solitude*, Ballantine Books, New York, 1989, p 174.
14 Egonu, 'The circumstances leading to the creation of the work', op cit.

Postscript

1 Uzo Egonu, exhibition flyer, University of Lancaster, 1974.
2 Egonu, ibid.
3 David Dabydeen, *Hogarth's Blacks: Images of Blacks in 18th Century English Art*, Dangaroo Press, 1985.
4 George Whittet, original English text of review for *Mudroon*, 1982. Artist's private papers.
5 'Reflections of Uzo Egonu: Contemporary Nigerian Artist, Interviewed by Hiltrud Streicher', unpublished manuscript, 1966, revised 1975.

SELECTED BIBLIOGRAPHY

Adekeye, A. 'Uzo Egonu of Nigeria', *African Arts*, Autumn 1973.

Adenaike, F. '''City of Caserta'' Cup for Nigerian Artist', *Daily Times*, 3 February 1972.

Afolabi, O. 'Uzo Egonu: Painting the Soul', *Nigerian Homenews*, 22-23 February 1990.

African Arts, 'First Word', Summer 1974.

African Arts, 'Uzo Egonu', Winter 1973.

Albright, T. 'A Pair of Print Shows — Having It Both Ways', *San Francisco Chronicle*, October 11, 1983.

Antiques Weekly, 'Contemporary African Arts', 16 August 1969.

Araeen, R. *The Other Story*, The South Bank Centre, London, 1989.

Bennett, G. 'BBC Art Competition 1970', *African Arts*, v, 1, 1971.

Bradshaw, L. 'Egonu', *Arts Review*, xviii, 18 September 1966.

Bradshaw, L. 'Uzo Egonu: An Appreciation' in *Egonu, The World in Perspective*, catalogue of exhibition, London 1968.

Brett, G. 'The New Africans', *The Times Saturday Review*, 9 August 1969.

Burland, C. 'Mellon, Egonu, Binney', *Arts Review*, 2 June 1973.

Chic Magazine, Untitled, 1 March 1968.

Dagbladet, 'Femte og sidste Inter-udstilling', 12 May 1972.

Daily Mirror, London, 17 July 1968.

Daily Nation, 'Work of Nigerian artist comes to town', Nairobi, 19 January 1971.

Daily Express, London, 16 July 1968.

Daily Times, 'Nigerian Artist Triumphs', Lagos, 14 July 1971.

Daily Times, 'Oil Painting for Ibiam', 11 June 1965.

Denvir, B. 'London Letter', *Art International*, xiii, October 1969.

Der Abend, 'Schwarze Nythen: Uzo Egonu stellt im neuen Afro-Centrum', 23 October 1972.

Der Tages Speigel, 'Ein kultuzentrum fur Africa', 8 November 1972.

Double Vision, 'Uzo Egonu', undated.

Duerden, D. 'Uzo Egonu', *Arts Review*, 20 July 1968.

Eastern Daily Express, 'For Art's Sake', 19 April 1965.

Ebele, A. 'Black Living Picasso', *West Africa*, 2 August 1982.

Egonu, U. 'Uzo Egonu Now 1986'. Publicity folder for the exhibition 'Stateless People', Royal Festival Hall, London, 1986.

Egonu, U. *The World in Perspective*, catalogue of exhibition, London, 1968.

Egonu, U. Exhibition of prints by Uzo Egonu, catalogue of exhibition, University of Nigeria, Nsukka, 1995.

Egonu, U. 'International Graphic Triennale', *Artist's Newsletter*, December 1983.

Egonu, U. 'About Myself and My Work', Artist's statement, 1970.

Elgon, J. 'Morning Show', *East African Standard*, Nairobi, January 1971.

'Federal Nigeria', Special issue dedicated to the Dakar Festival of Arts of *Negro Arts*, 9, 3&4, 1966.

Fraczak, A. 'The Biennale of Graphics From The Third World', *Project*, 6, 1980.

Gooding, M. 'Third World Biennale of Graphic Art', *Arts Review*, 18 July 1980.

Hampstead News, 'Uzo wins art contest — and chance of a trip to Kenya with his work', 16 October 1970.

Jegede, E. 'The modern African artist who is still loyal to tradition', *West Indian World*, 15 June 1993.

Kahlcke, W. 'Afrikanisches in Berlin: Uzo Egonu in Afro-Zentrum', 19 October 1972.

Kolner Stadt-Anzeiger, 'Wahl der Titelgrafik uberraschte Uzo Egonu', 12 October 1983.

Kolner Stadt-Anzeiger, 'Der Nigerianische kunstler Ezo Egonu im liberlum Zentrum', 18 January 1973.

Kolner Stadt-Anzeiger, 'Kunstler aus Nigeria zu Sylvester an der Erft', 30/31 December 1972.

Kolnische Aundschau, 'Nigerianischer maler verlebt seinem Festurlaub in Bedburg', 29 December 1972.

La Revue Moderne, 'Uzo Egonu', April 1975.

Moody, R. 'Uzo Egonu', *MagnetNews*, 10-23 April 1965.

Moss, C. 'Striving to shed European tradition', *EADT*, 28 August 1987.

Mullaly, T. 'Wide range of African art display', *The Daily Telegraph*, London, 11 August 1969.

Neue Presse Frankfurter Feuilleton, 'Einsam beim Essen; Afrikanischer Maler', 2 July 1985.

New Nigerian, 11 October 1966.

Nigeria Today, Office of the High Commissioner for Nigeria, London, March 1980.

Nri, M. N. 'Uzo Egonu: The Intricacies of Prints', *West Africa*, 30 January 1986.

The Observer, 'Blackpool's national show', 29 July 1979.

Onuorah, B. C. 'Let's boost our Arts', *Sunday Satellite*, Enugu, 20 January 1985.

Onuorah, B. C. 'Don On the Tragedy of Educated Nigerians', *Sunday Satellite*, Enugu, 20 January 1985.

Simpson, G. 'Uzo Egonu (Black Art Gallery)', *The Voice*, 25 January 1986.

Stroud News and Journal, 'Stroud will see work by Nigerian artist'. Gloucester, 12 November 1970.

The Voice, 'One Man's Vision', 25 January 1986.

The Voice, 'Uzo Prints', 26 January 1986.

The Weekly Gleaner, 'Uzo finds blend of paint and print', 31 January 1986.

The Teacher: Journal of the National Union of Teachers, London, 19 January 1966.

The Citizen, 'War inspired work by Ibo artist', Gloucester, 16 November 1970.

The Daily Telegraph and Morning Post, 'Tropical Art', London, 6 September 1966.

Tialobi, G. 'How Uzo Egonu, Nigeria's best-known artist in Europe earns his living', *The Punch*, 19 May 1978.

Udechukwu, O. *Okike 10th Anniversary: An Exhibition of Drawings, Prints, and Watercolours*', Nsukka, 29 April 1982.

Weingarten, H. 'Tasse Kaffee wirbt fur internatinale kunst', Kolner Stadt-Anzeiger, 9 September 1983.

Wembley News, 'Nigerian artist now lives in South Kenton', 29 October 1971.

Wembley Observer, 'Talented Artist from Nigeria', 20 October 1971.

West Africa, 'Matchet's Diary', 16 August 1969.

West Africa, 'Egonu exhibits', 13 January 1986.

West Africa, 'The Vision of Egonu', 11 June 1973.

West African Pilot, 'UAC Mounts Nigerian Display in London', 4 January 1972.

Westindian Digest, 'African Mirror in Islington', February 1986.

West Indian World, 'Egonu embraces a continent', 15 January 1986.

What's On in Nairobi, 'Nigerian Exhibits in Nairobi', Nairobi, 25-31 January 1971.

Williams, S. 'Contemporary African Art', *Antiques Weekly*, 23 August 1969.

Wolfram, E. 'Egonu, Zirner-Macdonogh, Crosland', *Arts Review*, 3-17 October 1964.

Wright, B. 'Eight Artists', *Arts Review*, 20 February - 6 March, 1965.

Wykes-Joyce, M. 'Summer Exhibition', *Arts Review*, xviii, 16 August 1966.

BIOGRAPHY

1931 Born, Onitsha, Nigeria.
1945 Came to England and studied at a private school, Little Snoring, Norfolk.
1949-52 Studied Fine Art, Design and Typography at Camberwell School of Art and Design, London.
1953 Lived in Paris for a year.
1958 Travelled in Finland for two months, and visited Sweden and Denmark.
1960 Commissioned by the Nigeria High Commission, London, for a symbolic painting depicting the country's independence the following year.
1963-68 Member of Free Painters and Sculptors Group, London.
1968-74 Textile design and book illustration. Commissioned by various publishers, and designs bought by textile companies.
1970-89 Member-Fellow of Printmakers Council, London.
1973 75 Member of Artistic Programme Sub-Committee for the Lagos FESTAC Committee.
1981 Served on the Jury of the International Poster Competition at UNESCO, Paris.
1993 Commissioned to paint a large work entitled *Universality* by International Maritime Satellite Organisation (INMARSAT) London.

EXHIBITIONS

Individual Shows

1964 Woodstock Gallery, London.
1966 Atelier Vincitore Gallery, Brighton, England.
Upper Grosvenor Galleries, London.
1967 Leicester University, Leicester, England.
1968 Upper Grosvenor Galleries, London.
Commonwealth Institute Gallery, Edinburgh, Scotland.
1970 George Room Gallery, Stroud, England.
1971 Gallery Africa, Nairobi, Kenya.
1972 Agisymba Galerie, Berlin, Germany.
1973 Commonwealth Institute Art Gallery, London.
1974 University of Lancaster, Lancaster, England.
1980 Liberales Zentrum, Art Gallery, Cologne, Germany.
1982 Bhonagree Gallery, Commonwealth Institute, London.
1985 Ana Gallery, University of Nigeria, Nsukka, Nigeria.
Galerie Neue Horizonte, Frankfurt/M., Germany.
1986 Royal Festival Hall, South Bank Centre, London.
Civic Centre, Exhibition Area, Harrow, London.
Black Art Gallery, London.

Mixed and Group Shows

1963 Free Painters Group, FBA Galleries, London.
'Winter Salon', Royal Institute Galleries, London.
1964 In Lagos, Port Harcourt and Enugu, Nigeria.
1965 Woodstock Gallery, London.
Royal Festival Hall, London.
National Museum of Wales, Cardiff.
1966 Camden Arts Centre, London.
Summer Exhibition, Upper Grosvenor Galleries, London.
Winter Exhibition, Upper Grosvenor Galleries, London.
First World Festival of Negro Arts, Dakar, Senegal.
1968 FBA Galleries, London.
Camden Arts Centre, London.
Contemporary African Art, Africa Centre, London.
'Artists for Czechoslovakia', Camden Arts Centre, London.
INTER FAUNA, 'Im Reich der Tiere', Ehrenhof, Dusseldorf, Germany.
City Art Gallery, Bristol, England.
Victoria Art Gallery, Bath, England.

'Artists of Eight Commonwealth Countries', City Art Gallery, Bristol, England.
High Wycombe Arts Festival Exhibition, High Wycombe, England.

1969 FBA Galleries, London.
Camden Arts Centre, London.
'Contemporary African Art', Camden Arts Centre, London.
Galerie Jules Salles, Nîmes, France.

1970 Trinity College, Dublin, Ireland.
Brentwood Festival, Brentwood, England.
BBC Morning Show Art Competition and Exhibition, London.
The Guildhall, London.

1970/71 Open Poster Contest and Exhibition for African Artists 'AFRICA RESPONDS', Organising Committee for the Games of the XXth Olympiad, Munich 1972, Germany.

1971 'Three Contemporary African Artists', Dorchester Hotel, London.
'Three Contemporary African Artists', United Africa House, London.
'Flower Painters of the World', Augustine Gallery, Holt, England.
'Les Arts en Europe 1971', Brussels, Belgium.
'Painting and Sculpture of Today 1971', Augustine
Gallery, Holt, Norfolk, England.
Concorso Internazionale di Pittura 'ITALIA 2000', Napoli, Italy.
Hachette Gallery, London.
British Week in Austria, Linz, Austria.

1972 'INTER 72' International Art Exhibition, Holstebro-Hallen, Holstebro, Denmark.
Camden Arts Centre, London.
Contemporary African Art Exhibition, Africa Centre, London.
Printmakers Council Print Exhibition, Oxford University Press, London.

1973 Bluecoat Gallery, Liverpool, England.
Art Exhibition, USA Army, Berlin, Germany.

1974 Kresge Art Gallery, Michigan State University, Michigan, USA.

1975 Three Dimensions Gallery, Berkeley, California, USA.
Commonwealth Society London 'African Fine Art Then and Now', London.

1977 'FESTAC', Lagos, Nigeria.

1978 Contemporary African Art, Maison de la Culture, André Malraux, Reims, France.
Edinburgh Festival, Edinburgh, Scotland.

1980 Galerie Exler & Co., Frankfurt/M, Germany.
International Book Fair, Frankfurt/M, Germany

1981 Dixon Gallery, London.
'Inter 81', 14th International Art Exhibition, Holstebro, Denmark.

1982 Westbourne Gallery, London.

1983 October Gallery, St Helena, California, USA.

1984 'Into the Open', Mappin Art Gallery, Sheffield, and UK tour.

1986 Brixton Art Gallery, London.
The Roundhouse, London.

1986/87 'Double Vision' Bradford Art Galleries & Museums, Bradford, and UK tour.

1989/91 'The Other Story', Hayward Gallery, London, and UK tour.
'The South of the World - The Other Contemporary Art', Galleria Civica d'Arte Contemporanea, Marsala, Sicily.

1992/3 '2nd Coming'. Outstanding contemporary art from ten years of major exhibitions 1980-1990, South London Art Gallery, London.
'Art for a Fairer World', Art Gallery and Museum, Kelvingrove, Glasgow, and touring.

1994 'Transport Breakers', Colonnade Gallery, Sotheby's, London.
Bluecoat Gallery, Liverpool.
Burlington New Gallery, London.

Participated in the international graphic biennales: Ibiza, Spain, 1972;
Frechen, Germany, 1972, 74, 76, 80, 83;
Bradford, UK, 1972, 74, 79, 86;
Fredrikstad, Norway, 1974, 76, 78, 80, 82, 84;
Kracow, Poland, 1974,76,80,84;
Ljubljana, 1975, 77, 79, 81.

PUBLIC COLLECTIONS

Victoria and Albert Museum, London.
The Arts Council of England.
National Museum of Modern Art, Poznan, Poland.
Bradford City Art Gallery and Museum, Bradford.
International Centre for Public Owned Enterprises, Ljubljana.
National Museum of Modern Art, Baghdad, Iraq.
Fylde Arts Association, Modern British Prints, Blackpool.
Inner London Education Authority, London.
Commonwealth Institute of Scotland, Edinburgh.
National Gallery of Modern Art, Lagos, Nigeria.
The National Collection of The National Council for Art and Culture, Lagos, Nigeria.
Raychem Corporation, Menlo Park, California, USA.
International Print Biennale, Kracow, Poland.
Kramer College, Leeds Education Authority, Leeds.
Galleria Civica D'Arte Contemporanea, Marsala, Sicily.
RWE-Energie A.G., Werk Frimmersdorf, Germany.